Sleeping on Islands

# Andrew Motion

---

# Sleeping on Islands

## A Life in Poetry

faber

First published in 2023
by Faber & Faber Ltd
The Bindery, 51 Hatton Garden
London, EC1N 8HN

Typeset by Faber & Faber Ltd
Printed in the UK by CPI Group (UK) Ltd, Croydon, CR0 4YY

Grateful acknowledgement is made for permission to reprint extracts from:
*The Fall of Rome*, Copyright © 1947 by W. H. Auden. Reprinted by permission of
Curtis Brown, Ltd. All rights reserved. *In Memory of W. B. Yeats*, Copyright © 1939 by
W. H. Auden. Reprinted by permission of Curtis Brown, Ltd. All rights reserved.
*The Letters of Robert Frost, Volume 1, 1886–1920*, edited by Donald Sheehy et al and
published by Harvard University Press. Reprinted by permission of the Robert Frost
Copyright Trust. 'The Otter' from *Field Work* by Seamus Heaney © The Estate of
Seamus Heaney. Reprinted by permission of Faber & Faber Ltd. 'An October Salmon'
from *Ted Hughes: Collected Poems* © The Estate of Ted Hughes. Reprinted by permission
of Faber & Faber Ltd. 'Aubade', 'Cut Grass' and 'Reference Back' from *Philip Larkin:
The Complete Poems* © The Estate of Philip Larkin. Reprinted by permission of Faber
& Faber Ltd. 'Brother Fire' by Louis MacNeice, from *Collected Poems*, reprinted by
permission of The Estate of Louis MacNeice . 'Meeting Point' by Louis MacNeice, from
*Collected Poems*, reprinted by permission of The Estate of Louis MacNeice. 'Fare Well'
by Walter de la Mare, reprinted by permission of The Literary Trustees of Walter de la
Mare and the Society of Authors as their Representative. *Selected Writings of Paul Valéry*,
copyright © 1950 by New Directions Publishing Corp, translation by Louis Varese.
Reprinted by permission of New Directions Publishing Corp.

A CIP record for this book
is available from the British Library

ISBN 978–0–571–37529–5

MIX
Paper | Supporting
responsible forestry
FSC® C171272

Printed and bound in the UK on FSC® certified paper in line with our continuing
commitment to ethical business practices, sustainability and the environment.
**For further information see faber.co.uk/environmental-policy**

2 4 6 8 10 9 7 5 3 1

For everyone here, and everyone not.

# Contents

# Preface

In 2006 I published *In the Blood: A Memoir of My Childhood*; it ends as I reach the age of seventeen. What follows here is a sequel, in the sense that it begins when I'm still seventeen, then moves forward across the next fifty years, before stopping in the spring of 2020. But it breaks the pattern of the earlier book in several ways. *In the Blood* is written in the historic present and sees everything from a child's point of view, in the hope of catching childhood's freshness and surprise. *Sleeping on Islands* has an adult point of view, is written in the past tense, and is also more selective: it concentrates mainly on my life in poetry, and on my meetings and friendships with other poets, most of them now dead. This means among other things that it has a more fragmented form than its predecessor – but so be it. Like most people, I find my memories are just that: fragments. Although as my title suggests, I prefer to think of them as islands.

AM
Baltimore
Spring 2022

# Part One

1970

When our summer term ended and school broke up, the three of us went home for a fortnight to earn some money, then met up again at Victoria station and caught the night train to France. We were sixth-formers, best friends, and this was our first big adventure – our proof of independence: Michael, who would soon be going to Cambridge and later become a doctor like both his parents; Sandy and I, who were a year younger, interested in painting (Sandy) and poetry (me), but with only the vaguest idea of how that interest might develop. A couple of days later, via Munich and the Alps and Athens, we landed on the island of Skyros in the Aegean, and pitched our camp under a fig tree on the beach near the jetty. Michael and I planned to sleep inside the tent, but Sandy didn't want to do that because he disapproved of our cigarettes. Fair enough, we thought, and stayed up to talk in the open for a while. Lay down, rather, because none of us had slept much during the journey, and now the splash of waves, the rotting seaweed smell, and the warm sea breeze were making us drowsy. There was a black moon overhead – a wheel of cheese we'd wedged in the branches to keep it from the ants. The real moon, the bone-white moon blazing in the sky beyond, was too bright to look at for long so I turned to the stars instead, feeling my heart quicken when I saw one ignite and tear across the darkness, drifting more steadily among the fixed constellations.

My mother had written to me at school every Monday and Thursday for ten years and I'd always thrown away her letters after reading them. Hundreds of letters. Thousands of lines. Millions of words. Now, because of the accident, I hoarded whatever scraps of her handwriting I came across: shopping lists tucked into cookbooks; a holiday postcard from Sicily, dropped down the back of a chest of drawers; her inscription in Rupert Brooke's *Collected Poems*, which she'd given me for my seventeenth birthday last autumn. 'Andrew from his Mother' it said on the flyleaf, in curly blue fountain-pen ink. I'd felt disappointed when I first saw what she'd written; it sounded too formal. But now I'd changed my mind and decided it was grown-up. Besides, look where it had led and look what it started.

The sunrise woke us, but we had to scrap breakfast because a thief had climbed into the fig tree during the night and stolen our wheel of cheese. Or had Sandy . . . ? But no, he couldn't have eaten as much as a whole cheese, and anyway it didn't matter. We still had our water and we'd be fine, even if the man in the cafe on the jetty didn't think so; he'd laughed at us yesterday when we told him about our plan to walk to Rupert Brooke's grave. In those shoes? he said, or words to that effect, rolling his eyes at our flip-flops. Did we realise what the ground was like on that part of the island? Did we even know where to look? Not really. All we had to go on were the notes I'd taken from Christopher Hassall's biography: after Brooke had died of septicaemia on board the troop transport the *Grantully Castle* as it sailed through the Aegean on 23 April 1915, his soldier friends rowed the body to Skyros, because that was the island nearest to the ship, landed in Tresboukis Bay, carried it a few hundred yards up a dry streambed, and buried it in an olive grove. A good place for a poet. Then they said a prayer and walked back down the sandy path to their rowing boat. A month later most of them were killed at Gallipoli.

------

My mother was vanishing, all the pictures in my head fading day by day, week by week – then suddenly whoosh, gone. Like when my father laid a fire in the sitting room and held up a sheet of newspaper to make it draw, and the flames leaped, and the paper stiffened, then rusted, then caught, then turned into a shining feather and floated up the chimney. Which was when my father climbed to his feet and brushed yesterday's ash off his knees.

------

The man in the cafe had known what he was talking about: there was no path to Brooke's grave, not even a track, just low hills of ancient lava wreckage, and thyme bushes made of knives. We hopped and swerved and stumbled for half a mile, then returned to camp with our ankles lacerated, rummaged in our backpacks for the socks and long trousers we'd worn when leaving England, tied strips of plastic bag round our feet to stop our flip-flops flip-flopping, and set off again. Five hours later we were still tramping, the sun now directly overhead and our brains scorched. There was no shade anywhere, not a single tree, and no kindness in the ground. I thought of Lawrence of Arabia – Peter O'Toole with his ice-blue eyes that never showed the heat – and remembered how he had ridden his camel back into the desert to rescue the boy he loved. Mirages and delirium. Then I thought about James Gardiner, the son of a teacher at school. James had died of heatstroke last year when he was travelling in Turkey before going to university. A red-faced boy, black hair, smiley, embarrassed even though his dad was popular. I didn't know the whole story, just how he fainted at the side of a road because nobody stopped while he was waiting to hitch a lift. Before James slipped away, he must have seen what I was seeing: the sun swinging across the sky like a light bulb in a cellar, and the sea pouring off the edge of the world.

———

I sat down in the shade of a boulder and my life backed away from me: these were my hands lying sunburned in my lap, but they might have belonged to anyone; and these were my friends peering down at me but seeming like ghosts. I dragged them into real time: Michael with his bustling squarish body, his false front tooth, which was darker than the others, his money belt, and complicated camera settings. And Sandy with his beefiness and curly rock-star hair. Sandy who felt like a brother, only more so. Sandy who was holding a flask to my mouth and telling me that he'd heard a shepherd rounding up sheep on the hills nearby, and was going to ask him about the grave: the shepherd was bound to know where it was.

———

My mother lay on a hospital bed with her hands folded across her stomach and her head propped on a high bank of pillows. Her nose and mouth were hidden by the oxygen mask, a clamp the colour of dirty snow, but the rest of her face was clear. Cheeks sunken. Eyes shut. Eyelids faintly flickering. The bruise at her temple had faded now, softening from deep raspberry red to mushy brown and violet, and the hair on her scalp – growing back after the operation – was darker than it used to be when she lived in the world. Did those tremors in her eyelids mean she was dreaming? Or was she awake in a way the rest of us didn't understand, and still thinking her thoughts? Could she tell, for instance, when my father left her bedside carrying that day's laundry, and her night alone began? Or had all time become the same for her, an endless present with no memories and nothing to ripple the surface?

———

Sandy disappeared – his shadow stretching and snapping alongside him – and his voice in the far distance skimmed over the thorn bushes as he yelled to the shepherd. Michael, meanwhile, patient and careful Michael, stayed close in the shade of the boulder, adjusting the brim of my hat to keep the sun out of my face. His own face looked scalded by the heat and his lips had cracked – he was rubbing cream on them. Did I want some? Why not. He squeezed a dab of white onto the tip of my forefinger and as I lifted it to my mouth, I saw my mother bending towards the mirror on her dressing table in the time before the accident, puckering her own mouth as she stroked with the angled tip of her lipstick. There. She slid a Kleenex between her lips and pressed them together. Done. Then came a rattle of stones and

Sandy walloped back. He'd found the shepherd – just a boy about our age; he hadn't spoken any English but he knew what the word 'Brooke' meant. 'Brooke! Brooke!' he'd said, pointing inland. Sandy reckoned the grave was only five minutes away.

———

Originally Brooke's friends buried him in the parched ground of the olive grove, piled lava blocks into a rough sarcophagus shape, then planted a plain wooden cross inscribed with his name and rank. Later, when the war was over, the Anglo-Hellenic League arranged for something more permanent. A white marble sarcophagus surrounded by green railings, a squat square pillar at each corner, and the encircling inscription, which we solemnly translated from Greek into English: 'Here lies Rupert Brooke, who died for the delivery of Constantinople from the Turks.' We'd been expecting this – the biography had told us about it. But the thing itself was still astonishing. So violently out of place. So lumpenly English in the olive grove's nimble light. Embarrassing, really – especially when it came to the inscription.

I bowed my head and stared at the dust beneath my feet: these weren't the sort of thoughts I should be having; I wanted something more exalted. Brooke might not have been a great poet – there might, I dimly realised, even have been something slightly repellent about his personality, and the way his death had been manipulated to turn him into a hero. But he was the most eye-catching of the small number of poets I'd read, and coming to Skyros was an act of faith. It demonstrated a realignment in myself, and my loyalty to a creed that had nothing to do with parents or home or upbringing.

The dust stirred as my weight shifted, and the scent of thyme

8

drifted through my head. Then I looked up again. A column of red soldier ants was marching out from a crack at the head of the sarcophagus, each one carrying a wizened-looking load the size of a peppercorn and disappearing with it into the shade. We'd got here just in time. We were seeing the last of Rupert Brooke.

———

It was early evening and we expected to reach our camp under the fig tree by nightfall. But after tramping a couple of miles we saw a storm blowing in from the sea and changed our plans. One minute the sun was quietly unravelling in a tangle of purple clouds, the next it had erupted in a gigantic saffron fireball, the next there was darkness and strong wind rushing to meet us. We tacked towards the coast, where the ground was more broken and gouged, hoping to come across another dry streambed where we could shelter for the night. And we did find a place – a gulley between steep lava walls, which ended in a cliff overlooking the sea. The wind was even fiercer by this time, howling over the top of our camp, whipping the waves below us into whitecaps, and blowing dust in our eyes. But that was all right: we were explorers, and this was the kind of thing explorers had to put up with. Sandy opened his rucksack with a little cough of self-congratulation, showing us that he'd packed our primus, as well as a can of beans, a can-opener, and a spoon. We slapped him on the back, suddenly ravenous, as thunder clouds ruptured overhead. A single crack like a prophecy, then a pause, then two, three, four sky-swallowing booms. And rain. Fat separate globules to start with, but soon a downpour, and the bare streambed beneath us turning back into a stream. We gave up the idea of using the primus, scrambled to the side of the gulley where the ground was still dry, then opened the can and took turns to dredge up a spoonful before passing it on.

———

My father was a brewer and commuted every weekday to an office in London. But he had always thought of himself as a country man and lived for his weekends and country pleasures – until my mother's accident. Now he was first and foremost a hospital visitor, stopping at my mother's bedside for an hour every evening on his way back from the station, before continuing on towards home. As his headlights bloomed then died inside the garage beside the house, I came down from my bedroom and waited for him in the hall. My brother Kit, two and a half years younger than me, was already sitting on the bench in the shadows, but we didn't speak. We knew what happened next. We looked at each other and waited for the crunch of footsteps.

Five years earlier, when my parents had first moved into this house, which stood at the edge of a village near the Essex/ Suffolk border, my mother had asked for panes of glass to be put in the top panels of the door, because she thought this hallway was too dark. She must have imagined multicolours and warm gules on the carpet. What she got was plain see-through squares, their edges bevelled like a mirror. Those edges caught the sunlight sometimes and refracted it in rainbows, but mostly it was simple white and yellow that came through. And now the shadow of my father's head as he paused on the front step, shifting his briefcase from his right hand to his left. The briefcase that he opened once he'd come indoors and greeted us: always gently formal, never a kiss on the cheek but instead a pat on the shoulder. The briefcase from which he now gingerly lifted the plastic bag containing the nightie that he'd collected from my mother's bedside cupboard in the hospital. The same routine every day. Just as every day he next took the plastic bag through to the boot room where we kept the washing machine, and held his breath while he tossed the nightie into the drum, and slammed the door, and put in the powder, and switched on the machine, before breathing freely again and marching through to the kitchen, where he poured himself two inches of Scotch. No wonder he seemed withdrawn from us, as we padded along behind him. He was suffocating in his own sadness.

———

Sandy and Michael and I finished eating, still sheltering on the higher ground beside the stream of storm water, and tipped back our heads to watch the sky perform. The whole island was flinching under the lash of lightning. Stroke after juddering stroke, and each one flashing a jigsaw of thorn tufts and thyme bushes. Monster-rocks and smooth creaturely flanks. A few olive trees hunched over like beggars. And the sea leaping and wincing away to our left – throwing its waves into the air, sliding in oily-looking slabs, dragging its beach-stones together. The gravelly sound reminded me that Achilles had lived on Skyros before leaving for the war against Troy. The keel of his ship must have sounded like that when it scraped into the water and he sailed away. Tonight there was nothing like a ship, just broken pieces of lightning and a procession of pictures. Brooke's friends rowing back to their ship after the burial. My father at home in the empty house, one hand clamped round his whisky glass and the other clenched in his lap. My mother beneath the clock on the wall at the end of her ward, its finger trembling as it waited to start a new minute. Then the pictures disappeared, and a stronger gust plunged into our camp, snatching up the empty food can. I heard it clatter through the darkness, flying over the edge of the cliff and down onto the stony beach, where it gleamed into the sea and drowned.

––––––

When the storm blew itself out and the sky deepened again, we searched for a patch of dry ground, then lay down to sleep. I clasped my hands behind my head, climbing up through the emptiness, wandering among the constellations. I was thinking about islands. How Skyros was an island, and England was part of an island that was surrounded by other islands, and how living with that kind of separation, of isolation even, was like being inside a poem. Because poems like islands could easily be joined and considered under one heading but were also self-contained and distinct. They were way stations and destinations at the same time. Did that mean I could talk about sleeping in a poem, in the same way that I could say that I was sleeping on an island? My mind was losing its footing, closing down, but I kept going. Sleeping on this island tonight meant losing consciousness. Sleeping in a poem meant entering a different sort of wakefulness, where the mind had no particular orders but instead followed its instincts, free-floating from territory to territory, trying to complete things which felt unfinished in the world, things which . . . But that was as far as I could get before my eyes closed.

––––––

We were only away from England a few weeks, but when I got back it was home and not Greece that felt like a foreign country.

Travelling had shaken what used to be solid ground. Or not so much shaken it as turned everything back to front, so that what had once seemed fresh and natural now felt stifling and strange. My father's friends with their booming voices and red faces and seething complaints about boys who looked like girls, and girls who looked like boys, and music that wasn't music: all these men had been through the war, and although they never talked about it, the shadow of battles fell across everything. Battles they'd won while still wearing uniform, and now were losing in the peace. It made them irritable and worse. I thought of my father's friend Anthony Round, a farmer who lived half an hour towards the coast; when we were visiting him and his family for lunch one Sunday, he'd suddenly jumped up from the table, fetched his twelve-bore from next door, opened the window, and shot a cat that was sunning itself in the yard outside. For no reason except that it was there. I wanted nothing to do with people like that. I retreated to my bedroom and shut the door, stalling and stewing while I waited for time to pass and the future to arrive.

———

'You need to take more exercise,' my father told me. 'You're liverish,' and every afternoon I stamped across the field outside the house and disappeared into the Ashground, where I moped and smoked and wrote in my notebook beneath the trees. It wasn't enough. Apparently I was still liverish. So I revived a routine I'd begun with my mother, and did the weekly food shop in Coggeshall, which was our nearest country town. In the old days I'd gone round to the butcher and baker and candlestick maker while my mother sat with Leslie, who cut and permed her hair. Now I visited Leslie alone, chatting to him for a minute or two between his appointments. We didn't have much to say to each other, but I enjoyed knowing that our friendship puzzled my father, and Leslie liked to hear how my mother was doing in hospital.

One day Leslie introduced me to his friend Mr Anderson: he thought I'd be interested in meeting him because Mr Anderson had just published a book. It was called *Foxed!* and was about a fox cub, which I thought was a pity, like the exclamation mark in the title. But never mind, Mr Anderson was the first proper writer I'd met, and he certainly looked the part: loose and gangling and sad, with long grey hair and a lean face. He asked me to come over to his house for tea, so that we could get to know each other better.

The life of the mind! This was more like it, I thought, especially when it turned out that Mr Anderson's house was really a cottage in the middle of a wood, where he lived with his friend Alex – it made them seem like characters in a story. When I arrived, Alex was lying on a sofa in front of the fire and lifted his hand as though he expected me to kiss it. When I didn't, he giggled. 'Poor baby,' said Mr Anderson, rattling down a tray of cups and saucers, and I wasn't sure which of us he meant, me or Alex. Then he started talking about his book. He'd found the fox cub while out walking, he said; it had somehow got separated from its mother and looked very mangey, so he'd decided to raise it himself. Things had gone well to start with: the cub drank milk from a bowl and took pieces of chicken from his fingers. But gradually it grew more and more difficult to control – it was a wild animal after all, and didn't understand that he was only trying to help. Eventually it ran away. Then the local hunt held one of their meets nearby, and Mr Anderson thought the hounds had probably eaten it. Like they'd also eaten the mother.

We drank our cups of tea and listened to the fire crackling, and after a while Alex changed the subject; he told us about his life as a dancer, and how one day he'd broken his foot, which was why he now spent most of the time lying down. I thought Mr Anderson might say 'Poor baby' again, but he didn't; he offered me a glass of wine and asked me to stay for supper.

I said my father was waiting for me and I had to get home, and Mr Anderson looked disappointed. 'Another day,' he said, and gave me a copy of his book as I stood up to leave. I thanked him and said I'd come back next week, but when I told my father where I'd been, he said he didn't like the sound of Mr Anderson, and that was the end of that. I never saw Mr Anderson again. But I never forgot the way he said 'Poor baby', or how the trees seemed to bend closer to the cottage while we talked, until they were scratching at the windows, or the faint purring sound when Alex ran his fingers through the fringe of his white scarf, talking about how his life with Mr Anderson used to be illegal but wasn't any more because the law had changed. Their fox might have disappeared, and they were both melancholy in their way, but deep down they also seemed like the most contented people I'd met for a long time.

———

When I saw the red spine of *Foxed!* shining on the shelf in my bedroom, it made me want to write a book myself. But what would it be about? The wish to say something seemed to have come before I knew which words I wanted to use, or what their subject might be. Although of course the answer was obvious: the only original thing in my life, the calamity that set me apart from everyone else, was my mother's accident. But I wasn't sure

I wanted to write about that, because I didn't want people to take pity on me, and didn't know how to connect it with the rest of life. Death had set my mother apart, stored her somewhere it could keep her constantly in view, and we didn't even have a name for this place. It wasn't still 'the accident' – that was over, if not done with. And it wasn't 'sickness' or 'illness' – they implied she had a disease, which wasn't true. Perhaps 'limbo' was the word? But even that didn't feel entirely right; it carried a whiff of religion – of dead souls waiting for judgement – and my mother wasn't a dead soul – not yet, anyway – and she certainly didn't deserve to be judged in that way.

The words tumbled round, and eventually it occurred to me that I might be able to settle them down if I wrote about death more generally. That way, I thought, I might see how it was actually a part of life, and not simply an explosion of life or the end of life. So I made a list of all the people I knew who'd already died, beginning with my great-grandmother Jessie. How small she'd looked when my mother drove me over to her house years ago to say goodbye – like a wizened child who'd got lost and collapsed in the enormous snowfield of her bed. And how like a painting everything was, in that room with the curtains drawn against the sun, and her white lace cap lopsided on her head, and her sharp little mousy fingernails scratching the palm of my hand.

Then Louise Oliphant, who sat next to me at primary school and was killed in a skiing accident, only I didn't hear about that until much later, so imagined she must be alive and living alongside me when all the time she was nowhere. Louise was a girl and therefore as rare in my early life as spice, but that wasn't the only reason I remembered her so well. It was also because she'd peed on the floor one day while still sitting at her desk in our classroom. That in itself wasn't remarkable: accidents of that sort happened now and then. What was surprising, to me at any rate, was that when I saw the flood creeping towards my sandals I wasn't in the least disgusted, but only wanted to kneel down beside her and hold her tight.

Then William Brooks at my next school, who had cancer; as a memento, his parents had given my English teacher a book their son had hollowed out to make a hiding place for a radio, radios being illegal. When my teacher showed it to me, he had tears in his eyes – the only time I saw him at a loss.

Then Mr Catchpole the maths master, with his bad skin and weird lunging walk: an unhappy man obviously, who fell in love with a boy he used to take golfing. Nobody knew exactly what happened next, but when the summer term ended Mr Catchpole went to his room on the top floor of the building where the unmarried masters lived, and killed himself. Nobody found him until nearly two months later and the autumn term had begun; nobody had missed him.

Then Major Gosling with his purple face and salt-and-pepper moustache, who was my father's commanding officer when their regiment landed in Normandy on D-Day. He was the man who got angry when my father drove his half-track off the landing craft onto the beach through three feet of water, then opened the lid of the vehicle and stood up while there were bullets still flying everywhere. 'Captain Motion!' the major had yelled. 'Do you want your bloody head shot off?' My father had turned around quite calmly and said that he was changing his trousers; if he was going to die, he wanted to be wearing dry trousers. Twenty-odd years later Major Gosling was the one shot – by accident apparently, when he climbed through a fence without checking the safety catch on his gun: the trigger snagged on a bramble. Well yes, my mother said, when my father told me that. Well yes.

———

Back at school, Sandy and Michael and I gave a talk about our trip to Skyros; we all wanted to boast about our adventures, and I wanted to advertise my new loyalties, and let people know that I had a new identity. My English teacher Peter Way, who had organised the event, and knew that I was now writing poems as well as reading them outside the classroom, asked the school's headmaster to come and listen: Denis Silk. According to my father, Silk's predecessor had been a lounge lizard, but Silk himself was definitely human, always frowning to make sure that everyone knew he was concentrating, then speaking slowly and urgently, as if each word were a seed that had to be pressed into our brains. When our talk about Skyros ended, he kept me behind and told me that although he was a head-master, and headmasters were supposed to be interested in rules and nothing else, he was actually very keen on poetry, war poetry in particular, and back in the day he'd known Siegfried Sassoon. They'd met playing cricket, apparently, and when Sassoon was an old man, and his doctor wouldn't let him drive any more, Silk had sometimes chauffeured him around. A Humber Snipe. The leafy lanes of Wiltshire. And not only that. Through Sassoon, Silk had also got to know Geoffrey Keynes, the younger brother of Maynard.

I could hardly believe what I was hearing. What little I already knew about writers had given me the idea that all the seriously good ones (the ones who didn't write books about foxes) were either long dead or somehow not a part of ordinary life. But here was someone who'd done the most humdrum thing – drive a car! – with a famous poet sitting beside him in the passenger seat. I looked down at Silk's hand, a large and meaty paw, well made for taking a difficult catch in the outfield, and thought how it must have shaken Sassoon's hand. If I shook it too, would something of Sassoon be passed on to me? A ridiculous idea, obviously, but it connected with something I'd begun to think about while I was standing beside Brooke's grave. The idea that as I turned towards poetry, and away from the life I'd inherited from my father, I was entering a world where time worked differently. Where living and dead people could communicate in an endless flow, and there was no clear boundary between real things and imagined things. Geoffrey, I knew, already lived in this somewhere. He'd been to school and university with Brooke, they'd been best friends, and ever since Brooke died, Geoffrey had been his literary executor. He was in his late seventies now and living in a village the other side of Cambridge. Perhaps if I could meet him, he'd be able to lead me further in the direction I wanted to go? Not that I said as much to Silk, and not that I had to. He gave one of his most earnest frowns, and suggested we drive over for lunch one weekend; it was time he saw old Geoffrey again, and the story of our Skyros adventure was bound to go down well.

―――――

As Silk's car began the journey east towards Geoffrey's house, I leaned my head against the window and let the vibration of the wheels fizz through me, reminding me that I was made of atoms. It was like star-gazing at our camp under the fig tree in Greece. I might fly into pieces at any moment. I might vanish altogether.

Then the front door of Lammas House swung open, and my head-photo of young Geoffrey suddenly warmed into life, coloured in, and creased into old age: thin white hair, bristly grey moustache, gaunt sun-browned face, slightly hunched back, and a bony hand with a heavy antique ring on the little finger, clasping my own hand. This wasn't poetry any more. This was flesh and blood. And alarming as well as marvellous, because although Geoffrey seemed pleased to see us, smiling, then lifting his hand to wipe his mouth, he also looked fierce. Like a sparrowhawk, I thought at first, then changed my mind. More like a thrush when it bounces across a lawn with its head tilted to one side, listening to what's happening underground before stabbing down with its beak and eating.

A collector.

Silk was a collector too – Staffordshire pottery: we'd stopped at an antiques place on the way over, and he'd bought a figure of W. G. Grace. But according to Silk this was nothing compared to Geoffrey: Geoffrey was a one-man museum. It meant I expected his house to be huge, but now that we were stepping inside, I could see that it was a family home – with no family in it any more. Three bedrooms upstairs at a guess, and everything downstairs small-scale except the dining room, which was two rooms knocked together. But Silk was right, there really were pictures everywhere – everywhere – including here in the hall, where Geoffrey was already pointing things out, grinning and sometimes spitting a little, as though he was seeing them for the first time and could hardly contain his excitement: William Blake's *Canterbury Pilgrims*, Stanley Spencer's *Coronation Cockatoo* and *John Donne Arriving in Heaven*, where Donne looked like a bat flying up through a trapdoor into an empty green field.

Geoffrey saw me gazing around and took this as a cue to

keep going, plunging further into the house and pointing busily to left and right. Here was a painting of Stonehenge by John Constable; here were William Cowper's pet hares Tiny and Puss, stitched in silk thread by Blake's wife Catherine; here were dozens of other Blake drawings, paintings, prints, and sketches, including *The Ghost of a Flea*, hanging in the breakfast room, where Geoffrey could keep an eye on it while he ate his porridge. Here was J. B. Pyne's *View of Old Exeter*, which Sassoon had written a poem about (a poem I could quote from, and did, nodding towards the 'clouds like safe investments floating by'). And here were books. Books in bedrooms, books along passageways, books in the bathroom (as long as they were paperbacks), books in the dining room, but mostly books in Geoffrey's study. Glass-fronted cases there because everything was rare and precious; the shelves were double-stacked.

'What would you like to see?'

I aimed as high as I knew, at my favourite of all poets: 'Keats.' And there they were: the 1816 *Poems*, and *Endymion*, and the book with the odes in it, all first editions.

I went again. 'Donne.' This time it was two copies, both first editions, and one perfect but the other with eighteenth-century scribbles inside it. 'Dull dull dull,' it said on one page, in rusty brown ink; and on another, 'Dr Donne is a dull ass.' Geoffrey snapped the book shut and laughed, then wiped his hand over his lips again. I realised he must have false teeth and they didn't fit very well; he had to keep checking they weren't falling out.

———

I turned aside for a moment and looked out of the window, thinking about the dead who had already sunk into the underworld, and the thousands of leaf-shadows flickering as they waited to be ferried across the River Styx. Then I turned back and ran my eye along the dark spines on Geoffrey's book-shelves, watching his hand swoop to pluck another and then another soul from the pit, before passing it over for me to admire. When I opened a page, the ancient black words looked so delicate on the whiteness, their survival felt like a miracle. How could something so nearly non-existent have made such lifelong demands on Geoffrey? And would they ask the same questions of me? If I gave my life to writing, would I always be in thrall, or would I be in charge? Geoffrey might not be a poet himself, but as the friend of poets – of every kind of writer – I thought he was bound to know the answers, and help me to open the door that separated my present existence from the future I could still see only in glimpses and glances. And if this guidance came in the form of friendship, so much the better. It would make ambition seem an intimate and deeply felt thing, not merely self-assertion, or cold-eyed calculation. At the same time, it helped me to manage my rapidly developing sense of privilege, and the guilt that it produced. Although I was reject-ing or modifying the life that my parents had imagined for me, and although I knew that my mother's accident was the tragic opposite of good luck, I also realised that my background and schooling made me exceptionally fortunate. I felt that by re-focusing this fortune and transforming it into friendship – with Geoffrey now, and perhaps with other mentor figures in the future – I was doing something to earn it. In ways that hadn't previously seemed possible, I was beginning to make my life my own, and take responsibility for it.

Geoffrey's wife Margaret was the sister of Gwen Raverat, which meant that she was a Darwin and a Wedgwood combined. Geoffrey wanted me to know that, and told me as he introduced us, but Margaret only smiled and shrugged. She looked like Mrs Tiggywinkle, with her grey hair in a bun, her soft round face, and her glasses twinkling in the depths of her sitting room across the hall from Geoffrey's study. Always rustling her papers and keeping things simple. Bloomsbury-simple, as I understood it. No central heating in her room and none in the rest of the house either. Bare boards and threadbare rugs everywhere, worn-through lino in the kitchen, and a small bilious Aga. Plain living and plain food. Even today, Sunday, now that we were sitting down to eat. Geoffrey was hacking lumps off a leg of lamb with a carving knife that looked as though he'd sharpened it every day of his life – the blade was thin and tarnished as a strip of burned paper. Geoffrey the doctor who'd been given his knighthood for surgery. Geoffrey stabbing with his glance and chopping with his impatient hands. The ghost of a flea hovering in the room behind him, with its mincing gait and devilish sideways glance.

—————

It didn't matter that Geoffrey was sixty years older than me – it just proved what I'd been saying about how time worked differently for people who cared about poems – and after that first visit, I stayed with him for a part of every school holiday; Lammas was only an hour's drive from my father's house. It was a strange friendship, though, and not only because of the quizzical looks that other people sometimes threw in our direction, when they thought about the difference between our ages. I liked books (or not) because of what was in them, and

Geoffrey liked books if they were rare. Although he did read a lot too, and not just old dead people. The first time I went to Lammas alone, I found Seamus Heaney's collection *Death of a Naturalist* lying on Geoffrey's desk. I'd already read it, and for once felt that I could surprise Geoffrey, not the other way around, because I'd recently met Heaney. Ted Hughes, too. I'd gone to London before Christmas to hear them both reading poems by Wordsworth. It was a kind of dare, like the trek to Brooke's grave, though on a smaller scale: I'd scarcely been to London before, except to see doctors and dentists, and I'd never been to a poetry reading. But I'd joined the Poetry Society, and they put on a Wordsworth evening at their headquarters in Earl's Court, because there was some kind of anniversary.

An upstairs room with a dozen people in the audience and a lot of empty chairs; I sat to one side, feeling embarrassed and half wishing that I hadn't come – until the reading began. Then Heaney read too fast and quietly for me to understand everything he was saying, but that didn't matter because his accent made up for it – the way it turned his words into a mixture of song and talk. And as for Hughes: his gleaming jaguar voice pounced on the words and shook them almost to death. 'She was an elfin pinnace; lustily/ I dipped my oars into the silent Lake,/ And as I rose upon the stroke, my Boat/ Went heaving through the water, like a Swan.' The surge of the water almost lifted me out of my seat.

When it was over, I went up to the podium, where the two of them were sitting at a little table, and asked if they'd sign copies of their books, which I'd brought with me: *Door into the Dark* and *Lupercal*. As they did this, I remembered looking at Silk's hand and thinking how it had shaken Sassoon's hand, and then at Geoffrey's hand while thinking how it had touched

Rupert Brooke. Now I watched Heaney's hand and Hughes's hand as they wrote their names in my books. Exaltation again. Rarefication. But ordinary and explicable as well. Heaney was wearing a nice heathery tweed suit that looked brand new – had he bought it specially to come to London? Hughes was much scruffier and had a razor cut on his chin, so he obviously hadn't shaved very carefully; he'd even missed a bit on one cheek. It didn't stop him being a kind of wizard, though. After they'd finished with me and I'd retreated to my chair, I watched other people in the audience take up their books for signing. Some of them, the women especially, actually seemed to curl up against Hughes while he wrote their names above his own. Did poetry always have this effect? Heaney had a little mob swarming around him, too, although the attention seemed to make him uncomfortable: he was smiling but leaning backwards, as if he wanted to avoid the heat of a fire.

---

Every time I went to Lammas, Geoffrey and I made a ritual of walking at some point through the gate at the end of the garden, where a track led across the corner of a field and ended in a clump of balsam poplars that Geoffrey had planted when he first came to live here years ago. Now the saplings were full-grown trees, and on summer evenings they released a delicious sweet scent that seeped across the country roundabout, and even reached into the house. Standing under their canopy, watching the sun flicker pale green and yellow, I felt the richness of Geoffrey's life even more powerfully than I did in his library. Beauty came towards him everywhere, or he tracked it down everywhere – even, as it turned out, in the little triangle of land I'd just walked across,

between the gate and these trees. Geoffrey told me that whenever the farmer went round with his plough in the autumn, he
followed it looking for flint arrowheads among the furrows,
and those he found he kept in a saucer on his desk: shiny black
leaves with their facets catching the light. Now, as we walked
back to the house for tea, we searched again but found nothing.
'Never mind,' said Geoffrey, with his dry barking laugh, 'they're
here somewhere,' then took me by the arm and pulled me closer,
kissing me. Darting, dry kisses, tight-lipped, with his moustache
prickling. I didn't say anything. I couldn't decide whether I liked
it, but I certainly didn't mind. Next morning, Geoffrey came into
my bedroom early with a cup of tea slopping in one hand, and
with his other hand he pulled down the bedclothes to look at me.
Not touching, just looking. Then he tugged the curtains open
and left me to drink my tea.

———

Another time Geoffrey announced at breakfast that we were
going to drive to Lavenham, half an hour away, because there
was someone he wanted me to meet. 'Who's that?' I asked,
but he wouldn't tell me; it was a surprise. Off we went from
Cambridgeshire into Suffolk, with Geoffrey revving and grinding as though his car was the only one allowed to use the roads
and there was no danger of us meeting anyone else coming the
other way. When we reached Lavenham we stopped to look at
the church, a masterpiece made of flint and light, then zoomed
on downhill again and swerved into the yard of an old mill house.
Here Geoffrey turned off the engine and faced towards me: had
I worked out who lived here yet? No, I hadn't, and I didn't like
it when he kept me in the dark; it made me feel stupid. Bright

white clapboard, larch trees bending overhead, and the murmur of a stream somewhere in the background. I still had no idea. And no idea again when we stepped indoors. These red-brick floors and damp walls – they gave nothing away, and neither did the woman with a strangely smooth face who suddenly appeared out of nowhere and pulled Geoffrey aside, whispering in his ear. I couldn't catch what they were saying but got the gist: we mustn't stay for long. Geoffrey nodded and led me through the hallway past an open kitchen door, then down some treacherous steps into a pantry: I saw shelves loaded with jam jars, a ham under a fly-guard like a fencing visor, and a shaft of sunlight boiling with dust. Dust that made me think the mill wheel must still be grinding away upstairs, spewing out chaff.

'This is Edmund Blunden,' Geoffrey said, pointing through the light-beam into a corner filled with shadows. Edmund Blunden? I knew he'd survived the war, I'd read his poems and his autobiography, but it had never crossed my mind that he might still be alive. Alive after a fashion, anyway: I saw a wild flushed face twisting out of the darkness – white hair, panicking eyes, skin tortured with blood vessels, mouth aghast – and stepped forward. Blunden's eyes narrowed. 'Who are you?' he said in a strangled shout, and I told him, holding out my right hand. Slowly he lifted his own hand, and the tips of his fingers were cold against my palm. Then the ruined face swivelled away, the shadows darkened again, and I followed Geoffrey back up the steps past the kitchen and outside into the light.

———

Geoffrey wanted me to apply to university in Cambridge, because Cambridge was close to Lammas and we'd be able to see each other every weekend. But my English teacher at school, Peter Way, had other ideas and told me to apply to Oxford instead – he'd been there himself and thought the English course would suit me better: it meant beginning at the beginning with the Anglo-Saxons, then going straight through to the Second World War and stopping. The complete story, just like that. Geoffrey was miffed but not seriously, and a few weeks before leaving home to begin my first term I went to stay with him again, coinciding with the annual village fete. It was all low-key and traditional: a lopsided tent where the publican's wife dressed up as a gypsy and read fortunes, a game of Smack the Rat, and in the centre of the village green a large marquee that even at a distance smelled thickly of roses and wet canvas.

As I followed him into the gloom of the tent, it suddenly occurred to me to ask, 'What did Rupert Brooke look like?' I don't understand what possessed me – it felt as though someone else had put the words into my mind – because I already knew perfectly well what Brooke looked like; I'd stared at photographs of him for years and had them off by heart. Besides, my timing was off: Geoffrey was distracted by the vegetable competition, hunching over the displays of carrots and onions to see if his own entries had won anything: he was always competitive, even about the little things.

Then out of nowhere Brooke sauntered up to us, brushed against Geoffrey's shoulder, and smiled directly into our faces, before lounging through the flap and disappearing. Six feet one and a half inches tall ('the same height as Christ'), floppy fair hair, loose-limbed, rosy skin, glancing approvingly to left and right. Geoffrey turned around and watched him go. 'He looked like that,' he said, giving a chuckle of disbelief. 'Exactly like that.'

# Part Two

---

## 1970–1976

A pattern was beginning to appear, like the beginning of a story. But to call it a story felt wrong. How could there be a story, when there was no reliable way of connecting one thing with the next? Life was random, wasn't it, a series of accidents? I wasn't sure. One minute it seemed so, and the next it felt as though an idea of structure emerged from events, or imposed itself on them, whether I liked it or not. Take poetry, for instance. I'd begun writing because it was a place to be private, because it helped me to deepen what I was feeling (and sometimes to understand myself better), and because it was about as unlike my father's world as anything I could imagine. Then my English teacher read what I'd done and encouraged me to keep going. Then I began reading more seriously and got my crush on Rupert Brooke – which led to Skyros, which led to Geoffrey, which led to yet more encouragement, which had now brought me to the point of leaving home for university, where no one in my father's family had been before. That all created a sort of pattern, didn't it? That sounded like the beginning of a story?

As a child I'd thought time must be like a broken mirror, because I could see my face – my idea of myself – flashing back at me from this piece or that piece of life, but otherwise disappearing in the cracks between each fragment. Now the pieces seemed to be better connected than I'd imagined, but I still felt that I was looking at reflections, never seeing the whole picture, never living inside the mirror. Was this something I'd inherited, or was it just me? There was no point asking my father, he'd only harrumph – it was too personal. And I couldn't ask my mother because she was still floating in her unconsciousness, not speaking. Which meant there was all the more reason for me to hurry up and leave home, and meet the sort of people who were supposed to be interested in questions like this.

Before that happened, I had another idea about stories. About my mother's story, in particular. When I thought of her life purely in terms of events, it contained not much before the accident: a quiet childhood in Beaconsfield as the daughter of a GP; a dim school and no chance of university (because she was a girl); a quick trip to South Africa to 'see the world'; a part-time job working as a typist in Pinewood Studios; then marriage to my father when she was twenty-three, two boys in quick succession, and a housebound life as a housewife, punctuated by illnesses of one kind and another. All insignificant in the great scheme of things, but all precious and fascinating to me because they were the facts of her life. Because they were her story.

Then came the accident, which looked at from one angle marked the end of her story but was really the beginning of another. Although this second story was different. It was a collection of moments in which time never moved to a steady beat with a steady step, but lurched, veered, stopped, started again, wandered. So who was to say what constituted a story and what didn't, and who was to decide on the true scale and importance of things? Did education, travel, love, and family matter more than shock, pain, disappointment, and grief? Or did I have to think differently about what had meaning in life and what didn't? Either everything was a story, or nothing was: it all depended on how I looked at the world. And on whether

I trusted facts – because facts could be fickle, as my mother also proved.

In the days immediately after her accident, my father and Kit and I had scrambled to find out what exactly had brought it about – but because no one had seen her fall, there were no completely reliable witnesses. The consensus was, she'd been riding her pony Serenade through a wood, the pony had stumbled as she came out into a field, she'd flopped forward but clung on to the pommel of the saddle, the rotation of the pony's shoulder-bone had knocked off her hard hat, and when she eventually let go of the saddle she landed on a cement track; the blow knocked her out, cracked her skull, and produced a blood clot on her brain which the doctors later removed; now she was in a coma.

It helped to know this sequence of events. We could imagine the scene, understand the connections between cause and effect, and gradually learned how to compress the story into a shape that made it repeatable. We found ways to live with it. But a while later, after I'd published an account of the accident somewhere, a man called Paul Smith wrote to me out of the blue saying that I'd got it wrong. My mother had been riding near a big house where he worked as a gamekeeper, and he'd seen it all. In the old days, there'd been a ha-ha dividing this house and its garden from the surrounding fields, and although this ha-ha had been filled in long ago, it had left a dip in the ground which was often lined with shadows. When Serenade had seen these shadows, she'd been spooked, reared up, and caught my mother off guard. My mother had tumbled backwards out of her saddle, and as she fell Serenade had instinctively kicked out, clipping my mother on the side of her head with the edge of her metal shoe. Smith said that he'd run forward and knelt

33

down beside her in the grass, but she was out cold, with blood dribbling from her ear; he'd raised the alarm and waited with her while someone else rang for an ambulance, and half an hour later she was taken away to hospital.

If this story was true, and I believed it was, did it matter that I now had to revise the version I'd been living with? In one sense it made no difference to anything, because the outcome was still the same: my mother was in hospital and unconscious. But in other ways it changed everything – not just the details of the setting, but the associations and the forces those details suggested. A big house and its surroundings instead of a wild wood. Less risk and more simple bad luck. A tumble with someone watching instead of a fall in solitude. But what did these differences amount to? I didn't know how to decide. Stories mattered and they didn't matter. They seemed coherent, but really they were shadows flickering in the grass.

It crossed my mind that I might be reluctant to think of lives as stories, because the story I knew better than any other, which was the story of my mother's present, was only going to end one way. In other words, the chain of events implied by the word 'story', which was also the organising principle in all the novels I'd read (admittedly not many), was bound to form a sequence that ended in death. Poems, on the other hand, which weren't so keen on telling tales in a consecutive way, were a means of confirming but also of weakening that connection. They were a way of accepting the inevitable, but also of arresting time or stepping outside time.

This paradox felt valuable because it was like my experience

of time itself. Which is to say: now that my childhood was end-
ing – was already over, perhaps – parts of it were hardening into
pictures that refused to fade. Sometimes these pictures troubled
me because I thought they were equivalent to the songs of the
Sirens and would lure me back to the past when it was the
future I wanted. More often they seemed like visions: things
that I had seen with my heart and not just my eyes – often very
small-seeming, very modest, very humdrum things, but marvellous nonetheless. Spots of time. A glimpse of the scullery
next to the kitchen in our old house, for instance, where years
ago my mother had washed sheets in the sink on laundry day,
then fed them through the mangle before scooping them up
in a kind of hug and taking them outside to hang on the line
by the greenhouse. Her hands were mottled with cold, and the
wet ghost of the sheets made an impression on the front of her
housecoat. After she'd gone out, the cracked wooden lips of the
mangle grinned at me with their idiotic bubbles.

Or the coal man presenting his sooty face outside the kitchen
window, touching his grimy cap to my mother and giving her
a thumbs up. Then the coal man opening the flap of the cellar,
heaving the sacks against his chest one by one, gripping them
by the corners to empty them, and nearly but not quite disappearing as the coal-lumps rumbled downwards into the dark,
leaving a wisp of slack that fled across the yard like a genie
escaping its bottle.

Or the trampled mud near the cattle trough in the far corner of the field adjacent to the house, where the top one or two
inches of water always froze solid in the winter, which meant
the cows couldn't drink from it. When I went to sort it out,
waving away the drooling mouths and coils of steamy breath,
I chipped round the edges of the ice because I wanted to take

it out in a single sheet, like the glass for a window-frame, then hold it up to the sun. But even when I managed that, it was impossible to see through; there were too many bubbles and ridges. I ended up chucking the ice sheet down onto the mud and watching it smash, which made the cattle buck and snort and shimmy away, then cautiously come back for a closer look, still breathing hard through their shiny noses.

Or the knife-grinder who once every autumn parked his bike on the tarmac outside the front door, propping its wheels off the ground so that the bike stood still while he turned the pedals to spin the sharpening device, which even though it was made of stone was called a steel. When the steel touched the knife-blades and made a dry scraping sound, the spark-trail fanned across my hand like mosquito bites.

Or my mother herself on her high bed; there was no oxygen mask any more, but other tubes still snaked into her body under the bedclothes, and the hole in her throat was held open by an industrial-looking white plastic washer. Sallow skin, sugary sweat, clamminess. A whiff of blocked drains. She'd turned into Sleeping Beauty and was waiting for the Prince to hack through the brambles and wake her with a kiss. Sleeping Beauty who'd been adrift for almost three years now, never speaking, but was still capable of giving those occasional little eye-tremors and hand-twitches to show that one day she might.

———

As soon as I'd become a reader, I imagined becoming a writer – and now that I was leaving school, I began to follow the scent of printer's ink. Geoffrey egged me on – everyone he knew had published something or other, so why not me too? And ambition played its part: if I was going to write at all, I wanted other people to read what I had to say, and hoped they'd recognise their feelings in my own. Recognise them, but also keep their distance. Poems, I thought, were a way of being sociable while remaining at one remove – and given my preferred ways of behaving, that mixture suited me very well. It also made it seem appropriate – and funny – that one of the magazines I subscribed to, which was called *Workshop*, was edited by a man whose name was Norman Hidden. Norman was kind to me, accepting the first poem I sent him, inviting me to submit more, offering to publish a little chapbook, then – as I left school and began my gap year – asking me to give a reading. My first reading! – upstairs in a pub off Oxford Street in London, playing second fiddle to the novelist B. S. Johnson, who was a friend of Norman's and had just published his loose-leaf 'book in a box' called *The Unfortunates*.

I mentioned all this to my father, thinking that he'd be proud of me, but he only looked bewildered. This wasn't surprising; my father was often bewildered these days – confused by life in general, and exhausted by his daily hospital visits, his commute to London, and the burden of managing things at home. To make life easier for himself, he'd decided to look for a housekeeper and, after scanning advertisements in the back pages of *The Lady*, had hired a brightly depressed divorcee: Patricia. But Patricia had soon left – she got fed up with working alone for hours on end – and then so did the second person he took on, and the third, and the fourth. Now an old family friend had come to look after him: Este. She was a loud, energetic, country-glamorous person who was much bouncier than my father, but they seemed to be getting along well. 'A poetry reading?' said Este, as I told her about Norman's plans while we were chatting around the fireplace in the sitting room at home. 'We'll come and hear you, won't we, Richard?' My father frowned and crossed his legs. 'Of course,' he said.

———

I arrived at the pub early, took one look at B. S. Johnson, and wanted to run away. Four-square and burly, with a well-managed quiff of dark hair and an expression that combined zeal with disdain, he looked to me like a clever version of Ronnie Kray, the bulkier of the notorious criminal twins. But the way he welcomed me was so gracious, and so tactfully engi-neered to suggest that we were equals under the spotlight, that I soon changed my mind – at least until we looked between the curtains at the back of the little stage, and saw in the audi-torium that only a handful of people had turned up. Then my nerves came surging back and changed into dread; all the jokes I'd prepared during the last few weeks (weeks, not days), all the links and asides which were meant to be charming in their self-deprecation, evaporated in an instant. Worst of all, my father and Este were sitting exactly in front of where I was due to stand and deliver, Este looking windswept and red in the face, my father with his thumbs tucked into his fists and his legs once again tightly crossed.

I stepped forward as though I expected to be burned at a stake and began reading so quietly that a voice kept calling out from the shadows, complaining that I was inaudible. It made me feel angry with myself, but at the same time it didn't matter. I no longer cared whether anyone could hear what I was saying; I just wanted the whole evening over and done with. Although Este at least seemed to feel otherwise. Whenever I got to the end of a poem, and also whenever she thought I'd got to the end of a poem, she clapped very loudly, then threw her head back as though she was about to shout something. Tally-ho, for instance. I dared not look at my father.

After a thousand years I finished and went to sit down beside them, so that we could listen to B. S. Johnson, who now that he was on stage had somehow concentrated into an even more compelling version of himself. That seemed like a lesson I should take to heart. As I also took to heart his self-confidence when he finished his reading, closed his box of loose pages, and picked up a large canvas bag containing copies of his books, which he was determined to sell. Out of courtesy, I think, he first approached the three of us, asking my father whether he'd like to buy a copy. I looked away. B. S. Johnson wasn't to know that my father had read only half a book in his life – a thriller by Hammond Innes called *The Lonely Skier*, which obviously hadn't been thrilling enough to hold his attention until the end. Still, B. S. Johnson didn't seem to mind when my father briskly told him no thank you. 'Nice chap,' my father muttered on the pavement outside, when we had said our goodbyes, then turned around and a taxi appeared just like that, ready to whisk him and Este away to the hotel where they were spending the night. He suddenly looked very dapper with his shining black hair and dark suit and paisley tie, opening the door for Este, then sliding in beside her. Really, I thought, my father could have been fun, if only life had been kinder to him.

---

I met Joanna halfway through my gap year between school and university: beautiful freckled high-cheekboned face, loose brown hair, Biba warpaint, ankle-length green corduroy coat, and a knuckleduster of finger-rings. But I had to wait. She'd already been at Oxford for a year, was obviously more interested in theatre than anything else, and now was going to live in Cambridge for the summer, rehearsing a production of *Julius Caesar*. I was about to disappear too, travelling to Turkey this time, and we arranged to meet again when I got back.

My mother opened her eyes: it was almost exactly three years since the accident. There was no prince with a magic kiss, no miracle drug, and no sudden life-changing word in her ear; just a nurse checking in as usual and finding that instead of dozing my mother was staring at the ceiling. Almost at once she started to speak, too – rootling in her skull, finding a voice in the muck and blood, and trying it out. It wasn't her old voice but a strange deep rasp, and for a while nobody could understand what she was saying. Then the doctors closed the hole in her throat, and the sounds became more familiar, and gradually turned into words.

My father rang to tell me all this: Joanna and I were living together in Oxford by now, in a flat in St John Street that was owned by a woman who claimed to be the exiled Queen of France, and next day I caught the train down to London, then back out to Essex again. My brother Kit was already there, sitting beside my mother's bed and holding her hand, but when he saw me coming into the ward he stood up and made way. I told him to stay put and pulled up a second chair, then leaned forward and whispered hello, hardly daring to look. Our mother's eyes were sunk very deep in her head, and seemed full and empty at the same time, like the eyes of a cat. Like a creature that had stared for a long time beyond the edge of life, and now couldn't refocus on life itself. But we kept looking. And kept looking. And something slowly changed – a small bright pinprick appeared in the depths of her pupils, then expanded as it came closer. I turned to my brother, wondering what he thought. Would the whole of our mother come back to us? Would she remember how to love us? Would she even remember who we were? Of course, Kit said, and he was right. A moment later her hand opened a little, and she called us by our names.

———

Kit had been born almost three years after me, and in the late stages of this second pregnancy my mother had fallen ill with brucellosis and spent almost a year in hospital; Kit and I were then looked after by Ruby, my grandmother's companion, who many years previously had been my mother's nanny. Although I had no conscious memory of this disruption, hearing about it later had made me suppose that I must have resented my brother to start with, blaming him for my mother's illness and departure. Why else were my earliest recollections of him so often stained by jealousy, or the guilty realisation that I'd been unkind to him? I remembered in particular a party for my sixth birthday, when my friend Adam – the son of a neighbour – had come round to play at our house; in the course of our ragging and rollicking Kit had hurt his shoulder. He was still complaining about it in the evening after Adam had gone home, sitting in his high chair and crying. But nobody suspected there was anything seriously wrong. Next morning, when he was still crying, my mother at last took him to the doctor, who sent him for an X-ray. He'd broken his arm.

Later, when Kit and I were sent away to boarding school, I took better care of him. But even as a teenager, I still felt that we had to compete for our mother's affection. Our mother was interested in poetry and painting, even if she'd never had much chance to prove it, and this made them even more attractive to me: becoming interested in them myself was a way of drawing closer to her. Kit, on the other hand, enjoyed the country pursuits that appealed to my father. Soon after I started at Oxford, he went to study at Cirencester Agricultural College; now he was working as a seed merchant – a career that he successfully pursued for the rest of his working life.

———

Eighteen months after we first met, Joanna and I got married: we knew that our tender age would upset some people and shock others, but that was partly the point. We wanted to set ourselves apart, not only to prove the quality of our feelings, but to poke the world in the eye. Exactly as we thought, and with a candour that we found perversely bracing, my father disapproved, my grandfather refused to come to the wedding (but later changed his mind), and several of our friends wondered why we wanted to embrace such a moth-eaten institution as marriage. We largely ignored my father and grandfather and did what we could to convince sceptical friends that our decision made us rebels, not conformists. In truth, we didn't care much either way: love was all we needed, and as far as we were concerned, our lack of experience was simply an opportunity to prove our resourcefulness. Anyway, among the doubters and finger-waggers, there were plenty of people who actively encouraged us – including Joanna's mother Zoe, who was excited by our spirit of adventure, and my own mother: she wanted to see me settled. If she realised that our decision was partly a result of her accident, and my need to make a precociously definite bid for stability, she kept the thought to herself.

———

Joanna and I wanted to live in the countryside, and as I came to the end of my second year at Oxford, we began exploring villages that lay near the city. Eventually we landed in Toot Baldon – the name was comical, but the place looked exactly right for two people who wanted time alone with each other: half a dozen houses with their roofs pulled down over their eyes, an empty pub smelling of Dettol, and a cattle grid leading to a muddy track that stretched ahead of us between an avenue of mature chestnut trees. This track ended in another cattle grid and, as we clanked across, we saw ahead of us a clump of gigantic elms, a chapel surrounded by a graveyard, and a large, dark, rambling Victorian house that we thought must originally have been the rectory. The owner was standing at the front door. Is this where there was a flat to rent? It was.

We were shown into a makeshift downstairs kitchen, then climbed up past the bathroom to the top floor and crouched into a long V-shaped corridor under the eaves. There was a little bedroom at the end with windows that looked into the high branches of the elm trees, and a sitting room opposite with sloping walls like a boat. I stood in the prow and stared across the valley at a church half hidden in a fuzz of greenery: Garsington, where Ottoline Morrell had held her Bloomsbury

Group court. Then I faced right towards the Chilterns and noticed a deep white scar in the chalk: that must be where they were building the new motorway to London. Echoes and silence. Closeness and distance. Secrecy but a lookout post. We could hardly believe our luck.

———

I stood back from my mother's bed as a couple of nurses bustled in to turn her. 'Nearly done, Gillian,' they said, gasping and heaving. 'Nearly there now.' I'd explained to them that although her name was Gillian, everyone called her Gilly, but they never remembered. 'There you are, Gillian,' they repeated, straightening from her bed and rubbing the small of their backs. 'You're always such a good girl, aren't you? Such a good girl.' My mother nodded. She didn't have so many words to spare that she was willing to dip into her store every time someone spoke to her. 'Thank you,' I said, and off they went while I sat down again at the bedside. My mother winked at me, half smiled, and as she slipped back into her doze her mouth sagged open. She looked like a shark – that senile gape.

———

I went back to Edward Thomas. I'd read one or two of his poems at school but hadn't thought much of them then – I preferred poets who made more noise, painted in brighter colours, and used larger gestures. Now that I was living in the country, I began to retune my eyes and ears and found that I could receive his quiet-speaking voice more clearly. Also, I was surrounded by a lot of the things that Thomas had written about – or versions of them, at least – and this meant that my page-time and my life-time began to draw more closely together. Thomas's chalk pit and badger mound, his leaves like fish fossils in the surface of a path, his dusty nettles standing in the corner of a farmyard, all felt like familiar and palpable things, not just like the ingredients of a poem. This told me that while I might have left my home behind me, the sounds and sights of my childhood were indelible. I realised that if I could keep them intact and stop them getting confused with the things I actually wanted to lose, I'd have treasure inside me for the rest of my life. This made Thomas more interesting to me, and more thought-provoking, than any other writer I'd come across; reading him was like falling in love with a dead man – which might have been embarrassing if Thomas himself hadn't been so melancholy. But sadness seemed to give his words an additional authority and dignified the feelings I had for him. Gave them such depth, in fact, they bore almost no resemblance to those I'd previously had for Rupert Brooke.

———

The words I most wanted to use in my own poems were always just out of reach. I could see them hovering at a dream-distance, but could never stretch far enough into my mind, never cross over some barrier in myself. Then one evening I did cross over: I was writing a poem about my mother's clothes, remembering how my father still kept some of them in a trunk in the attic, and although my poem was really nothing more than a quick yelp, for a few lines I felt that I was writing down something that already existed in my mind. I finished and stared at the page. How had I just described it to myself? 'Something that already existed.' Because what I'd felt while writing those lines had nothing to do with plotting and planning. It was more like retrieving something. More like remembering than inventing. This seemed unlikely, but the longer I thought about it, the better it made sense – because my greatest pleasures as a reader also seemed like forms of recognition. When I was enjoying a poem, I almost never felt, 'That's new to me!', but rather, 'That's right! That's it!' – as though something I'd previously known only in outline, or known and forgotten again, had at last been completed and returned to me. Completed in ways that made the world seem more nearly finished, even though in a sense my own self had been annihilated in the process.

———

Edward Thomas made his living for years by writing what he reckoned were potboilers, and one of them was called *Feminine Influence on the Poets*, which Joanna and I thought was enough to put anyone off reading it. The subject interested me, though, partly because it was a way of thinking about my own case. I'd started to dabble in verses before the accident, but it was obvious that my mother's fall had turned me into a poet, and also obvious that she'd become a kind of black hole that swallowed every other subject I might want to write about. Now there was a danger of it swallowing my personality as well – since to a great extent that also depended on the accident and its effects.

I found my copy of Emily Dickinson's poems and turned to the one beginning 'That sacred Closet when you sweep –/ Entitled "Memory" –':

August the Dust of that Domain –
Unchallenged – let it lie –
You cannot supersede itself
But it can silence you –

Then I closed the book again, went back to my desk, opened my notebook, and heard my own words jabbering towards me. Something about sorrow, something about injustice, and something about guilt. Something about writing and wounds, too. Paper cuts. I closed my eyes and saw my mother staring up at me from her bank of pillows – visiting hour had just ended and I was about to leave her again. Her eyes beseeched me: stay. Then they blinked and gave me permission to go. I slunk off down the corridor feeling ashamed of myself. Really, I thought, I still took everything from my mother, even now: such conviction as her suffering gave me in thinking about the world; the pity associated with her tragedy.

———

On weekend mornings Joanna and I lay in bed late listening to the murmurs of the house-family below, then tuned them out and concentrated on each other. Afterwards I rolled aside and watched the rooks rising like ash in the elm-tops outside our bedroom window. Their nests were a mess, black twigs scrambled together, but they held steady when the wind blew, and on days like these, pale blue days when the sky flowed smoothly, they rode the air-current like leaves on a stream. Easily adrift. Swerving and swaying. With the rooks continually giving each other orders, quarrelling and making up, then levitating from the elm-tops with their wings held rigid, before sinking down sideways into the field. There they were now, stalking through the grass like preachers, pausing among the cowpats and dock clumps, hectoring worms and bugs, advancing in lines, then abandoning their plans and levitating again, settling back on their nests to eye the world below, just as they'd done when Edward Thomas saw them:

> Over the land freckled with snow half-thawed
> The speculating rooks at their nests cawed
> And saw from elm-tops, delicate as flower of grass,
> What we below could not see, Winter pass.

———

Joanna asked me about the anxiety of influence – she meant the influence of other poets and of Edward Thomas especially, not just feminine influence. All those quotes that now poured through me constantly – the dead voices and the living voices combining. Her question made me feel that being influenced might be like cheating. Don't copy anything! Make it new! But in truth I didn't feel guilty like that. I welcomed influence. It wasn't just that I wanted to know what other people thought, and how they'd found voices for those thoughts. It was also because poetry had led me such a long way from home and the things I first knew, I felt glad to have people guiding me. Especially if the guide was like Thomas, who was a very good poet but not an overwhelming one. Reading Thomas was like walking arm in arm with a ghost who was also a close companion.

And not only that. Thomas's poems had a completely fresh feel for me – every line seeming as though it had just come indoors from a tramp through the fields, when in fact they'd all been bolted together with a combination of his own and other people's words. Wordsworth and Keats and John Clare, mostly. Not to mention Thomas Hardy and Robert Frost. So Edward Thomas obviously hadn't felt anxious about influence either. He used other poets as a way of being himself. And he didn't think of dead poets as being lifeless, but as people who shared the same aims and frustrations as himself. It meant that for Thomas to quote them, refer to them, keep them in mind, was really no different from talking to a friend. As I felt I was doing myself, when I was reading.

I flipped through more memory-pages, looking for another example of what I was trying to say, and remembered the time when I'd been ill and living at home five years before – the time when I'd first begun to write poems. It was early summer, I was furloughed from school but no longer bed-bound, and my mother had dragged what we optimistically called the sunbed into the garden and unfolded it in the shade of the laurel bush. I was reading Andrew Marvell and drifting in a dazzle of pleasure and semi-understanding – a kaleidoscope feeling: dark leaves, heat splinters, grass sloping away to the ash tree and the open field beyond. Which felt more real, the garden or 'The Garden'? My own green thoughts in a green shade, or those on the page? A. M. or A. M.? There was no difference, that was the point. No difference because no barrier, just the atoms of the world surging continuously into and out of each other, shapeshifting. Real life and ghost life keeping company.

———

Why poetry, though – poetry in particular? Why not rock climbing or birdwatching, or something that resembled gainful employment? The reasons all stuck their hands in the air and shouted at once. Poetry because I thought of it as the voice of suffering; poetry because it might preserve my mother's life in words that survived her; poetry to escape the past and prove my independence; poetry because it had particular charisma, which I thought would probably subside in time, but for now blazed with an irresistible beauty; poetry because its forms were always an invitation to feel more deeply and think more carefully; poetry because it prized compression and distillation in a world of deliquescence; poetry because it belonged to everyone; poetry because it was a cousin of nonsense and told the truth slantways; poetry because when I was left to my own devices I heard sounds in my head – rhythms and musical phrases – that subsided only when I translated them into language; poetry because it was solitary; poetry because it made solitude communicative; poetry because of the way Byron described it in his *Journal* – 'The feeling of a Former world and a Future'; poetry because I didn't have to give any of these reasons or excuses – because I didn't think of poetry as being first and foremost a form of meaning, but a way of being.

---

My mother begged my father to let her live at home and not in the hospital, imploring him with her googly eyes and rusty words. My father wanted to say yes, but the doctors told him it would never happen: her injuries were too serious, she needed constant nursing, she couldn't care for herself, she still had her catheter. And it was true. My mother could scratch her nose now, turn her head a little, raise a fork to her mouth just about, but that was all. How would my father manage?

My father protested. He could take out a loan and hire builders to put up an extension on one side of the house, where nurses might live and take it in turns to look after my mother. He could buy a Ford Transit and adapt it to make room for a stretcher, so he could drive her to and from the hospital if need be. But even when he'd done both these things, the doctors still said no. It would be too dangerous. My mother caught pneumonia every few months – she'd always done that, ever since the accident – and she'd die if she didn't get proper care soon enough.

My father wrung his hands. My mother went on pleading, her sunken eyes glittering, her voice frosting over.

———

How to be modern, that was the question. How to love the mighty dead and let their voices soak into me, without also giving the impression that I thought nothing needed to be changed since the last Romantics had died. My childhood made the question loom especially large, because I couldn't think about my father's world without feeling that I'd been born either too early or too late, I couldn't decide. It wasn't as though my father was rich or grand – my father was precarious, although he made a good job of disguising it. But as I kept reminding myself, my upbringing had still been privileged, there was no doubt: the chances it had offered; the connections. Then there was the whole business of growing up in the countryside, when for the first time in history most people were living in towns. What kind of echo would my memories have for those who'd never seen a peewit, and didn't care what a fish-rise looked like, and had never walked past a clump of thistles as their down blew into the setting sun? Could I write about these things in my Now, without seeming as though I felt nothing but nostalgia for a vanished Then?

I thought about Ted Hughes and Seamus Heaney: they were both country people and they'd found a way to deal with it – Hughes by turning Yorkshire and Devon into a kind of slaughterhouse where even a thrush bouncing across the lawn looked like an assassin, and Heaney by making County Derry into a compost pit where blackberries and turf-lumps and corn dollies were all squashed together with bullets and rifle grease. But my own place? My mid-1960s rural Essex? Not much modernising there. More often, in fact, a sense of people trying to stop modernisation or drive it backwards.

It was the same problem that had bothered me from the first: how to keep the connection between poetry and suffering, but stretch it so that I could write about more than my mother in hospital. So that I could treat the accident as not simply a tragic tumble, but an example of how the rapacious Earth wanted to drag everyone down into its underworld. If I managed that, I thought, it would show that my mother's story was a kind of metaphor as well as a thing in itself, and at the same time prove that I was someone who had uprooted myself and now belonged nowhere. Was that modern enough? I thought about how Edward Thomas had described himself as 'a superfluous man', and thought I knew what he meant. I remembered the phrase in *Macbeth* that Joanna especially liked: that violence has become a 'modern ecstasy'. Modern in this case meaning everyday. Modern meaning recurring. Modern meaning regardless of time and place and circumstance.

---

I decided to pay my mother a surprise visit but when I reached her ward, the curtains were drawn shut around her bed and a scrum of doctors and nurses was boiling inside them. What was wrong? I launched forward, but the matron stopped me, putting her hand on my arm: my mother was having an epileptic fit. 'She's not epileptic,' I said. The matron explained: head injuries sometimes cause epilepsy, and that's what was happening here. I looked towards the bedcurtains again, saw them part for a moment, and caught a glimpse of squid-eyes bulging in my mother's face, froth bubbling around a strap in her mouth, her paralysed legs drumming on the sheet, and her rigid back arching. It was like watching stone bend. Then matron led me away to a waiting room and sat with me until my mother was sedated and sleeping. When I went back to her bedside, her face was shiny with sweat and her lips strangely tangled, as though something she wanted to say had got halfway through her mouth, then turned round and died. I kissed her, tiptoed away, and drove back to Joanna.

———

Ever since the accident, feelings that I thought should have been opposite seemed to exist side by side: pleasure and sadness, relief and anxiety, hope and regret. Even here, in our hideaway flat: we felt safe, but knew we'd have to leave sooner or later. To dull the blow that I knew must be coming, and to reinforce the sense – or the illusion – that I was in control of my life, I began to look on the place as somewhere I'd already lost. I must never forget, I told myself, staring from the high window that faced towards the Chilterns, or walking through the fields and lanes round about. I must never forget what I've felt and read and seen here for the first time. Never forget Joanna in the long grass with her hands brushing through the seed heads, or the hawthorn tunnel in the hedge below the house and its sickly blossom smell, or the washed-out wood of the gate where the tunnel ends, or the fencepost shaved by its latch where the wood is soft as feathers. Never forget the bend in the path beside the oak tree covered with ivy, or the dew on cow parsley that grows there in the shade, or the loose bar in the cattle grid where the chestnut avenue begins, and the Friesians approach with strings of grass-juice swaying from their mouths. Never forget the low corridor under the eaves, and my desk in the boat-room sailing endlessly towards the horizon.

———

Joanna loved everything by and about Louis MacNeice – the first book she gave me was his *Collected Poems*, and I soaked it up because every page felt like a part of her, or a way into her mind, or a description of our life together: 'Time was away and somewhere else./ The waiter did not come, the clock/ Forgot them and the radio waltz/ Came out like water from a rock:/ Time was away and somewhere else.' Then she discovered that MacNeice's friend Eric Dodds, E. R. Dodds who'd written *The Greeks and the Irrational*, taught at the University of Birmingham with MacNeice during the 1930s, then became Regius Professor of Greek at Oxford, had retired to Old Marston, a village on the edge of the city. Why didn't we write and ask if we could pay him a visit?

We knew from the address (Cromwell House) that Dodds lived where the Treaty of Oxford had been signed during the English Civil War, and when we got there it looked as though the generals and politicians had just left: a low-ceilinged sitting room, thickly latticed windows, stone floors, threadbare rugs, and no central heating but a big open fireplace with a blaze smelling of ash and rosemary. Mrs Dodds was wearing a bobbly black overcoat and lying on a chaise longue, and once we'd shaken her hand, Dodds led us through to his study at the back of the house, where he sat us side by side on a tight little sofa and scrutinised us through his shaggy eyebrows, sucking on his pipe. Irish tweed suit, Irish crew-necked jersey beneath the jacket, soft Irish voice. Shinily bald head. Friendly but cautious. Maybe a little lonely. He had the face of a sage-child but no children of his own, and no students any more either, just the books of his lifetime. Books towering to the ceiling behind him and books crammed onto shelves all around.

It was difficult, though, talking about the dead like this – I already knew as much from my conversations with Geoffrey, and wasn't sure what I expected to feel. A sense of personal connection with MacNeice, obviously, but what form might that take? A story about him that wasn't generally known, so that we could feel blessed by privileged information? Or something less tangible, something like ghost-contact and physical proximity with a shadow? And why did we want this, exactly? Because we liked his poems, of course. But also – in my case anyway – because I wanted a sense of companionship, albeit with another dead man. It turned out to be a tall order, even though I knew Dodds was interested in what he called 'supernormal phenomena'. No matter how much he wanted to bring his friend back into the room, he could never quite conjure him up, never quite haul him over the Styx and into the fresh air above ground. He talked about MacNeice's loose voice with the drink sloshing through it, about the handsome camel face

and the gallantry, about the jokes and cleverness and reckless-
ness that made women fall for him. And all the time MacNeice
stayed in the grave.

But it was tantalising as well as disappointing, and over the
next several months we made several more visits and gradually became friends. At which point Dodds said that although
he lived quietly these days, he still liked to go to dinner sometimes in his old college, Christ Church, and wondered whether
Joanna and I would mind keeping his wife company while he
was out. Of course we wouldn't mind. Although when the taxi
took Dodds off to his dinner, and the three of us settled round
the fire, sitting close to the flames because the house was like a
fridge, Mrs Dodds said that she didn't want any idle chit-chat,
she'd much rather we read to her. *Tono-Bungay*. She handed
over an ancient hardback, and I set off with the fire burning one
side of my face while she burrowed into her overcoat, listening
intently. As I came towards the end of the chapter, I noticed that
someone down there at the foot of the page was kissing someone and decided to skip ahead, thinking Mrs Dodds would be
embarrassed. As I made my edit she interrupted me, her voice
quavering but stern: I'd missed something and needed to go
back. She remembered the kiss from the last time she'd read
*Tono-Bungay*; she'd been looking forward to it.

———

I'd seen it announced in the local paper, but Dodds confirmed
it: W. H. Auden was returning to Oxford, to live in a cottage
that belonged to Christ Church. I knew the one – pale yellow
stone, recently cleaned; I saw it from the pavement whenever I
walked along St Aldate's.

This was exciting news. I revered Auden and had already read plenty of stories about the previous times he'd lived in the city: as a student in the 1930s, when he cast his spell over Stephen Spender and John Betjeman and the rest of them; then when he was Professor of Poetry, sitting in the Cadena Cafe so tyro poets could touch the hem of his garment. Now he was almost mythical: the greatest living poet. That alone was reason enough to want to meet him – admiration, mixed with curiosity. But there was something else as well, though I found it difficult to say what it was, because it meant accepting an element in my character that I found awkward to acknowledge. It wasn't just that I wanted to learn from Auden. I also thought that knowing him would be a kind of endorsement. My need for a mentor, in other words, coincided with my need for approbation, and the more distinguished the mentor, the more valuable the approbation.

Dodds warned me: Auden was an old man now and starting to get confused. I didn't want to believe this, but soon saw it for myself, when I went to a reading that he gave to the university Poetry Society. From my chair near the back of the audience I saw him shuffle into the room like a tramp (he was wearing carpet slippers) and spill his water, then heard him read in a monotone without saying anything about how the poems had been written or where or when. I couldn't have cared less. He was here, that was the thing, here in the same room – although looking so like the photographs of himself, he might as well have stayed in his cottage and sent along a body double. That wedge of boyish and strangely dry-looking hair; those slippers and crumpled clothes. The voice: flat American 'a's and every word kippered by cigarette smoke – 'Miles and miles of golden moss/ Silently and very fast'. And the famous face, stealing attention

57

from the poems. The face as fissured as a limestone pavement. The face that was extraordinary and commanding, although when he smiled it was also full of kindness and shyness.

———

Dodds took me to dinner in Christ Church and introduced me to Auden, who asked me to sit next to him – which felt wrong until I realised (though found it hard to believe) that no one else wanted to do that. The other college tutors and professors seated around the table had seen Auden every night since he came back to live amongst them, and I could tell from their sour expressions that they were already fed up with him. After a while I could see why. When Auden talked, he abruptly laid down the law about every subject that entered the conversation and several that didn't; he repeated himself; he interrupted others and didn't listen to them; he looked a mess and made a mess; he was already drunk when he sat down to start eating and got steadily squiffier course by course. But I still couldn't have cared less. It wasn't just that the stories were new to me and I hadn't yet had the chance to feel bored by them; it was simply that Auden was Auden. Not my 'hero', exactly – I'd never wanted to apply that term to any of the people I admired, because it made me sound more gawping and passive than I felt. But certainly the living writer I most admired, and the one whose advice I most wanted. And would soon have, it seemed, because as dinner ended Auden asked me to send him some of my poems (I must have squeezed in the fact that I wrote them, while he held forth), and asked – ordered – me to come round to the cottage so that he could tell me what he thought. Next Thursday at four?

Dodds said that Auden was very strict about punctuality, and if I wanted to make a good impression I'd better arrive on time. The following Thursday I waited on the doorstep of his cottage until the bell in the cathedral nearby was actually chiming four, then knocked as its echoes died away. Auden opened the door a crack, looking as though he'd just crawled out of bed, then puffed upstairs and led the way into the sitting room. My head-camera started recording immediately, thinking I'd never see any of this again: Auden waddling ahead of me like an enormous toad; the pale wood floor; shelves against the far wall, bulging with books and papers; two saggy black leather armchairs on opposite sides of a low table in the middle of the room; the table also heaped with books and papers, including the poems I'd dropped off a couple of days before (now smeared with cigarette ash and stained with dried-out glass-bottom rings); Hockney etchings on the walls – mostly boys sitting on small chairs and staring into space, but one of them Auden himself, looking toad-like here, too. The same Auden who was now asking me whether I'd like a cup of coffee, then shuffling off to the kitchen across the hall to make it, then shuffling back and crumpling into his crumpled chair, while I perched in mine opposite and tried to look as keen as I felt, although the chair made that tricky: it seized me and flung me backwards, so I couldn't help seeming insultingly relaxed.

Write about what you know, Auden said, in his flat pontifical voice. Try different verse forms, Welsh forms for instance, Gerard Manley Hopkins explored them. Make things up but don't tell lies about Nature, you must always obey natural laws.

Several of the poems I'd dropped off were about my mother, and Auden seemed especially interested in them. In the poems as poems, but also in the accident. How long had my mother been unconscious? What could she remember and what had she forgotten? Would she ever come home? The interrogation was all very brisk and clipped, scientific almost, but the curiosity felt real – although more like a doctor than a poet. And that was fine: in fact it made everything easier, because it helped me to control feelings that might otherwise have been confusing. Then we moved on from grief and hospitals and talked about other writers – who I liked and who I didn't. Auden was pleased when I told him about my feelings for Edward Thomas, he liked him too, but he often mentioned people I hadn't read yet – Hannah Arendt, for instance, and Goethe. That was embarrassing because it reminded me how little I knew, despite the hours I spent hunched over books every day. But it was also heartening. Surely Auden wouldn't be mentioning these people to me if he didn't think I was worth it?

At six o'clock exactly (I could hear the cathedral clock again) Auden made us both a martini, we drank it, and that was that: now he must leave for supper in hall, and I must go and find Joanna. But same time next week, Auden said, and send round some more poems over the weekend? Of course. Just like that we settled into a routine, and as soon as it was established, like everything else in Auden's life, it didn't change – although once Stephen Spender was there too, and I felt almost embarrassed by the way Auden told his friend what to do and think. Not that Spender seemed to mind. He just sat there laughing – flushed and awkward like a big white-haired child – and whenever he tried to get a word in edgeways, Auden pushed it away. Which only made Spender laugh some more. Auden wasn't like a doctor, suddenly, he was more like a schoolmaster – then switched to being something else again, the next time I went. After we'd talked, and precisely as the clock reached six, he stood up and closed the door to the landing, revealing in the process a Hockney drawing that had previously been hidden behind it. This one showed a naked boy leaning forward with his forearms resting on his knees and his cock nestling between his thighs. Auden smiled at the boy, then turned to me and asked me what I'd like. Martini, I said, ignoring the idea that he might have meant something else, and that I'd missed a trick by not enquiring what. Not realising, either – or not until later, anyway – that if I'd given a different answer, I might have seen that a situation in which I assumed I was a more or less passive recipient of poetic wisdom was actually one in which I had more control than I realised.

———

Every time I left Auden's cottage and went back to my normal life, I felt that my feet weren't quite touching the ground. It was partly thanks to what Auden had told me, which always seemed important. But it was mainly and simply because I'd been in the presence. Physical contact. Thinking: this is the hand that wrote those marvellous poems; this is the head that thought the thoughts. Before I'd met him, I'd been inclined to believe that poems were bolts from the blue that had very little to do with everyday things like work and tax and haircuts and clothes and crossing the road safely and weather. But merely by existing, by proving that he was flesh and blood, Auden showed me otherwise. He proved – no, he let me feel on my pulses – that poems are not weird visitations, or ornaments stuck on the surface of life, but part of life's daily bread. Exceptional when they're good, but still daily bread.

———

Then it was September, a dark cold day, and I reached across Joanna and turned on the radio in our bedroom overlooking the elm trees, so that we could listen to the early-morning news. The newscaster said that Auden had died. I immediately climbed out of bed and drove into Oxford to buy the papers, then brought them back and read the obits, feeling tearful and hollow. Why, though? Why so upset? Auden had been kind to me – had shown, in fact, that 'irresistible inclination towards being good and doing good' that I would soon read about in Hannah Arendt's elegiac tribute to him. But we'd only known each other for a few months, and never exchanged confidences: we weren't close. And although I thought the world of Auden's poems, I knew in my heart that his death hadn't broken an especially rich flow of late work – the recent poems had been smart and charming and sad, but their power had a much lower voltage than the earlier ones. On top of that, his death wasn't exactly unexpected: Auden was sixty-six, but all that smoking and drinking made him seem older; his insides must have been completely furred up.

I remembered the night almost exactly five years earlier, when I'd been watching the news at home with my father, and the announcer had said that Siegfried Sassoon was dead. There was his photograph on the screen – the handsome face with the jug-handle ears – and just for a second I'd felt as though a friend had gone. Now it was the same with Auden, only much more so, not just because I'd met Auden and been encouraged by him, but for another reason as well. Poets might or might not turn into bores. They might or might not keep writing good poems to the end of their lives. But when they die, the simple fact that they can't write any more changes their work for ever; it rips it out of their own time and throws it forward into eternity.

I folded up the newspapers and stared through the window of our sitting room, watching the clouds pass and treetops sway. This was what the world looked like without Auden in it. This was the world where all the still-living poets moved a little closer to their own extinction. Then I went to my bookshelf and found the *Collected Poems*. Unpublished things would come to light, I told myself, and so would new facts about Auden's life. Opinions about his work would change. But today, for the first time, I had to talk in the past tense about the man who wrote them. He had become his admirers.

> Now he is scattered among a hundred cities
> And wholly given over to unfamiliar affections,
> To find his happiness in another kind of wood
> And be punished under a foreign code of conscience.
> The words of a dead man
> Are modified in the guts of the living.

As I finished my first degree and began writing my M.Litt. thesis – about Edward Thomas – Joanna and I moved into the city: my mother had given me half her savings, and we bought a little house by the Thames near Folly Bridge: it cost £8,000. As long as we'd stayed in our countryside sky-boat, the sense that our time there would last for ever had been matched by the feeling that everything was too good to last. Now, suddenly, the balance of opposites was broken and the village raced into the future without us. The elm trees caught Dutch elm disease and had to be cut down, the rooks made their airy bounce and vanished, the rectory changed hands and the new owner poured concrete along the track under the chestnuts, and the pub became the kind of place that people visit on the weekend.

It took me back to the old questions: was I – was everyone – born just too late or just too early to have the life they most wanted? Did everyone feel their present was uninhabitable, or only enjoyable in snatches? That was certainly how it seemed to me, although there was nothing I could do about it except keep going, thinking that if ever I stopped moving I'd fall through the surface of time and disappear. Joanna might still be working at Oxfam, but she'd been promoted and now made occasional working visits to India, where she'd been born. I hunkered down in the library every day from nine to five, took on some undergraduate teaching, and met once a term with my supervisor, John Fuller. John had a reputation for fostering poets – James Fenton and Alan Hollinghurst and Mick Imlah, for instance – but it was hard to see how he managed it. His own poems were very clever and stylish, and so was his conversation, but mostly he sat still and listened, with his back to a big window so his face was hard to read. That was his secret, I decided: he kept himself semi-visible, never crowded anyone, conspired with people and encouraged them, but gave us all enough space to grow into our own natural shapes.

I was still sending poems to magazines, had a few accepted, and then Faber published me and a handful of others in one of their *Introduction* anthologies; when my first copy arrived I rushed through it in a dazzle, flickering between excitement and envy and anxiety, certain that the poems by Tom Paulin were the best of the bunch. I'd never heard of Tom before, but an author's note told me that he was teaching at the University of Nottingham, and after we'd met at the launch party, he asked me to visit. Tom was a little older than me, he had a job and a wife and two young children, and the difference between our temperaments was plain to see. Tom was opinionated, quick-witted, and apparently much more self-confident than I'd ever felt. Nevertheless, I could see that I'd fallen in with someone who belonged to my own generation of the poetry family, and this was exhilarating. Once I'd climbed out of my train at Nottingham and into Tom's orange Citroën, then arrived at his large quiet house with fir trees dusting the kitchen windows, I was already so spellbound by his vinegar Belfast accent, I'd begun to sound like an intermittent Ulsterman myself. Listening to Tom was like hearing an ecstatic preacher on a hilltop – entranced one minute and lugubrious the next – always exaggerating, sweeping, condemning, uplifting. And always *minding* – minding more about poems than anyone I'd met, and allowing me to feel that I could show more boldly how much I minded about them as well.

Tom helped me to understand that I needed to be more realistic about the way I responded to older poets, and more accepting, in particular, of the way ambition combined with the appetite to learn from them. It was just as well – because now, suddenly, everyone I met seemed either to be a poet themselves or the friend of poets. This made the world feel smaller and larger at the same time, and both were good. Smaller because it was easier for me to know my place, and larger because it encouraged me to stretch my wings.

Then Faber's chairman, Charles Monteith, asked me to a drinks party in the garden of his flat in St John's Wood, to meet Robert Lowell. It was like talking to Auden for the first time: every cell in my body remembered the poems by him that I loved, and this almost stopped me from thinking straight. Although Lowell, like Auden, immediately came to the rescue. He might have looked barmy, with his eyes swivelling behind his smeary glasses, and his Einstein hair, and his dirty clothes and fingernails, but he was kind. Smiley in a shy way, and corkscrewing around himself when he talked, as though he was always on the point of turning into a tornado. Standing beside the tall leylandii that shaded Charles's garden, we found ourselves talking about place names for some reason, and I told Lowell that American names sounded romantic to English ears. Oh, said Lowell, like what? Maine and Nantucket and Madaket and Martha's Vineyard and Boston Common, I said, partly to suck up but meaning it as well. They really did sound glamorous to me; the whole idea of America sounded glamorous – the distances and the freedom and the sense of devil-may-care. Lowell grinned and said he thought English names were romantic too, then reeled off a few – Stoke Poges and St John's Wood and Sturminster Newton. But what about songs?, I replied, feeling astonished that the conversation was still going. American songs made names sound romantic as well. 'Twenty-four Hours from Tulsa', for instance: that had an unforgettable yearning feel to it. But twenty-four hours from Toot Baldon? Then Lowell's friend and editor Jonathan Raban appeared, and it was almost a relief to know that my time was up.

———

Not just poets in London, but poets in Oxford, too, wanting to share poems and talk about them. Jon Stallworthy, for instance, who was a friend of Geoffrey's and therefore should have been a friend of mine as well, but always seemed a little distant and controlling: he couldn't have been jealous, could he? And Peter Levi, who'd recently given up being a Jesuit because he'd fallen in love with a woman outside his Order and decided to marry her: whenever I saw him, his gown was fluttering behind him as though he were still leaping over a wall. And John Wain, with his blue sailor's cap and his reckless booming voice: he was reputed to be a friend of Philip Larkin, but it was hard to believe that the Hermit of Hull would want to spend much time with someone who made such a racket and filled the back bar of the King's Arms with such extravagantly impressionistic judgements. And Wain's acolyte Sally Purcell, with her pale clever face, her poems about witches and warlocks, and the small stuffed dinosaur she carried with her everywhere. And Neil Rhodes, with his shrewd dry talk and wildness lurking under his insouciance. And that man with long black hair whose name I could never remember, who wrote a sonnet sequence containing the portentous phrases that Joanna and I kept quoting to each other: 'We admired Nick's Afghan bag', and 'The city sits like a melon on an anthill'. And Andrew Harvey, who lived in the ether of All Souls, but descended once a day to cross the road to my own college and leave a poem in my mailbox – a poem I could never read because Andrew's handwriting was so bad.

———

And Anne Stevenson, who had a residency at Lady Margaret Hall, which was Joanna's old college, and had just published two books at once: *Travelling Behind Glass* and *Correspondences*. I bought them both and turned over their pages as though I was reading holy writ, then was introduced to her by Joanna's former tutor, Mary Jacobus, and we started meeting once a week for poetry talk. Anne was pale-skinned and intense and already a little deaf, which meant we had to sit close together so that she could hear my muttering, and her expertise was strangely shot through with uncertainty, which made the advice she gave me feel all the more approachable. Especially her advice that when I was writing I should ride my body as well as my mind. Bring them close to each other so that my mind could work like a body does, through its senses. I cudgelled into the small hours, gnawing at my fingernails and chain-smoking, until Joanna got fed up and went to bed alone. It was a dangerous business, this obsessing over the best way to make words work, but that didn't stop me from making it the centre of my existence.

———

And Craig Raine, who was nine years older than me and seemed to be ninety-nine years more self-assured, despite the fact that he was always namechecking his famous friends: Julian and Martin, Ian and Hitch. Craig sidled up to the desk in the Bodleian Library where I was immersed in Edward

Thomas and spoke to me out of the side of his mouth, inviting me for a cup of tea in the covered market nearby; he made tea sound like the hardest liquor imaginable. When we were done and I returned to my seat, I thought it might as well have been. I'd never laughed so much, never heard someone talk about sex so much, and never met someone who showed so often and so proudly that he read everything through a kind of mental microscope, seeing even its smallest pieces of machinery. I'd hardly said anything myself, but that didn't seem to matter. Craig only wanted to talk ('Now listen, love . . .').

A few days later Joanna and I went to supper in Craig's flat and met Li, Craig's wife, who had just had a little girl, Nina. It became a regular thing, this supper-meeting, and usually followed the same pattern: get drunk; disagree about Edward Thomas (Craig liked him much less than I did); and listen to Craig cackling away about sex, and James Joyce, and sex, and his famous friends, and sex. Once, wobbling home late on my bike, I was knocked to the ground by a car, but luckily the police saw it happen and knew it wasn't my fault, so they didn't breathalyse me, they just asked me whether I was hurt. 'Not really, officer,' I said, rubbing my knee. 'Well, sir,' the policeman said, in the special language he'd learned at training college in Hendon. 'Well, sir, I must still request that you roll up your trouser leg in order to ascertain the extent of your injuries.' I told him that I'd be happy to do that but needed to explain that I'd had an operation for arthritis a few years before, and my kneecaps had been removed: I didn't want the policeman to think they'd been scythed off in the accident. 'Never mind, sir,' the policeman said, as calmly as if I'd just told him what time it was. 'I've seen everything.' I was very glad to hear that; I knew Craig would like it.

And Alan Hollinghurst. I'd heard about Alan from John Fuller, because Alan was taught by John as an undergraduate. Now he was also working on his thesis in the library, writing about E. M. Forster and Ronald Firbank and L. P. Hartley – and writing his own poems as well. One of them had won the university poetry prize, the Newdigate, and I'd read it and liked it and sent a note to Alan saying so. (When I won it the following year, I told Alan I was a quick learner who was also a slow starter.) Next thing I knew, we were sitting opposite one another at a low table in the King's Arms, drinking Guinness. Neither of us likes Guinness much, so we must have been nervous when we ordered, but the moment we started talking everything felt easy – as though we'd known each other all our lives. Our backgrounds weren't exactly the same, but near enough. Our schools weren't the same, but near enough. We thought the same things were good, and the same things were funny, and the same things were annoying, and the same things were ridiculous, and the same things were beautiful, and the same things were sad. We both wanted to spend our lives writing, and neither of us felt sure how to manage that – we were working on it. But there was also enough difference between us to make us interesting to one another. Alan knew a great deal more than I did about classical music, and architecture, and fiction, but less about contemporary poetry. And Alan might have seemed shy, with his wire-frame specs, his lock of chestnut hair falling across his forehead, his modesties and amusing deprecations, but he was also completely self-possessed, quietly but determinedly living as he wanted to live, and not as others chose. That, among many other things, made him seem exemplary to me.

Ian Hamilton published some of my poems in the magazine he edited, the *New Review*, along with others by Anne Stevenson, and wrote to say that he wanted to meet us. Ian had the reputation of being hard to please, so this was exciting. Exciting, too, to be invited to the Pillars of Hercules, which was the pub next door to the magazine's office in Soho – a poetical holy of holies, as far as I was concerned.

We arrived early and ordered white wine, then Ian slid in, instantly recognisable: the unnervingly neat schoolboy sweep of hair across his forehead, which must have been cool when he was young but now looked like a wig; the square face, wounded and pugilistic; the side-of-the-mouth drawl (that's where Craig got it). 'What are you drinking?' he asked, raising one eyebrow. 'White wine.' 'White wine?' Ian made it sound like Ovaltine but forgave us, handed me some books to review, and invited me back a month later. This time it was lunch in an Italian restaurant, although no one ate anything, they just ordered without looking at the menu, then smoked and drank and stubbed out their cigarettes in the food. Ian and Clive James and three other men – I'd seen several women in the magazine's office, wearing heavy make-up and short skirts, but Ian hadn't asked them to come along, and the women didn't seem to expect it. I felt sorry about that; their absence reminded me that Ian and his friends belonged to a different generation from my own, where this kind of exclusion was par for the course. As it was, I didn't say a word, not a single word, and spent the whole meal feeling like a frog at the bottom of a well, staring upwards at the light.

When I was still outside looking in, the poetry world had seemed gigantic. Now I was squeezing through the gate, it turned out to be like a walled town where everyone knew or recognised everyone else, because they all derived from the same small cultural gene pool, and scurried through the narrow streets pushing each other into the gutter or lifting them out of it in a permanent battle for survival. Gossiping and grudging. Competing and complaining. Although when Michael Longley came to read at Oxford, it was clear from the first moment that he wasn't a begrudger – not in the least. While Craig and I talked to him after the event, he promised to check out our poems, and soon afterwards invited us to read in Belfast, where he met us at the airport and drove us into town. I sank down in my seat as we swerved past the ruins of a bombed-out cinema, but Michael told us that we'd be OK provided we were sensible. Craig gave his merry cackle and wrote down images in his notebook: in the plane after crossing the Irish Sea he'd already decided that the city looked like 'a radio/ with its back ripped off'. I thought that was brilliant, even better than mist being like the sky tired of flight in 'A Martian Sends a Postcard Home', which I'd reckoned must be a poem for children when he first showed it to me in Oxford.

The other poets there – Paul Muldoon, Ciaran Carson, James Simmons – seemed friendly enough, but it was hard to tell: there was something about their courtesy that made it seem like an invitation to disaster. It was only five o'clock when they took us to a bar in the centre of town before the reading, and enthusiastically set about helping us to get drunk. If the intention was to bolster our confidence, it didn't work: when the reading began a couple of hours later, and despite my saturation, I still felt very nervous – it was only the second time I'd performed my poems in public. Craig was nervous too, he must have been, because he dropped his poems as he began talking and they whooshed over the floor, which meant he had to spend his first few minutes scrabbling them back into order, looking as though he was bowing down to the audience. My own reading, although I'd practised every night for about a month, telling myself to speak up, SPEAK UP, was still mostly inaudible – people kept shouting at me out of the darkness, objecting that they couldn't hear, like those voices I'd heard during my evening with B. S. Johnson. They didn't sound unhappy, though, and I soon understood why. This wasn't a poetry reading, it was a competition, Belfast versus Oxford, and Belfast was winning by miles. It made me feel so awkward, Craig told me when I eventually sat down that I looked like Siegfried Sassoon. I wasn't surprised. I felt like Siegfried Sassoon – a long time dead.

And even more so when we went back to Michael's house afterwards and sprawled around in the half-light listening to Billie Holiday. 'Strange fruit, strange fruit,' Michael murmured, shushing the room with his open hand, as though he was conducting an orchestra, then waving the talk forward again, his wife Edna glimmering beside him. There were other women in the shadows too, and I thought this must be the kind of party I'd read about, where people got drunk and slipped away to anonymous rooms together. Is that what I'd like to do myself? I was lying on the floor now, propped on one elbow, and gazed round the room trying to focus. But I'd had too much to drink, the faces all slid together and melted, the Belfast accent made everything seem as though it was galloping beyond the horizon, and before I could answer my own question, I closed my eyes and fell asleep.

# Part Three

---

# 1976–1978

I finished my M.Litt. and applied for a job teaching English at the University of Hull. The university of *where?*, several of my friends asked incredulously – but that was the point. After six years in Oxford, I was feeling stifled by its privilege. Grateful for it, inevitably, but also convinced that my future lay in a less pampered environment. In any case, Philip Larkin lived in Hull. He'd run the university library for the past twenty years, I'd loved his poems ever since first reading them at school, and I thought that if our paths were ever going to cross, it would be more likely to happen in his home town than anywhere else.

That, at least, was how I put it to anyone who asked, but I knew it wasn't the whole story. The possibility of meeting Larkin was the latest example of an impulse that had grown in me ever since I first started reading poems. Initially it had led me to Brooke's grave, then to my friendship with Geoffrey, and then to my meetings with Auden. But this time there were differences as well as similarities. My crush on Brooke was in a sense the result of my background: he was one of the few twentieth-century poets whose name meant anything to anyone in the world I'd grown up in – thanks less to his work than his glamorous reputation ('the handsomest young man in England', one of his contemporaries had called him). In the same sort of way, and despite being a vastly better poet, Auden was also someone whom my circumstances had chosen for me: he lived up the road in the city where I went to university. But my hopes of meeting Larkin stemmed from a much better-informed kind of choice. He might have been already on his way to becoming a gloomy kind of national treasure, but he was famously stand-offish, and he lived in one of the loneliest parts of the country, where, as he said himself, 'Only salesmen and relations come'. This meant that in order to meet him I had to refuse the paths out of Oxford that most of my contemporaries were taking (almost all of which led them to London), and strike out on my own. But supposing I got to Hull and never met Larkin, or met him only once and we didn't get on: would that mean I'd steered my life into a side alley, when I wanted to walk the sunlit highway? I resisted the idea and told myself I could always live in Hull for a short while, then get a job somewhere else. On the other hand, suppose I saw Larkin on a regular basis and even – an unlikely prospect, given his reputation – became a friend? Would that mean my own reputation would grow by association, and disproportionately fast because Larkin was so inaccessible? I shoved that idea out of my mind as well, and reminded myself that there were other reasons for going to Hull, besides Larkin and poetry. It was a salary. It was the North. It would do me good to live in ways I hadn't been raised to expect.

---

When I was offered the job, Joanna and I were faced with a choice: should we both up sticks, or reorganise our lives to include a gigantic commute? The moment we started talking about it, we realised what the answer must be. Joanna's own work and her friends were in Oxford, she didn't want to migrate to a city she'd never seen, and I didn't want to abandon entirely the life that I already had. That meant I should move to Hull alone, and every weekend we'd take it in turns to travel the 150-odd miles that were about to separate us. It would be difficult, but the alternative was to split up – and neither of us wanted to do that. As far as we were concerned, our marriage had been a kind of rebellion in the first place, and this was its second unconventional stage. It was 1976; people didn't have to play by the old rules any longer.

On my last day in Oxford, I went into my college to say goodbye to my tutor and was stopped at the lodge by the porter, Douglas. 'Is that it, Mr Motion?' he asked. 'Leaving us now, are you?' 'Yes,' I said. Douglas paused, stepped thoughtfully backwards, and looked me up and down as though I were a horse that he'd trained, which was now up for sale. 'Well, off you go, then,' he said at last. 'And I'll say one thing. For a bloody poet you've got your feet on the ground.'

It felt like the highest compliment I'd ever been paid by anyone, and I repeated it gratefully to myself as I gathered my books and clothes and bed linen, and the little upright desk my grandmother had left me, loaded them into a Transit van, then said goodbye to Joanna and drove them up to Hull. Three and a half hours. That wasn't going to be much fun every fortnight. But when I arrived, I could see that travelling would be the least of my problems.

A month previously I'd made a recce visit and rented a flat five minutes from the university in a long brick canyon inauspiciously called De Grey Street. It had seemed OK then – sitting room, bathroom, and bedroom, and a kitchen window that overlooked a railway embankment where two or three times a day the local goods train rattled into view, gave a mournful hoot, then trundled away again. Now, as I began unpacking in the early-autumn rain, I could see the place was a disaster. No central heating, and already clammy-cold. Vomitous sucked barley-sugar carpet running riot everywhere except the kitchen. No proper bed but a mattress on the floor. North-facing and sunless. Gigantic dust-smelling, stain-covered, hippopotamus-grey, undisguisable three-piece suite in the sitting room. Putrefying wood smell in the bedroom. Wallpaper peeling off the walls. Chest of drawers with broken handles. Broken fan heater. Broken kettle. Broken everything. I'd come to Hull partly because I wanted life to feel more 'real', but this was more reality than I could easily bear. Crouched on the carnivorous sofa, surrounded by the salvage of happier days, I felt paralysed: lonely for the first time in my life, and hopelessly out of my depth.

---

My mother was moved into a special unit for the long-term sick; it was called the Link, to suggest a connection between hospital and home, but the doctors knew that patients who came here would never leave. Every expense had been spared: the plywood floors bounced, the windows refused to open, the doors slammed, and no one had any privacy. Still, there was room for a dozen beds and only two of them were occupied: my mother in one and Lucy directly opposite. Lucy was a teenager who'd been hit by a car when she tried to run across the A12. She must have been beautiful once; now her unconscious face was hard to look at, and my mother looked at her all day, every day.

Hull came to me in pieces. Boiled-looking back-to-back ter-
raced houses near De Grey Street, with kids ragging at corners.
Queues of unemployed men and women outside the job centre,
standing like cattle with their backs to the wind. Snickets with
Victorian gas lamps still flickering in the misty evenings; the
stink of fish from the glue factory; smashed glass in the bus
stops; bomb craters and waste ground in the city centre as
though the Luftwaffe had just left.

But that wasn't the only story the city had to tell. There was
also the older part of town, the Land of Green Ginger, where the
River Hull cuts into the Humber. Here there were handsome
grey-brick buildings and cobbled lanes; an offshoot of the Dutch
embassy, because this far east Holland is closer than London;
the dark and warren-y pub where Joseph Conrad drank; the
Slave Museum; the Wilberforce house; exotic-looking customs
and excise offices; romantically decayed pumping stations; a
battered terminal where the ferry toiled to New Holland on
the opposite shore; tug boats and tankers and the rump of the
fishing fleet.

Slowly I began to understand. Hull was sometimes beautiful,
sometimes bereft, and always bloody-minded – it was the city
that told King Charles to fuck off in the Civil War. Now it still
said fuck off to most new arrivals, myself included.

---

I wheeled my mother's stretcher-bed outside and we sat together
in the sun; there was a patch of grass between the Link and
the boiler shed. I told her about Hull, how I'd made difficulties

for myself by moving there, and she smiled and gurgled and sometimes murmured a husky question. In the end we both fell silent, and I watched the summer breeze pick at her blanket, or stared through the window of the boiler shed and followed the contortions of its silver pipes and dials, its shining brackets and tubes. It made me feel sleepy, and when my eyes closed, I could hear my mother screaming. When I opened them again, and turned to face her, I found that she'd fallen asleep.

———

I looked at the map of east Yorkshire, decided Spurn Point at the mouth of the Humber was the loneliest place in this lonely part of the world, and told myself to drive out there. That way I could confront the changed facts of my life and see more clearly what they might become.

I set off early on a Sunday, sunlight crackling around me like silver foil, and Hull soon fell away behind, the road emptying as it wound past ground staked out for new estates, then dwindling into a lane that skewered the old quiet farmland. I slowed down sometimes to look at churches and war memorials, or big mushroom-farmhouses, or fallen clouds of cow parsley, or the church in Wellfleet where Andrew Marvell was born – locked – then the other church at Patrington where the spire is punctuated by clover-shaped holes to let the wind through. The Queen of Holderness. Then I was past all that, into the edge-land where there were no more churches, no more houses or trees or hedges, only dead flat fields where the wind made galaxy patterns in the wheat.

———

Lucy had died and my mother was alone in the Link, every day identical to the one before and the one after: doctors prescribing medicine (thirty-something pills every twenty-four hours); a priest nagging about the value of suffering; my melancholy father hunching through the evening visiting hour; nurses turning and wiping and bathing her. And still her body wouldn't accept what had happened to it; still she ached and bled. I thought of Larkin's poem 'An Arundel Tomb', and its earl and countess 'cast in stone'. My mother was an effigy as well: her skin marble-smooth, her identity gradually eroding.

———

I parked where the earth proper turned into sand and looked at the map again, running my finger along the dangle of Spurn Point and into the mouth of the Humber; it would take me half an hour to walk to the end, I reckoned, and then I'd be at the loneliest point of all, with the North Sea on one side and the river on the other.

An hour later I was still walking – blocked from the sea on my right by a high bank of dunes, with viewing places here and there because high tides had blasted a way through. I stopped beside one of them and looked towards the waves – but there was too much stun-flash and glitter, so I kept going. And kept going. Past scoops of yellow sand pitted with raindrops and spray. Past dunes with their topknots quivering as the wind streamed over them. Past a disappointing run of stagnant pools where the water looked like burned metal. Past a stumpy lighthouse and a lifeboat station. The boat was crouched at the top of its wooden ramp and ready to go, but there was nobody there. Nobody to sail the boat, and no one who needed to be rescued.

A place that was nothing and nowhere and endless – that's what I'd expected and that's what I wanted. Absolution. A plain white canvas where I could sketch a new beginning. But when the land ran out, at the very end of Spurn, finality turned out to be nothing like a blank. I stood with my back to the wind, resisting its shove and bluster, and took it all in: the sky splitting open; whitecaps falling over themselves where the sea current mashed together with the river current; hundreds of seagulls wheeling and squabbling and screaming as they plunged and stabbed for fish. Beyond them, lying offshore in a tidy queue with their engines churning, six enormous tankers were waiting for the tide to turn so that they could enter the river and complete their journey to the docks in Goole and Immingham and Hull.

I folded my arms, the wind still rocking me on my heels, and kept staring. This was my vision, then, this panorama. Not emptiness after all, but occupation – the iron business of the world. Towering hulls and cargo battlements. Mystery and mass and profit. So be it. I continued staring for a while, then turned aside and began tramping back towards the car.

———

While I was still in Oxford, writing my thesis, I'd also been publishing poems in magazines at a regular rate, and by the time I moved to Hull I'd organised them into a book I wanted to call *The Pleasure Steamers*: the title poem was about the river cruisers that I'd passed every day when I crossed Folly Bridge on my way to the library. Knowing next to nothing about poetry publishing, and not having an agent, I'd sent the typescript to several editors at once – including Michael Schmidt, who had

founded Carcanet Press seven years previously in 1969, soon
after graduating from Oxford, and was now running it from
the village of South Hinksey, just outside the city. Michael and I
had never met, although he'd printed some of my poems in the
magazine he ran alongside the press, and from these intermittent contacts I'd got the impression that he was more enthusias-
tic than organised, and more interested in writing as such than
he was in the mechanics of publishing in general and publicity
in particular. For all these reasons, I felt a little sceptical about
his operation, and might have preferred a more establishment
outfit to take me on. But at the same time, I liked Michael's
independence, and when he replied within a week of receiving
my poems, and said that he wanted to publish them, my delight
easily overcame my doubts. I was twenty-three and thought
time was on my side. If things didn't work out with Michael, I
could always try elsewhere.

Weeks passed without another word from him. I left Oxford
for Hull. I told myself not to worry that there was no sign of a
contract, or any editorial comment on the poems, or any conversation about design or how to promote the book. Then one
rainy Saturday morning the postman rang my front doorbell
and handed over a Jiffy bag with a finished copy of the book
inside it. I pulled it out in a state of bewilderment. A plain
powder-blue-lettering jacket: it looked like the kind of thing
that appeared in bookshops on the remainder tables. More
troubling was the thought that these fifty-odd pages were all I
had to show for the last three years of late nights. I didn't mind
the language seeming simple – I'd spent long hours trying to
make it like that, believing that if the surfaces of the poems
were clear, then readers would be able to look through them
into the complicated tangles of feeling that lay beneath, in

the same way that I felt myself able to do when I was reading Edward Thomas, and Hardy, and Larkin, and the other poets I liked best. But what about those complexities beneath? Did any such things in fact exist? The book was in three parts – an opening section of occasional poems, a middle section containing the long narrative poem that had won the Newdigate Prize, and a final section made up of poems about my mother. As I'd been writing, I'd felt myself to be squaring up to the world in all its aspects. Now it seemed that I'd only been . . . well, what, exactly? I couldn't decide because I found it almost impossible to read what was written on the pages before my eyes. Was it embarrassment that prevented me? Disappointment? No doubt a bit of both – but there was something else as well. Something like a feeling of depletion. I was looking at the record of experiences that I'd meant to intensify, but in fact had diminished as I handed them over to others.

When I next saw Joanna, I gave her this first copy, which seemed only right: the book was dedicated to her and she'd seen all the poems through their early drafts, often giving me advice that I sorely needed. I'd calmed down by this time, and could see more clearly where the book failed and where it succeeded. I had a better sense of its themes, too. My mother, obviously, had been my overriding concern – the fact of the accident, the misery of her hospital existence, and the efforts that my father and brother and I had made to understand what had happened to her. But there was a second and equally large theme in the book, which I now began to notice for the first time. A great many of the poems had to do with different kinds of migration – dislocation, uprooting, deracination. I realised that long before my marriage had started to unravel, I'd been assuming its decay was inevitable. But whose fault was that? Our own? And if so, did that mean I was simply naive and careless, or actually self-destructive? The latter, I suspected, and turned again to thinking about the accident. Perhaps it had led me to try and control life's various forms of conclusion by pre-empting them.

---

I was the first new appointment in the English department since – none of my colleagues could remember, or preferred not to. They were like a still pool and I was a pebble that had been chucked into it, making ripples and annoying them. There were resentments and suspicions. I had suspicions too, and incompetence. I didn't understand this world, I knew next to nothing about the North, I felt at odds with everyone whenever I opened my mouth. What was that growing on my head? Fur err. Even when I made jokes about it, I still sounded like a snob. I wasn't used to having colleagues, either, just as I wasn't used to teaching half the things I was expected to teach. Victorian fiction? I'd read the series of European Poets in Translation that Penguin published in the sixties, and seen my favourite among them, Zbigniew Herbert, attacking 'the hypocrisy that a novel invokes. It is a fabrication, a make-believe kind of life, it results in mundane truths. Too many words. A poem, however, is a condensed experience.' Whether Herbert had meant this literally or not I didn't know, but I'd taken it at face value, and completed my undergraduate course without writing about a single fiction writer. I thought that if I started reading novels, I'd be betraying poetry.

But there was no bullshit in Hull, and as I began to appreciate that, I climbed down off my high horse, read more widely, and became an advocate for what I'd previously denied myself. In the process, and more cautiously, I also began to make friends. With Bruce Woodcock, whose office was next door to my own; with Marion Shaw, who also worked in the English Department, and knew Hull inside out because she'd been born there and never left; and with John Chappell, whose mouth embarrassingly flooded with saliva when he talked, so was easy to imitate and underestimate. John was meant to be my academic supervisor, and did occasionally stick his head round my door while I was teaching to ask if everything was all right – although his best question was: would I like to meet Philip Larkin?

———

I'd often seen photographs of Larkin and thought I knew what to expect. Balding and deaf. Black glasses, dark death-suit, watch-chain. But when John introduced us, in the bar of Staff House one weekday lunchtime, I was still taken aback. For one thing there was an odd feeling of self-parody about Larkin, as though he'd made a cartoon of himself and was hiding inside it. For another, he was a lot bigger than I'd realised – taller, heavier, more looming. More ancient-seeming as well. Only fifty-five, a year younger than my father (and thirty years older than me), but slower, more hesitant, more thoroughly damped down and cut off. Born old, perhaps, which was certainly what the poems wanted to suggest. But also worn down by the years, and unhappy. Overweight. The skin of his face pasty, his hand moist in our handshake.

I prattled away: Oxford (where Larkin had been a student himself); Hull and what I thought of it; teaching and how that was working out; Edward Thomas and my thesis, which I was now turning into a book. Larkin had been craning forward, cupping one hand behind his ear – it was just courtesy, a polite little performance of interest. Although when he heard the word 'thesis', it went into his head like a sprinkle of dust and he sneezed, then took a swig of beer to settle himself. But that promptly went down his throat the wrong way and made him splutter. Suddenly, instead of chatting politely, we were both in a muddle, Larkin struggling to catch his breath, and me slapping him on the back. It took a while for him to recover, and when he eventually removed his glasses to wipe his eyes, I saw two little sore patches either side of his nose, where the frames rubbed him. I thought: he's the best poet alive and famous for being a recluse, but here I am seeing him as though he's just got out of bed.

'You'd think I'd know how to drink a pint of beer by now,' Larkin said, heaving and sighing, then blowing his nose with a large white handkerchief.

I wanted to say, 'Yes, you would think that,' but sidestepped and told him instead that my father was a brewer, as though it might give the impression that I'd spent my entire life surrounded by people choking on beer, and the odd splutter here and there was nothing unusual.

'A brewer!' Larkin almost shouted, and his eyes, focusing behind their glasses again, lit up: it seemed that he liked the idea of my coming from stock that produced something people actually want – alcohol – rather than something they can take or leave – poetry.

———

Joanna and I stuck to our plan and every fortnight one of us would drive to the other's city. In my times alone I explored Hull or drove into the Yorkshire Wolds and wandered through oak woods in the somnolent estates, where the pigeons applauded my arrival, then left me alone. I visited Castle Howard with a new arrival in the department, Angela Leighton, and stood beside her at the Temple of the Four Winds, listening to the sounds of the sky. I caught the Humber ferry and scooted south through Lincolnshire between mile after mile of cabbage fields, then disappeared into the labyrinth of lanes around Somersby, d where I talked to the ghost of Tennyson. I spent another weekend in Essex, and visited my mother. These days, whenever I peeped round the side of the door into her ward before she knew I was watching, I could see that her chin was dropping lower and lower onto her chest and her eyes were sinking further and further into her head. Her light was burning out.

---

The *Hull Daily Mail* organised a poetry competition to mark the opening of the Humber Bridge – there would be an adults' section and a children's section – and the editor asked Larkin to be one of the judges and me to be the other: maybe this editor thought one of us had lived in Hull too long to say no, and the other not long enough. In any case, it was only an hour's work – probably a visit to Larkin's office after lunch one day. But Larkin had a different idea and invited me to come round to his house after supper: we'd do the judging over a drink.

I didn't know anyone who'd been inside Larkin's house, but the poems gave me an idea of what I might find. Not Mr Bleaney's room exactly, with flowered curtains, thin and frayed, falling to within five inches of the sill, but certainly simple. Bachelor tidiness. Odds and ends of specially chosen junk. All the same, when I'd made my way into the little enclave of streets opposite the university – a kind of un-gated gated community for senior staff and business people – I could hardly believe that I'd got the right address. 105 Newland Park (now much altered by subsequent owners) was a severely plain house: sore-looking pink-red brick, and a pollarded tree by the front gate, like the stump in a Brueghel picture. Had Larkin simply not noticed, or didn't he care? Neither thing could be true; his poems were full of beautiful things and they were all beautifully seen: high-builded clouds; the lion-faced sun; trees coming into leaf like something almost being said. It was more likely, I thought, that he felt something hidden from him had chosen it – proving that he was right to expect disappointment at every turn of his life.

Larkin opened the door looking both more and less like himself than he did at the university: jacket off, red braces, tie loose, mug of gin and tonic in one hand; his face, which always seemed severe in photographs, was flushed and smiling. A broad smile, like a child, but nervous too. He swayed slightly, ushering me into the dark hall and saying I must call him Philip now, not Dr Larkin. That would take a bit of getting used to, but there was no time to think about it now; I'd been distracted by a decorative plate hanging on the wall at the foot of the stairs. 'Prepare to Meet Thy God', it said: I couldn't decide whether it was funny or sad to realise that must be what Philip saw first thing every morning. Both, no doubt. In the same way that I'd often found it difficult to separate sad things from funny things in his poems.

When we reached the sitting room I went on noticing; it was like walking into Auden's sitting room three years earlier: I thought that I'd never see any of this again and wanted to remember it for ever. Thick green carpet; dark green William

Morris wallpaper; a paler green sofa against one wall, beneath what looked like – what was – a small Gainsborough oil painting of some cattle lying under a tree; a gas fire and a large clock above it, the hand permanently trembling like the one in my mother's ward; a window covered with a Venetian blind, but glimpses of garden-darkness through the slats; a G-plan chair with its back to this window – rough green cotton and bare wooden arms; an annex to the right where two more armchairs were drawn up to face a turned-off television set with a pot plant balanced on its head; and beyond that a small kitchen – gas stove, white cupboards, Formica-topped table.

And books. Books on shelves either side of the chimney breast where the gas fire was purring: Owen, Rossetti, Hardy, Barnes, Tennyson, the Powys family. Books about jazz above a small record player and a large collection of records – they were mostly jazz, too, but lying face up there was also a recording of *Macbeth* starring Alec Guinness. And notebooks in a separate little glass-fronted cabinet on the way through to the kitchen; were they the ones that Larkin – Philip – used for writing poems?

I drank a glass of white wine, then switched to gin, and we began judging the poems – the adults' section first, because Philip said that in his view children's poems were often better than poems by adults, and he wanted to end on a high note. I took the point – something about the innocent eye – but couldn't help wondering how many children's poems, or children, come to that, Philip had actually seen. After all, this was the man who'd referred to children as 'little scum', upbraiding them for 'their noise, their nastiness, their boasting, their back-answers, their cruelty, their silliness'. But that was something else I mustn't think about now. We were meant to be concentrating on poems, looking for something about how the new bridge across the Humber would join up things that had previously been separated, blah blah. Philip went next door to fill up our drinks. When he came back, he put on some Duke Ellington and capered round the room, sloshing a quill of gin onto the carpet. 'I could win this,' he said, beaming. 'I put my luncheon in the fridge,/ And go and look at Humber Bridge.'

When the judging was done, we listened to the beginning of *Macbeth* and chatted until Philip fell asleep in his chair. Almost immediately he woke up again and apologised, saying not to worry, he often did that. But it was obviously time for me to go. I looked round the room once more – the gas fire, the dark walls, the books, the carpet, and the wallpaper – and thought it seemed as if Philip had made himself a burrow. A place where he could hide, inside a city that had turned its back on the world. I also thought it was a shame he was so well known, because otherwise, if this evening was anything to go by, we might soon become friends. And that would mean, among other things, that I could override those questions about acquaintance as evidence of ambition, which had bothered me when I first applied for the job in Hull.

It was December, and Philip's mother had died: he told me at lunchtime when we were drinking in the Staff House bar – he'd been to church and prayed for her. He sounded sheepish as he said this, as well as melancholy, then swallowed some more beer and pulled himself together. He'd finished a new poem, he told me, and bulged his eyes – it was something he'd been working on for years but until now hadn't been able to finish.

He didn't say outright that his mother's death had made the completion possible, but he certainly implied as much.

I told him how pleased I was, and Philip shook his head. 'Yes,' he said, 'normally I feel like a chicken that can't lay eggs any longer.' He stared ruefully into his beer, then roused himself – politeness, despite his reputation as a misery guts, was always paramount. Almost always, anyway. 'What about you?' he asked. 'Are you writing anything?' Then he glanced at me sideways; I got the impression that if I said yes, he'd have thought it was merely proof of incontinence.

'Nothing much,' I told him, which happened to be true. After finishing *The Pleasure Steamers*, I'd felt a key turn in my mind and lock out poems for a while. The explanation was partly practical: I needed to finish turning my thesis on Edward Thomas into a book, and respraying academic prose was time-consuming. But it also had something to do with a feeling of blockage. Philip's mother's death had helped to free him for one last brilliant cry of despair. My own mother's half-life still flooded my imagination so completely, I couldn't see beyond her to any new subjects. I wanted to. I wanted to start writing about Hull, and Spurn Point, and my walks in the pigeon-clattering woods on the East Riding. But every time I turned to these things my mother's hand reached out to bar the way.

Perhaps there was now another obstacle as well, nothing like as grievous, but substantial all the same. Because I was spending more time with Philip, the example of his austerity had become more commanding – for good, in the sense that it made me write more carefully, but for ill in the sense that it made me feel any sort of doodling and experimentation was likely to be a waste of time. A masterpiece or nothing! If I'd been invited to look inside Philip's own notebooks, I'd have seen that until fairly recently he'd been as keen on trial and error as the next poet. But the brevity of his published books, and the decade that passed between the publication of each, had given the impression that he was parsimonious, rather than severely judicious. Besides, there was the question of my independence. Although I still felt as I'd always done about 'influence' – more welcoming than anxious – I understood the difference between admiration and imitation. And greatly as I admired Philip's poems, I'd never doubted that our emotional landscapes were significantly different. War-shadows had fallen across his childhood in ways they hadn't across mine – more exactly and more definitely; his political sympathies lay much further to the right than mine; his suspicions or disapprovals of 'abroad' bore no resemblance to my own feelings about life outside England; his 'difficulties with girls' were fed by the prejudices of a distinctly older generation; he resorted to satire more often than I did; and his melancholy was fiercer, more straightforwardly death-dreading. Also, I was more interested in modernist writers than he was, and more willing than he'd ever been to head in the direction I thought they were pointing. How to be sceptical and adventurous at the same time, and how to be lucid while acknowledging the mysteries of life – these were the questions that most bothered me, and I needed to think more about them. Before I started writing poems again, I had to pause and stand back.

A week or so later, Philip's new poem appeared in the *Times Literary Supplement*. It was called 'Aubade', which means dawn poem. Most aubades say something about feeling glad to see the new day and new sunlight, but not this one. This one says: 'In time the curtain-edges will grow light./ Till then I see what's really always there:/ Unresting death, a whole day nearer now,/ Making all thought impossible but how/ And where and when I shall myself die.' The next time we met, during the following January, I told Philip the poem had moved me so much it had come close to spoiling my Christmas – in the best possible way. Philip laughed and mentioned Judy Egerton, a friend from his time in Belfast during the early 1950s. She'd written to him one year saying how much she hated Christmas, knowing that he'd understand what she meant. He wrote back saying indeed he did. She then wrote saying thanks, but her Christmas was worse than his, because she was about to lose her job, her husband had left home, and her children were no longer speaking to her. Philip wrote to her a second time: ah yes, he said, but 'mine is happening to me'.

My mother caught pneumonia again, so I drove down from Hull to keep watch at her bedside. There had been scares like this before, several of them, but I didn't want to take a chance. I held her hand and listened to the oxygen hissing up its tube and into the mask clamped across her face; every time she exhaled, a little puff of shit-smell fanned into the room. Had I reached the point where I actually wanted her to die, so that she would be spared more suffering? I couldn't hold the question in my head for long; it was too large and too painful. Most of the time, and despite everything, it was obvious that she herself still wanted to live, because she still wanted to show every possible sign of love and mothering. But when she was like this, drifting and comatose, I had no idea what she wished for. Her labouring might simply be proof of a body's hunger for survival, no matter what it had to endure.

A couple of days later my mother surfaced again, lying mutely on her bed and staring at the ceiling. But she rallied a little, as she'd always done before, and next Sunday my father and brother and I collected her in the van and brought her home for lunch, manhandling her stretcher through the hallway and parking it at the end of the dining-room table. Her shit-smell swarmed under a smudge of talcum. Her swollen and calcified feet, poking out from her tartan rug, were tilted as usual, as though she was permanently practising how to stand on tiptoe. I moved to her side, rearranged the rug to cover her, then sat back down. Susan watched from the doorway – Susan, the most recent of my father's housekeepers, now that Este had left. She'd cooked chicken and peas, and my mother was using her one sort-of-usable hand to scoop some of the peas onto her fork. But her hand was shaking so badly, the peas fell off. She tried again. The peas rolled off again. She tried again. Could I help? No, my mother whispered, she wanted to do it herself. This time the peas bounced off her plate onto the carpet and the dog ate them.

———

Was I waiting to live full-time with Joanna again, or did we want to continue with our experiment? The latter, apparently, which meant among other things that the longer I stayed in Hull, the stranger it felt to be around people who were securely paired off. Or who seemed to be securely paired off, anyway – because when I quizzed them about it, a lot of them seemed to be living like characters in a John Updike novel. Maybe it had something to do with the city being isolated: people felt they could have fun and keep secrets because no one was looking. Or maybe they were just spicing up their lives by inventing fantasies, even when they weren't actually doing much.

I talked about it with Marion, my friend in the English Department – we were spending a lot of time together now, and she had an accepting sort of mind that was hard to shock. She told me Hull had always been like this and launched into a story. While she was growing up here during the war she'd had tuberculosis and lived for years in a clinic on the outskirts of the city, sleeping at night on the balcony so that she could breathe fresh air into her lungs. One night she asked the nurse why there'd been two sunsets earlier that evening, and the nurse said that wasn't right: the first sunset had been the real one, and the second one was the docks burning because the Germans had bombed them. Then Marion checked herself and said that wasn't what she'd meant to tell me. What she'd meant to say was: even in the hospital, people were at it like rabbits. In fact, after the war she actually married one of the other patients, Leon. But their life fell to bits when she went to university as a mature student. Now Leon lived in Whitby and was running an antiques shop, putting ships in bottles. Marion herself was a senior lecturer and married for the second time, although in a semi-detached kind of way.

We slipped off together to the Lake District for a few days – I'd never been there before and almost burst out laughing when we arrived. It was so kitsch! Like a gigantic biscuit-tin lid. Not that I said as much when we booked into our hotel, or even next morning, when I saw a red squirrel jumping through the silver birch trees at the foot of Loughrigg, where we began our climb.

We took it slowly and Marion told me about her mother, who'd left instructions in her will that she wanted to be cremated. After the service Marion had brought the ashes here to the Lakes, which her mother loved to visit. She carried the urn to a lonely spot with a good wide view, unscrewed the top, and reverently shook out the ashes. But as they wafted across the ground, a flock of starlings flew down and ate every last one. Marion laughed as she remembered this – she had a lovely skirling chuckle. She said she didn't mind in the least and knew her mother wouldn't have minded either: her mother had a soft spot for starlings. They're clever, she said; her cousin Edwin had one in his garden that knew how to make a sound like the phone ringing, and he was always having to dash indoors to check.

We were standing at the summit now, gazing down the heathery slope towards the lake of black water below, pressing into the wind. My biscuit-tin snobbery had disappeared, and I felt happy – conscious that for a moment at least I was standing where I wanted to stand, in company I wanted to keep. So it must have been something like exuberance that prompted what happened next, which was my right foot lifting to rest against a nearby stone, then pushing until the stone began to roll forward.

I knew immediately that I'd made a mistake – the bad kind that quickly multiplies and expands. And sure enough, as the stone set off and gathered speed, it dislodged other larger stones, so within a few seconds there was a whole rabble of them clicking away downhill, a mini-avalanche of pebbles, rocks, and boulders bouncing through the heather and heading towards the path, where other unsuspecting hikers were now striding towards us. Really, though, what had I been thinking a moment ago? Was it in fact exuberance, or was it a form of despair – because although I liked Marion very much, I hated the rest of my life and wanted to smash it to pieces? I crouched down on my haunches with my hands over my eyes, waiting for disaster.

But the stones all missed their target – if there had ever been a target. Through the gaps in my fingers, I saw the hikers below me skip out of the way, then lift their angry faces, shouting accusingly while the stones continued their riot down the hill, leaping and frisking and spinning and turning somersaults until they disappeared into the same little wood where I'd seen the red squirrel, thrashing through the leaves and at last slamming into the tree trunks and stopping dead. Just for a moment I had the feeling – the silvery whoosh of relief – that my own life was the one that had been spared. Then my mind swivelled back to the others again. If the avalanche had struck the hikers, it would certainly have hurt them. Killed them, even. And then I would have been accused of manslaughter and punished. Sent to prison, perhaps. Instead of which – this next-to-nothing. A fist waving in the distance. An aggrieved bellow. Then a disbelieving laugh and the hikers striding forward again. 'I'm sorry,' I told Marion. 'I don't know what happened there.' But that wasn't true. I knew perfectly well what had happened. I had uncovered something destructive in myself. Something which, in its appetite for ruin, signified impatience with the hard facts of existence, and attraction to the irresponsible freedoms of a ghost – a spectre that couldn't be held responsible for its own actions.

---

I was teaching Wordsworth, talking about one of the so-called Lucy poems, 'She dwelt among the untrodden ways':

She dwelt among the untrodden ways
    Beside the springs of Dove,
A Maid whom there were none to praise
    And very few to love.

A violet by a mossy stone
    Half hidden from the eye!
Fair as a star, when only one
    Is shining in the sky.

She lived unknown, and few could know
    When Lucy ceased to be;
But she is in her grave, and, oh,
    The difference to me!

One of the students in my class, cleverer than the others, took me to task for liking it so much. The words were too simple, she said. 'Oh,/ The difference to me!' A child of five could have written that; it was babyish. I did what I could to make her think otherwise, but the student snorted and stalked out of my office – I thought I might not see her again.

Next week she didn't show up for class. It was a pity; I'd liked teaching her. But the week after that she was back again, haunted-looking. She stayed behind at the end of the class and when I asked her what was the matter, she apologised for her previous absence: her mother had died, and she'd been home for the funeral. All the time she'd been away, she said, she hadn't been able to get the phrase 'oh, the difference to me' out of her head. She said that she felt the 'o' of 'oh' had been filled in.

In another class, one of the students said she thought that all poems were varieties of love poem – they held out their hand to the reader, asking for the affection of individual attention and advertising a general feeling of tenderness towards the world. I said that I liked the idea, but there seemed to be something potentially sentimental about it – as though a poet who believed such a thing might also feel a compulsion to please their readers at all costs. In one sense, my response was a form of self-defence: for reasons I couldn't entirely understand, I'd almost never written a love poem. Did I lack the quickness of mind and generosity of spirit to find a way past the inevitable clichés? Or did I doubt the durability of love, and therefore feel reluctant to write anything that might suggest otherwise?

In a sense, my reply to the student was simply a kind of throat-clearing, and once I'd allowed myself another moment to think, I gave her a different answer. I said that while love might be part of the impulse that brought poems into the world, my own experience had persuaded me that death was the stronger force. For that reason, I thought all poems were a form of elegy rather than varieties of love poetry. Obviously so, when they commemorated someone dead ('Lycidas', 'Adonais', Hardy's *Poems of 1912–13*); less obviously, but just as decisively, when they were not specifically concerned with mortality, but simply noticing the passage of time. Which thanks to their intrinsic nature they cannot help but do. Either by design or by implication, every poem on every subject insists: 'I saw this and now I don't see it any more,' or it reminds the reader, 'This particular thing/feeling/moment existed and now it doesn't.' Which is to say: poems are conscious of time before they are conscious of anything, and because time passes, and carries everything towards its end, they are both its flag-bearer and apologist. Its enemy, as well. Because poems snatch people and events from the current of minutes passing, and fix them in forms that defy time. This is the sense in which all poems are elegies. They are a way of grieving which is also a way of surviving – and within that paradoxical and enormous compass, every other subject is subordinate. Including even love.

———

Joanna had a change of heart, decided that she wanted us to live together, and got a job in the Admin building at the university. So we rented out the house in Oxford to Alan and our mutual friend Stephen Pickles, said good riddance to De Grey Street, and arranged to house-sit for a colleague of mine in the English Department who was moving to Canada for a year. Kirk Ella. A zombie suburb of Hull, as it turned out, where cars bumbled past our kitchen window at walking speed, schoolchildren passed in silent crocodiles, and neighbours spoke across their fences in whispers, if they spoke at all. Most of the time, Kirk Ella lay frozen in a day-long, night-long sepulchral hush. Fir trees and Russian vines. Leaded lights and net curtains.

Still, there was enough room for us to have people to supper now, and when Philip came, he met Joanna for the first time. It occurred to me, watching them talk by the gas fire after we'd eaten, that if Philip had been younger, he might have fallen in love with her. She was everything he liked: independent and clever and funny and beautiful – and she'd read a lot. No wonder he was laughing more than usual. Then I saw Philip notice a bookmark that someone had given us, propped on the mantelpiece. It was inscribed with a quote on it from Logan Pearsall Smith: 'Some people say life's the thing, but I prefer reading.'

Suddenly Philip was no longer laughing. 'What absolute balls,' he said impatiently, spinning on his heel. 'Life's definitely the thing, not books. Life.' It was a surprise to see him so heated, then no surprise at all: it was never the case that he'd given up on life, rather that he felt life had given up on him.

———

This was the pattern with Philip now: supper at home from time to time, occasional meals in the local Indian, and lunch once a week or so in the Staff House bar: not much to drink for me because I had to teach, but two or three pints for Philip, who liked to nap in the afternoon, with Betty the loaf-haired secretary guarding the door to his office. We talked about university business a good deal – gossip and grievances – but about poetry too: who had published what, who was any good (almost nobody, Philip thought, although Gavin Ewart got a pass), and who was best among the mighty dead. I always thought I knew who he was going to praise – Barnes, Rossetti, Hardy, Owen, Betjeman, Stevie Smith – but sometimes he surprised me. One day he quoted from memory a long section of Auden's 'Letter to a Wound', the part about the rectal fissure that Auden suffered during an encounter with a sailor. Another time, talking about Oscar Wilde, Philip told me the story of a recently widowed woman who'd been wretched for months, until Wilde made her laugh. Art as consolation, I thought. Like booze. One day, when I admitted that I was feeling low, Philip leaned forward and asked solicitously, 'Are you drinking enough?' Probably not, I told him. He recommended a glass of port at breakfast. 'I find it very comforting.'

Then there were the times he asked me round to Newland

Park: evenings drinking and chatting; afternoons watching sport on the telly with the volume cranked up, so that his
hearing aids could pick up the commentary. Cricket in summer, and rugby in winter, with the plant pot shaking on top of
the set, and Philip shouting 'Get it out! Get it out!' as the ball
squirted along the line of the three-quarters. Did he feel pater-
nal towards me? There was an element of that, unlikely as it
seemed, and I felt grateful for it. But it wasn't the whole truth.
It was mostly a matter of kindness. When he was propping up
the bar in the Staff House Philip often sounded blokeish, and
he had a reputation for being stern as well as idiosyncratic in
the pursuit of university business. But really his curmudgeon-
liness was a facade. Not meaningless and not entirely a pre-
tence – he meant it when he railed against annoying children,
or the obscurities of modernism. But his bluster was also a way
of protecting himself. His childhood stammer may have all but
disappeared (he still occasionally made what he called his 'bush-
man's click', as he swallowed his own verbal stumbles), but the
shyness of which it had originally been a part still remained
('shyness', he told me once, is 'the great under-appreciated force
in human behaviour'). It sharpened the edge of everything he
thought and felt and said, giving his personality its streak of
coarseness as well as its swath of sensitivity. And it was combined with a convulsive kind of truthfulness, which meant that
he always said exactly what he believed, even when (or because)
he knew it might upset people. He was honest with himself to
a fault, and this honesty was a crucial ingredient in the genesis
and authority of his poems.

It could also make him objectionable to anyone who didn't
share his views. During one of our earliest encounters, he told
me that he sometimes ended his letters to Kingsley Amis, and

his conversations with other friends like Robert Conquest and Monica Jones, by saying 'Fuck Oxfam', where anyone else might have said 'Cheers', or simply 'Goodbye'. I made a face when he told me this, and began to explain that because Joanna actually worked for Oxfam, I couldn't . . . But he apologised before I could finish my sentence, and from that moment on we steered clear of such salutations, as well as anything resembling the misogyny and racism that I would later find sprinkled through his letters. It meant that I knew nothing about their extent until after his death, although I guessed that they existed, because all our conversations, friendly as they became, had a slight but definite sense of limitation. The difference between our ages and achievements had something to do with it – but there was this as well: for all our shared poetic enthusiasms, and despite certain affinities in our temperaments, we lived at widely separated points on the political spectrum. For the sake of our friendship, we chose not to make an issue of this.

———

Kirk Ella was more comfortable than De Grey Street, but its silence felt like suffocation. And living full-time with Joanna might have ended my previous solitude, but it also brought complications: gaps had opened in our life that neither of us wanted to close. I knew what needed to happen. I must leave Hull and move south again, either to London or back to Oxford. But just as I'd done when first arriving in Hull, I felt paralysed, unable to twist my life into a new shape. I drove back to Spurn Point and stared past the river-mouth ships into the North Sea: it was winter now but uncannily calm and bright, and as the waves died against the shore they gave feeble little shudders,

their thin ice-skins crackling in the foam. Why would no saviour rise from the depths and take charge of my existence? I
despised myself for wanting such a thing – it made me feel
that I'd allowed my mother's immobility to become the guarantee of my own. But I knew that until her situation changed,
I was bound to follow the example she couldn't help but give.
The waves continued to make their brittle advance, and their
equally brittle retreat, and I watched them until my head was
numb with cold. Then I drove back to Kirk Ella and sat down
in the sitting room, staring through the picture window and
watching the frost tighten its grip on the garden.

As darkness fell the temperature plummeted, and by the
time Joanna and I went to bed the pipes had frozen. Paralysis
again, and again nothing to be done, so we rolled over facing
in opposite directions, and fell asleep. Then it was four o'clock
in the morning and Joanna was shaking me awake, telling me
that water was seeping through the ceiling above us: there must
have been a thaw in the small hours, and a pipe had burst. Or
more than just one. I scrambled upright, tugged down the steps
into the attic, and fumbled through the darkness under the
eaves, Joanna following with a torch. The beam flickered, our
shadows leaped around us, and there it was – no kind of saviour
but certainly a sign: burst pipes spurting among bare timbers,
their joints blown apart; little jets and large fierce slatherings.
Was there a plumber nearby? We had no idea. Where was the
stopcock? No idea about that either. Six years before, one of our
greatest pleasures had been lying in bed together, watching the
rooks sway in their high elm-nests beyond our windows in Toot
Baldon. Now we were perched on the joists like roosting birds
ourselves, clutching the pipes as icy water squeezed between
our fingers, then plunged into the house below. I imagined it

prising wallpaper off the walls, drenching beds, spoiling pictures, soaking into books, and saturating carpets. I thought of
our landlord in Canada, and how I'd have to ring him in the
morning and tell him that his house had been ruined. I wanted
to turn into water myself, to fall down through darkness and
disappear.

---

I talked to Philip about my life with Joanna, and he told me
about his routines with and without Monica — Monica Jones,
the dedicatee of *The Less Deceived*. He'd often mentioned her
before, but never given much detail — complaining once that
she'd taken a first edition of one of Evelyn Waugh's novels from
his shelves and read it while lying in the bath, which spoiled the
pages, or groaning affectionately about the holidays they took
together every summer. Now he admitted that as well as seeing
each other most weekends, they spoke on the telephone every
evening, sometimes for hours. Philip thought it might be one of
the reasons why he didn't write poems any more: phone time
and drinking time had taken over his end-of-day writing time.

Then Philip brought Monica into the Staff Bar because she'd
come to stay for a few days — she wasn't exactly a secret within
the university, just someone he kept in the background. He
introduced her somewhat bashfully, as though he was reminding me of someone I'd already met, which in a sense I had. This
was the complicated 'darling' of the poems; the shadowy shape
on the adjacent pillow of 'Talking in Bed'. But page-meetings
were nothing compared to shaking the hand of the real-life
woman, and I scrutinised her while trying not to stare. A gin
drinker, evidently, even at one o'clock. Dressy but dishevelled.

Eccentric. Big glasses blurred with fingerprints and a wet-looking mouth. Fishnet stockings, slightly grubby white silk shirt, and tartan skirt. Haphazard lipstick and a smear on her front tooth. Everything about her looked slightly skew-whiff but sexy, like a woman in a sixties film, when the old boundaries were starting to give way. And a bluestocking, asking me tricky questions. What did I think of Walter Scott? And George Crabbe – surely I must like him, as a fellow East Anglian? And what about the 1850 version of *The Prelude*? People were always saying it was much worse than the 1805 version, but was it, in fact? It was obvious what she was doing. Assessing me, just as I'd been assessing her. Seeing if I was fit to be Philip's friend.

Joanna and I were milling around in the kitchen, pouring drinks and beginning to make supper, when the phone rang in the hall. Joanna answered, sitting down on the bottom step of the stairs. It was my father. I worked that out immediately, listening between the words of the Joan Armatrading song that was playing in the sitting room opposite. And when I saw Joanna running her hand through her hair, and heard her saying, 'I'm so sorry, Richard, I'm so sorry,' I knew what my father had just told her. My mother had died.

What had I been telling myself about salvation and the shape of a life? It all seemed like nonsense now. There had only ever been one sign that I was looking out for, and it had nothing to do with the icy North Sea, and burst pipes, and ruined rooms. It was this. But now that it had come, and although I'd been waiting to see it for almost as long as I could remember, I felt nothing. Nothing, except a deep incompetence. Like someone who for year after year had been facing a long journey, but endlessly put off packing the things that I needed to take with me, and now had to scramble everything together at the last minute. I couldn't find my feelings! Where had I put them?

Joanna was beckoning to me, holding out the phone while my father's voice choked into empty space, but I stared beyond her into the garden, watching silhouettes of the leylandii sway in the moonlight. I'd always thought leylandii were horrible trees – just giant weeds really; if this were my own house, I'd have cut them down. Then I heard a voice at the back of my mind saying, 'Oh – Oh, the difference to me' – and the black ink of the evening rushed in to flood the empty pool of the capital letter.

———

I drove down from Hull to my father's house, and Joanna arrived a few days later, in time for the funeral. I felt beside myself: it's the phrase people use when they lose control, but I meant it literally. I was separated from myself, as though I'd become my own shadow and was watching myself from a distance, coldly observing and functioning with a strange automatic practicality. All the more so because my father – I'd never seen him like this before – was completely at a loss. That was another cliché, and also perfectly true. My father, who was normally so reliable, such a good soldier, suddenly couldn't make decisions, didn't want to see anyone, was even more silent and withdrawn than usual. Very well, I thought: I'll take charge. I talked to the undertaker and selected the coffin; I met the parish priest and chose the hymns and prayers for the funeral service; I rang the local Sue Ryder charity and arranged for them to collect my mother's clothes – the clothes that had been hanging unused in her cupboard all this time, or lying folded in the trunk in the attic, because throwing them away would have meant finally accepting that she was never going to wear them again. Did my father want to give the eulogy at the service? No. Very well, I'd do that too. I shocked myself with my own efficiency. Although I was trying to help, it looked as though I was hurrying my mother out of our lives. And in a way I was; I wanted to be in the aftermath of her death, not still caught in its storm.

———

Visitors called and left us with more worn-out language: my mother's death was a merciful release. I understood why they said it, they only meant to be kind, but at the same time I objected: who were they to decide whether her life had been worth living? I'd asked myself the same question only the other day, when my mother was still warm and breathing, and now that she was dead my feelings remained the same: my mother herself had been the only person entitled to choose her fate, and for nine years she had chosen to live, because she loved her family more than she hated her own distress.

But in the end it turned out that even she couldn't cheat the grave indefinitely. No, that wasn't right. I didn't mean 'cheat', I meant resist. Even she couldn't resist the grave indefinitely. In which case mercy didn't come into it, and release was not the word.

———

My father roused from his trance and said the hospital had rung to ask whether any of us wanted to see my mother's body – he quickly added that he didn't want to go himself, he preferred to remember her alive. My father was definite about this, and I didn't like to disagree with him: we were both so reluctant to confront one another at the best of times, it would have seemed as though we were having a row if I'd gone my own way at this worst of times. And yet when I followed suit, and told him that I didn't want to see her either, I immediately regretted it, and realised that I'd go on regretting it for ever. My mother's death had already been hideously protracted; now it would feel endless.

Still, the decision comforted my father as I'd hoped it would, and gradually he began to climb out of himself. When the hearse carrying her coffin arrived outside our front door, looking as out of place as a whale in a country stream, he shooed me and Kit briskly into his own car so that we could form a little procession down to the church. On the way, he pointed out a new house that had been built next to the village hall, and said how well he thought it fitted in. When we came to the main street and a man who lived in one of the cottages stepped forward and swept off his cap to hold it over his heart, my father said how good it was of him: 'Everyone loved your mother,' he said. 'Everyone.' My brother and I nodded our heads as the hearse continued its imperturbable slide down the slope, and by the time it had docked near the lychgate, the world had melted.

The church and graveyard stand on a shelf of flat ground, with a view across the River Blackwater towards farmland on the opposite side. My father straightened out of the car and gazed across the fields at a flock of peewits wheeling above the plough; his face looked wide open and oddly relaxed, tears oozing from his eyes with no effort of restraint, as though he was leaking an endless supply. Then he turned back to the hearse and his face closed again. My own face had already shut; my tears were dry. My brother was the same. None of us wanted anything to do with the congregation milling up the pathway into the porch; we needed to keep our feelings to ourselves – not just our sadness, but the anger that suddenly stirred alongside it. Where had these people been when my mother was lying unvisited in her dismal ward? Only a very few of them had come to see her; the rest forgot or pushed her to the side of their minds. Hitherto I'd felt some sympathy for them: I knew how distressing it could be to visit her. But today I despised them and wanted them gone. Which was impossible, because today was as much for others as it was for me and my father and Kit. So I lifted my head and said nothing. I walked impassively beside my father, with my brother and Joanna following, as the undertakers carried my mother's coffin into the church. I watched them lay the coffin on a pair of plain wooden trestles in the nave as calmly as if I were seeing porters install an item in an exhibition.

Then the service began – and immediately was almost over. Time collapsed. One minute I was hurrying through all the scenes of my life during my mother's illness – days when I'd missed her at school, and in Greece, and Turkey, and Oxford, and Toot Baldon, and Hull – and the next minute I was trapped in the crowded church, incapable of thinking about anything except her ruined body inside the coffin. My feelings had buckled, too – I couldn't keep hold of them or decipher them properly. I wanted today over and done with, and the world quiet again, but I also needed today to last for ever. I wanted Limbo, in fact. Limbo was where I'd been living since childhood, and where I knew how to survive, and Limbo was where I wanted to stay.

I crouched down in the pew, noticing how distinctly my father gave the responses and thinking that was a good sign, because it showed that he had taken charge again. And when I walked to the pulpit to give the address, my own voice also held steady and I felt proud of that. Then I saw Sandy's face among the other pale bubbles floating below me. I'd just been thinking about our travels together in Greece, and how he'd come to my rescue with his water bottle when I was in trouble with the heat, how he was always helping me one way or another, and I suspected for a moment that I might be hallucinating. But of course he was there. Sandy was Sandy. My oldest friend and the only one who remembered my mother in her time before the accident. These days he was living on a boat by Chelsea Bridge, and had recently broken his arm when the crank-handle he used to start the engine had swung back at him. I could see the plaster now, blistering white among the dark suits and overcoats. Dear Sandy, who was younger than me but always seemed like my older brother. The sight of him with tears running down his face, stoical Sandy of all people, made me lose my own way.

Which is the last thing I can remember about that day. Nothing about the coffin being carried out of the church and put in the ground near the graves of my great-grandfather and great-grandmother; nothing about the wake afterwards; nothing about how long I stayed with my father before driving back to Hull. I'd always prided myself on my memory, and deliberately cultivated it after the accident, as a way of keeping my mother present and my childhood intact. But now a blank had opened in my mind – a complete absence of time, after years when it felt as though time had been churning at a standstill. I stared into the emptiness, willing whatever had disappeared to come back again, and eventually I began to remember. There was my mother's coffin, gleaming deep down in the trench of her grave. And there on the lid was the small brass plaque inscribed with her name: Catherine Gillian Motion. No one had ever called her Catherine; she'd always been Gilly, not Gillian, as I'd kept telling her nurses; and Motion was her married name, not her birth name. I corrected myself. There was her name which was not her name. Her self which was not her self.

# Part Four

---

## 1978–1993

I'd wanted a saviour to rescue me when I squinted into the sun at Spurn Point, and imagined an Angel of Mercy. What came instead was the Angel of Death, and a year after my mother's funeral it led me to resign from my job in Hull and move back to Oxford. Stephen Pickles, the friend who'd been sharing my house there with Alan, was moving to London and I took his place. Joanna decided to stay in Hull for the time being, and we resumed our alternate-weekend routine, with the homeplaces switched around this time.

---

I opened the front door and looked outside: tall Victorian ter-raced houses opposite, where an unhappy-looking doctor lived with his pretty wife – Alan thought she was about to leave him and run off; the Thames to the right, bulging between stone embankments; and beyond that the bridge with its red-brick folly, its white statues in dark niches, then the wiry trees of Christ Church Meadow. The old question came back to me: had I been born too late, or born too soon? I still couldn't decide. On a patch of waste ground beyond the doctor's house, a property company was planning a new hotel, and men were prowling about in hard yellow hats, staring into theodolites. Whatever this new-old life turned out to be like, nothing was going to stay the same for long.

I went back indoors and sat down with Alan at the table in our dining room – the round walnut table that I'd inherited from my grandmother, my mother's mother. When my mother had been a child, she'd jabbed the point of her protractor into the wood and dragged round the sharp nib of the pen attached to it, scratching a circle in the surface. There was the scar, still perfectly clear – a dark central dot, surrounded by a small perfect circle; as I traced it with my fingertip and felt the little bump, a jolt ran through me like electricity.

———

We'd been talking about Tennyson, and now Alan was reading aloud: 'Audley Court'. It was a story but a lyric as well, about two men who eat a picnic and muse about the world and their girlfriends. Although when they get to the musing part, the men are really singing about each other:

> 'Sleep, Ellen Aubrey, sleep, and dream of me:
> Sleep, Ellen, folded in thy sister's arm,
> And sleeping, haply dream her arm is mine.
>     'Sleep, Ellen, folded in Emelia's arm;
> Emelia, fairer than all else but thou,
> For thou art fairer than all else that is.'

The poem was a kind of touchstone for us – a way of proving that we liked the same writers, but also that we shared a taste for things that were full-on beautiful while also oblique or re-directed. Relish the English language – use all of it! But also set it at an angle to its subjects, so as to catch the deep truths that lie in implication. So that unsaid notions can be recorded, as well as notions clearly stated. That was our ideal. Like the moment in Philip's poem 'The Whitsun Weddings', where he says that 'sun destroys/ The interest of what's happening in the shade'. We wanted to notice things that lived in obscurity, or things that preferred to be – had to be – discreetly reserved, as well as things that enjoyed the light.

> 'Sleep, breathing health and peace upon her breast:
> Sleep, breathing love and trust against her lip:
> I go tonight: I come tomorrow morn.
>  'I go, but I return: I would I were
> The pilot of the darkness and the dream.
> Sleep, Ellen Aubrey, love, and dream of me.'

For the first time in my life, I was free to give days the shape I chose, rather than having to chop and change myself to fit in with someone else's structures. But it turned out that I liked structures, as I'd begun to discover when I first lived with Joanna. Back then, in our sky-boat under the eaves, our daytime had been given over to work-work (Joanna commuting to her desk in the Oxfam office, me in the library writing my weekly undergraduate essays), and the evening to ourselves. Now I discovered that early mornings suited me best, because in the early mornings a vigilant part of my mind was still in touch with my dream-mind, and this meant that the balance between my conscious and unconscious was steadier than it became at later times of day. I knew that if I wrote too much out of the conscious mind, the part that was most readerly and prone to give explanations, I'd produce poems that made sense but lacked a necessary element of mystery; equally, I knew that if I wrote too much out of the unconscious mind, I'd dredge up things that might mean a lot to me, but probably nothing to anyone else. So: keep them in harmony; allow them to modify and inform one another. That was the idea, anyway – and that's why I began to make it my habit to wake up early, allow as few distractions as possible to jangle me before I reached my desk, and then convince myself to stay there until the middle of the day, when my energy began to flag and my concentration to drift. After that, I might sometimes go back and tinker with what I'd written, but more probably I'd set myself to do other kinds of work – teaching work, reviewing work, work that made money, which poetry never could or would.

The freelance life! In some ways it was less free than any I'd known before, but it set a pattern that was never to change. It didn't mean that I expected to write a new poem every day – of course not – but it did mean that I wrote regularly and kept myself fit for writing, in much the same way that an athlete might keep themselves in shape by going to the gym.

Alan understood this and felt much the same – while I sat downstairs crouched over my notebook, he worked upstairs in his room overlooking the back garden, writing a novel that was the precursor to *The Swimming Pool Library*. Joanna understood it too. But Joanna also thought that if I spent the entirety of my new life working, I'd not only deprive myself of possible subjects, but also waste the chance for adventure that I'd made for myself by leaving Hull. Besides, shouldn't we make one last attempt to re-establish our marriage, before it became an even more obviously diminished thing? We both thought so and made a plan to spend a part of the winter in India, where she'd been born and brought up: she wanted to show me her childhood places, and I wanted to see them. It felt risky in all sorts of ways, but as we made our plans the gods encouraged us: a poem that I'd recently written won the Arvon/*Observer* Prize, and that paid for our tickets. When I told Philip we were going, and hinted that I might want to write about it afterwards, he sent me a quatrain of his own: 'Beware the travelogue my son,/ The palms that wave, the pigs that grunt./ Eschew the dreadful jub-jub bird,/ And shun the local word for cunt.'

———

Early-morning woodsmoke and sci-fi ziggurats in Delhi, then on to Jaipur, Agra, Lucknow, Fatehpur Sikri. Buses in dust clouds. Bony fish-picnics and Diplomat whisky. A Christmas party with cotton wool glued to a tree by hands that had never felt snow. Then Varanasi, the holy city, and dead sheep rotating in the current. A shaman stripped to the waist and chanting as he poured water over his head using a battered silver dish.

And finally the house in Kanpur where Joanna had lived as a child, when Kanpur was still Cawnpore. A patchily white-washed Victorian labyrinth, with fans twirling and the fossil print of mop heads on wide stone floors. Shabby. Crumbling. Colonial-disturbing and colonial-elegiac. We slept in twin beds, not touching but happy enough. And at the same time not happy enough. As the house fell silent and the moon rose, I could hear the Ganges scooping along its course below our window, toppling handfuls of mud into the current. Soft little crashes, then the water running smoothly and quietly again. There was a sweet-smelling candle to keep away the mosqui-toes, but even with that burning, and blankets pulled up to my chin, the skin of my face kept prickling – miniature airy wings and feet, I thought, and fell asleep regardless. In the morning my face, Joanna's face, our bedclothes, the floor, all the furniture in the room, was speckled with flakes of whitewash that had floated down from the ceiling in the night. We lay still for a while like ghosts, and were still like ghosts when we got out of our beds and began the next day.

———

My mother had been to the Oxford house once, when my father drove her across the country for my wedding to Joanna. Now I kept a picture of her above my desk, propped against a shelf of books. A full-face watercolour miniature, three inches by two inches, which had been painted when she was a child, and which I'd inherited when her own mother died. The colours had long since faded – the yellow hair and light brown V-necked jumper, and the shadow falling across the left-hand side of her face. But I could still read her expression, her anxious half-smile and eagerness to please. And I could still see the blue in her eyes – the eyes which stared into the future and knew nothing of her life to come.

Had she and my father ever talked about the possibility of his marrying again, supposing the worst were to happen to her? I had no idea; it wasn't the kind of thing that either of them would have mentioned to me. More particularly, had she realised that for years my father had been sleeping with Susan, the last of the housekeepers that he'd recruited from the back pages of *The Lady*? It seemed possible, because my mother understood very well how lonely my father had become. But I doubted that she would ever have thought he might marry Susan, since she would have struggled to believe that my father, who was snobbish about these things, could settle for someone who came from a very different kind of background (Susan had been married to a publican before her divorce), and who had two young children in tow: my father was generally scornful of children, having never really been allowed to live as one himself.

But none of this mattered now, just as it also didn't matter, apparently, that most of my father's friends (who were also snobs) didn't like Susan and as a result saw much less of him than they'd done in the old days. In fact, when the phone rang on the desk in the front room of the Oxford house, and my father told me that he and Susan had got married earlier that same day, I realised that this unpopularity was something my father welcomed. He didn't want to destroy the entire edifice of his former life, but welcomed the idea of living more quietly than he'd done before, with a woman who loved him to the exclusion of everyone and everything else. The fact that he'd found a way to do that made me happy for him. At the same time, I wished that Susan didn't so obviously feel that Kit and I were a threat to their existence, simply because we were embodiments of the past that she wanted my father to leave behind. It meant that I began to see my father even less often than I'd done for the past several years, and that we both felt even more constrained when we did meet.

———

Philip wrote; he was due to spend a weekend in Oxford – he was a visiting Fellow at All Souls College – and asked if we could meet for lunch: there was something he needed to ask me. We ate at my mother's round table and soon got down to business:

Philip wanted to remake his will and add the name of someone younger than Monica and Anthony Thwaite, whom he'd already installed as his literary executors, so that he could more clearly imagine the long-term future of his estate. Executing was thankless work, he said, and meant a lot of drudgery while also being out of pocket – but would I become the third literary executor?

I put down my knife and fork and told him, 'Don't die,' which made him laugh, then said I'd be honoured. But I made a condition. If Philip wanted to destroy anything – papers and so on – he would have to do it himself, because if I was his executor I'd try to preserve as much as possible. 'Don't worry,' Philip said. 'When I see the grim reaper coming up the front path, I'll go to the bottom of the back garden like Thomas Hardy, and have a bonfire.' I looked through the window to my left, along the tight path beside the kitchen and into my own back yard, where I was growing vegetables. I imagined smoke curling between the leaves of the potatoes and runner beans, and dark lines of fire crawling across a page covered in Philip's handwriting: would he really be willing to do that? Actually destroy things, rather than simply toy with the idea? I turned away and changed the subject: I didn't like talking about death and its consequences, and for Philip it was insufferable.

Nevertheless, once lunch was over and Philip had left, I couldn't help making a summary of what he'd said, and what it meant for the future. Philip was overweight, alcoholic, and didn't take any exercise, yet he was still a relatively young man: sixty-one. Which meant that he should live for another – what – twenty years? And that in turn meant we should be able keep things as they were for a good long time yet. Meeting in Oxford whenever he was visiting All Souls. Or in Hull when I went back there to see Joanna. Or in London when Philip had to attend one of his library committees or Arts Council meetings. For someone so often described as a hermit, he was a surprisingly energetic traveller.

—————

I still saw myself as someone who hung back, and often I was like that. At other times I felt opinionated and impatient, wanting to change the status quo – and that was my mood when I applied for the vacant post of editor of the *Poetry Review*, the magazine of the Poetry Society in London. Although the *Review* had never been less than venerable, I thought it needed shaking up.

I was interviewed and appointed, then began driving once a week to the Society's dilapidated HQ in Earl's Court Square, where I spent the day alone in a room the size of a coffin, eating sandwiches out of a paper bag. For some pages I called in favours (a review by Philip of Sylvia Plath's *Collected Poems*), and for others I tried to point the magazine in a more diverse direction, which I hoped would show the changes in my tastes and opinions that had led me away from Oxford, and that my life in Hull had confirmed. I enjoyed it: the excitement of backing my own judgement, and the chance to expand the boundaries of the poetic establishment that I had inherited when I first started writing. But where were the parties? And where were the descendants of those beautiful people I'd read about in books about Cyril Connolly? I thought I'd glimpsed them when I'd been to see Ian Hamilton; I must have been imagining things.

—————

I'd applied for the editorship at the *Review* believing that a poetry magazine becomes most dynamic when its editor's taste is most definite – citing Connolly and Hamilton again. Sometimes editors will make judgements and include work that puzzles their readers – but ideally this puzzlement is welcome because it means that old assumptions are being tested and new territories explored: readers, if they trust their editor, enjoy being led as well as entertained.

In my own case, I wanted to show this decisiveness for the benefit of others but realised that in order to do so I must also challenge myself. This reflected the ambitions I had for my own writing. Since the publication of *The Pleasure Steamers* three years earlier, and especially since the death of my mother, I'd become increasingly interested in broadening the ways in which I thought about lyric. Specifically, I wanted to resist the idea that I only produced poems when I stumbled over a rock of intimate feeling (love, grief, loneliness) and let out some kind of rhythmical yelp. Instead, I wanted to cultivate a more deliberate approach: to write narrative poems that on the face of it had nothing to do with the circumstances of my own life – and were therefore proof of range and variety – but nevertheless continued to draw on my reserves of strong feeling. To be introvert and extrovert at the same time.

It was slow work. There seemed to be something irreconcilable in the relationship between lyric and story, as though the extrapolated facts of the latter were somehow inimical to the elisions and impulses of the former; facts were too inevitably lumpen, too ploddingly 'and then, and then', whereas lyric was untethered, free-floating, timeless. Perhaps, I thought, building on the ideas that Alan and I had been talking about, there was a way round this problem – a kind of Jamesian lyric that depended as much on implication and things that didn't happen as it did on things that were overt.

I'd begun trying to put these thoughts into practice while writing *Independence*, the book-length poem I'd written soon after returning from India, which studiously ignored Philip's advice to lay off the jub-jub bird. Now I began dredging my past and adapting my reading to look for incidents that I thought might also be suitable cases for treatment. The forms of these poems were similar to those I'd used before – mostly stanzaic and written in unrhymed free verse – and so was their language: conversational and simple-seeming. Back in the day, when I'd been writing my thesis about Edward Thomas, Craig had always insisted that quiet ways of writing were a kind of poetic suicide: nobody could hear poems unless their effects were roughly equivalent to the choir-blasts of the 'Hallelujah Chorus'. But I'd never agreed with this and hoped that by continuing to speak quietly I'd eventually persuade people to shut up and listen.

Eventually, when I'd written enough to make a short book, I gathered these story-poems together in a collection called *Secret Narratives*: the title, I hoped, would summarise the various paradoxes I was trying to embrace. Like *Independence*, it was published by James Fenton's brother Tom, who had recently founded the Salamander Press at his home in Edinburgh; he'd already published James, and Craig, and John Fuller. I was sorry to break my ties with Michael Schmidt, but since I'd still only met him a handful of times, and we barely knew each other, the separation was relatively painless. Besides, Tom made beautiful books, and being on his list meant that I was among friends.

The *Poetry Review* paid a pittance, and I needed to earn more money. Writing poetry obviously wasn't going to help, so what about biography? I read it by the yard now – why not write it? Why not write about Elizabeth Bishop, in fact; I liked her poems very much, she wasn't nearly as well known in England as she deserved to be, and surely a Life would help to put that right? I sent a proposal to her English publishers, Chatto and Windus.

The brass neck of youth. And the ignorance. I didn't even know that Chatto had recently appointed a new managing director: Carmen Callil, who'd previously helped to found Virago. But it wasn't Carmen that replied to my letter, it was the chairman of Chatto, Hugo Brunner; he said we should talk things over, and invited me to his office in William IV Street, off Trafalgar Square in the centre of London.

I had a stomach ache when I arrived, which seemed appropriate when I climbed from the street into a building that itself was as circuitous as an intestine. A winding and dimly lit corridor, obscure offshoots, mysterious cubbyholes, and everything shadowy although the offices were arranged round a central atrium. And in the offices themselves: corpse-grey lino, threadbare curtains, vast unwieldy typewriters hunched on splintery desks. Also, a very ancient-looking hairbrush on the shelf under the mirror in the lavatory – had that belonged to Cecil Day Lewis or Leonard Woolf, when they were directors of Chatto in the old days? And if so, was that their hair still clogging the bristles? 'We spend very little on the building,' Hugo said in his soft patrician voice, when I eventually found my way to his door.

'We like to give the impression that everything we earn goes to our authors.'

But not this author, apparently. Hugo explained that Bishop's biography couldn't be commissioned yet because her executor, Alice Methfessel, wouldn't allow it. Was there anyone else I wanted to write about? At this point a tremendous squawk-ing broke out along the corridor from Hugo's office: 'Is he here yet, darling? Send him along!' I already knew that Carmen was Australian, and recognised that as an Australian voice, so assumed it must be her. Hugo, who seemed a very unlikely sort of darling in his four-piece handmade suit, made a sour face but surrendered in an instant. He steered me through an enfil-ade of rooms where cowed-looking young people were shuf-fling mounds of paper, introduced me to an office muddle of art deco, Biedermeier and junk-shop kitsch, then creaked away in his gleaming shoes.

Carmen was almost invisible behind a battlement of books and manuscripts, but the spiral of cigarette smoke gave her away. A quizzical amused face, curly black hair, and energy glowing around her like a halo. I thought that if I hadn't already given up on the idea of writing about Bishop I might be tongue-tied – but as it was, I felt fine. I didn't want or expect anything from Carmen; I just thought she looked clever and fun, and immediately liked her.

We began by talking about Bishop, but Carmen soon got bored of that and changed the subject. 'Does the name Lambert mean anything to you, darling?' she asked. I told her that I'd read Anthony Powell's *A Dance to the Music of Time* and under-stood that the character of Hugh Moreland was modelled on Constant Lambert – whose compositions I also knew a bit; we'd sung 'The Rio Grande' at school. Carmen beamed at me.

It turned out that Powell's enormous novel was a talisman for her: she automatically approved of people who admired it, told me as much, and went on to say (which I didn't know) that Constant's father had been a well-known painter in Australia at the turn of the century, and his son . . . But I suddenly remembered. His son Kit had discovered and then managed The Who; he'd died only a year or so ago.

I asked why she was talking about the Lamberts but already knew the answer. She was looking for someone to write a book about the family – a three-generation biography – and wondered if I was interested? I said yes more or less immediately, feeling like a novice skier launching off the summit of the Holmenkollbakken, and got up to go because Carmen seemed to think that was now that; she'd contact my agent and make an offer. But she called me back to my chair. She said that she'd noticed the changes I'd made at the *Poetry Review*, and if I could promise to do the same sort of thing at Chatto, why didn't I take over as poetry editor when the present one, D. J. Enright, left at the end of the month? It would mean spending a couple of days a week in the office, and doing some reading and report-writing at home. Five minutes later I was back on William IV Street. My stomach ache had gone.

———

Soon after I started working at Chatto, Alan got a job working at the *Times Literary Supplement* and moved to London. On the day he left, we walked up St Aldate's together and said goodbye at Carfax in the centre of town. It wasn't a real goodbye, we'd see each other soon, but it was clearly the end of our shared life, and I felt very sorry about that. Six months later, fed up with living surrounded by the memories of our time together, I sold the house by the river and also moved to London – to a place between Shepherd's Bush and Turnham Green, with a scrap-metal yard across the road in front and a timber yard behind. It wasn't ideal, but it was London. London which I hardly knew, but where I thought I might finally lose the left-behind feeling that had dogged me since leaving home, and the cut-off feeling that had preoccupied me in Hull.

———

I threw myself into my research for the Lamberts book, flying to Australia to learn about George Lambert, burrowing in English libraries and personal archives. I threw myself into my duties at Chatto, too – Carmen made anything less than complete work commitment feel like skiving. That made her an exciting boss but also a demanding one, particularly since she thrived on turmoil – firing off orders, then changing her mind, insisting on what seemed to be impossibilities, speaking in a whirl of mixed metaphors and mangled proverbs. You can take a horse to water, but you can't make it gather moss. A bird in the hand always blames his tools. A stitch in time butters no parsnips. Sometimes it was hilarious, energising, creative. Often, it was nerve-wracking. Most people in the office lived in a state of permanently high anxiety; at least one had a nervous breakdown; and another – after hiding her pregnancy because she thought Carmen might sack her – eventually went into labour in an upstairs lavatory.

———

I finished writing about George Lambert; I was still only going in to Chatto a couple of days a week, so the rest of my time was free for me to work on the book. Then I started doing research for the second part, and interviewed people who'd known George's son Constant. I contacted Margot Fonteyn, who'd had an affair with Constant in her early days, but her assistant brushed me off, saying that Dame Margot couldn't remember anything that would interest me. I had tea with Ninette de Valois, who spoke so primly about the evolution of English ballet, it was like listening to a mother superior. I went for a drink with Frederick Ashton and asked him what had made Constant such a good conductor. 'Very good sense of tempi,' Ashton said, looking at the ceiling with a nostalgic smile. 'Very good rapport with the dancers. Very large cock.'

———

Carmen had passions, and her latest one was for musical boxes, so after we'd had supper together in her house one evening, she showed me her most recent acquisition. We were standing side by side in summery heat and tipsiness, night-time quiet pouring in through the open door to the garden, the kaleidoscope of Carmen's treasures and tchotchkes twirling across the walls around us. She opened the lid of the musical box and the barrel rotated, little metal tongues clicking over the spikes and a tune beginning. We leaned closer together to listen, and our shoulders touched. I could smell her hair. Then the tune began to slow down, drooping into a comical woozy sound, and Carmen found the key to make it speed up again.

She worked the key into the slot and started winding, both of us still staring into the box, admiring its ingenious machinery, inhaling the sweet cedar smell. Carmen took a firmer grip on the box with her left hand and kept turning the key with her right. I looked at the small hairs on her bare arm, at her red fingernails, at her watch and her skin swelling round the edge of the strap. Should I say something? No; we were complicit in something that might be nothing, that was all. And Carmen stayed quiet, too. She just kept turning the key, although the machinery was protesting now – I could hear the spring groaning and the metal tongues slipping. 'You'll . . .' Break it, I was going to say, but that's not what happened. In a miraculous transfer, the tension left the musical box and entered her watch – entered it so violently, the face cracked from side to side.

I stepped back, and Carmen put down the box. We breathed. I ran my hand over my own face to make sure that hadn't splintered as well. Then we said goodnight, and I left.

---

George Lambert was done; Constant was done; and now it was time for Kit. But how? With George there'd been plenty of letters and memoirs and archives to look at, but only a handful of people to interview. With Constant there'd been fewer documents and more people. With Kit there were only people – not a single letter so far as I could find, and nothing like an archive. But the people were brilliant, and Pete Townshend in particular. Pete volunteered to come across town to my house in Shepherd's Bush, where he plonked himself onto the sofa like an old friend and talked for hours; he said that he'd loved Kit, felt The Who would never have reached so high or gone so far without him, and wanted to share everything he could remember. And he remembered a lot, not just the high spots and low points of Kit's life, but the way Kit managed things from day to day, while at the same time channelling Constant's classical training into ambitions that eventually led to *Tommy* and *Quadrophenia*.

There was one detail Pete couldn't recall – it was only little, but important for the story. So he recommended that I contact Andy Newman, better known as Thunderclap Newman, who'd taught Pete at art school, was also managed by Kit, and in 1969 went to number one with a song that I remembered, called 'Something in the Air'. Thunderclap had a good memory, Pete said; he was a responsible kind of guy and he'd be pleased to help.

Thunderclap now worked as a plumber in Turnham Green, so I arranged to meet him there, in an Arts and Crafts pub called the Tabard. When I arrived, I recognised him instantly – in fact, I thought Thunderclap might even be dressed in the same boiler suit that he'd worn on *Top of the Pops* a dozen or so years ago, with the difference that he now had a bolshy-looking chihuahua tucked under his arm like a bagpipe. Very bolshy, evidently. When we shook hands, Thunderclap adjusted the position of his elbow, and the chihuahua peed hard and accurately into the salad bar. Never mind, though. Nobody else saw. We sat down, and I explained about the missing detail in my book and the importance of a definite date. Thunderclap slowly nodded, delaying his answer for a profound moment. 'Yes,' he said at last. 'I can certainly help you with that, Andrew. Glad to. It was around the mid-sixties.'

Carmen fired the editorial director and asked me to take over: it was a much bigger job than poetry editor, meant keeping an eye on the whole list and not just a part of it, and involved a great deal more commissioning and contracting, a lot more wining and dining of authors, and a much closer working relationship with Carmen: effectively, I would be her right-hand man. Even thinking about it as a possibility gave me that ski-jump feeling again – the sense that I was about to lose control of my own life, and see it overwhelmed by chores and deadlines.

At the same time, I also knew there were a lot of things that I'd enjoy about the work: hadn't a part of me always wanted to back my judgement with action – hence the *Poetry Review*, and the work that I'd been doing for the Chatto poetry list? Working as editorial director, I thought, would mean that I had a greater chance to champion the diverse causes I believed in, especially since I knew Carmen would strongly support my efforts in such a direction. I'd have to toughen up, though: Philip was always warning me about confusing courtesy with evasion. And not just toughen up to deal with the world of agents, contracts, and publicity. Toughen up to protect my poems as well. I'd now have a great deal less time for the wool-gathering that poems required, and would also risk disturbing the necessary mental balance of conscious and unconscious forces. There'd been a similar problem when I was teaching in Hull: my work in class-rooms required me to emphasise the fully conscious part of my mind, whereas writing poems in solitude in De Grey Street, or in the houses I'd shared with Joanna, had meant trying to stimulate the opposite part of my brain – so that my unconscious could provide its deep-seated contributions. Switching from one to the other had been difficult then, but now, with evenings full of manuscripts to read, publication parties to attend, authors and agents to entertain, it was about to become virtually impossible. Still, I told myself, I don't have to live like this indefinitely, and in the short term at least it's a challenge I can't refuse. It'll do me good. It'll take me out of myself and into the world.

———

Was I a busy person who was also lazy? I'd often wondered. Now I was certainly busy – meeting and cajoling, flying to New York to meet agents and publishers, costing and commissioning, reading and editing, drying tears, driving with Carmen to the Frankfurt Book Fair (branches slashing across the windscreen, Carmen shout-asking, 'Am I close enough to the kerb, darling?'). I wanted to be good at the job and I worked hard – but as I did so, I soon began to feel that my other self, my self in retirement, was suffocating. It wasn't that I'd lost faith in my poems or couldn't hear my own voice among the cacophony of others now filling my head; it was purely and simply a matter of time. Free time. Down time. Dream time. Good writing, after all, depends on nothing as much as it does on something. I promised myself that one day I'd get back to it – but not quite yet. For now, I'd write when I could, and otherwise concentrate on work-work. If that meant I felt more doubtful about my own poems than I wanted to admit, I pushed the thought aside. In any case, I told myself, a reasonable dose of self-doubt had never done anyone any harm.

———

Jan came to work as an editor at Chatto and I began to fall in love with her the first time we met. Her parents lived near my father, so she knew all my childhood places, but she also seemed exotic – she'd spent her own childhood in Iran, spoke Russian, had travelled round South America and spent some time with Borges. No wonder she looked confident, her beautiful lioness eyes staring down the world. But she was hesitant too, wise to trouble and wary of it – touching her hair while she talked, rubbing her thumb against the inside of her middle finger. It wasn't shyness exactly. More like a form of thoughtfulness that made scrutiny a vantage point and explained her depth of understanding.

I told Joanna what had happened, and soon afterwards we filed for divorce. A year later Jan and I got married, and during the next eighteen months we had three children: a son, Jesse, and then twins – Sidonie and Lucas, a girl and a boy born fourteen minutes apart.

———

Philip sent us a cheque as a wedding present, and Jan and I went to the salvage yard on Essex Road, looking for something to buy; we ended up with two small marble urns for the garden, and thought Philip would like to know how we'd spent his money: I'd write to him and tell him. But when we got the urns home and looked at them again, we realised they were funeral monuments. Given what Philip felt about age, and then the only end of age, we reckoned he might think we were pulling his leg. Maybe the better thing to do was simply write and thank him for the cheque.

———

Chatto was bought by Random House and our offices moved from William IV Street to Bedford Square in Bloomsbury; I went to check things over during the weekend of the upheaval, and as the last of several heavily laden pantechnicons pulled away, leaving generations of distinguished ghosts free to pace to and fro across the bare lino until the place was renovated and turned into a wine bar, I paused to think of them enjoying the quiet: Leonard Woolf and James Strachey and Charles Scott Moncrieff and Norah Smallwood. Then I looked at the facade of the grand old building for the last time. I'd recently edited a collection of sexually explicit poems by Fiona Pitt-Kethley; there on the wall beside the front door, someone had written in lipstick: *Fiona Pitt-Kethley is a virgin*. History, I thought, and not for the first time, is nothing if not selective.

Now my work-window overlooked the famous senatorial plane trees in Bedford Square. They'd stood there for three hundred years – Keats must have passed them on his way from Hampstead into the centre of town; Edward Thomas must have seen them on his way to meet friends in St Martin's Lane; they'd survived the Blitz. The office itself gave me the same feeling of stored-up time. A sweeping staircase, tall ceilings with pretty mouldings, Carmen's room like a kitsch version of Ottoline Morrell's erstwhile salon around the corner in Gower Street – long windows and a marble fireplace, but here the mantelpiece was cluttered with pictures of cats and hedgehogs, as well as party invitations.

———

I was walking down the staircase in Bedford Square behind Iris Murdoch and Jeremy Lewis, her editor, who were on their way to lunch to celebrate the new novel that Iris had just delivered. There wouldn't be any editing, there never was for Iris any more; Jeremy just marked up the pages and took the manuscript along to the production team on a velvet cushion. Jeremy's hair-thatch lay in its usual dark yellow slabs, which sprang and shook as he walked. Iris's hair was a proper bird's nest, as though before coming here she'd been rubbing her head to and fro in a cot for hours, like a baby.

———

Five years earlier, when I was still living in Hull, I'd liked a picture by William Roberts in the city art gallery, the Ferens: *Christ Driving the Moneychangers from the Temple*. It showed some men stripped to the waist, carrying ledgers between the pillars of a large hot-looking building, and the blue floor beneath their feet made me think of swimming pools. When I sent a postcard of the picture to Alan, I crossed out the real title and wrote 'Or: stealing the books from the swimming pool library'. Alan was starting a new novel at the time, and now he'd finished and wanted to call it *The Swimming Pool Library*. I roared through the typescript overnight, thought it was the best first novel I'd ever read, and rang Alan the next morning. Chatto published the book six months later.

———

Jeremy bought a new novel by A. S. Byatt, another of his authors, into the Chatto weekly editorial meeting. Antonia's previous books had all been well received but sold only modestly, and this new one, Jeremy said, was even less commercial than the others. Could be a disaster, in fact; he thought the kindest thing would be to reject it, and let Antonia see if a different publisher was able to do a better job for her. Carmen lit another reeking cigarillo and asked what it was called. '*Possession*,' Jeremy said with a sigh. 'What's it about?' 'Victorian things,' he said, then added doomily that it had a lot of poetry in it: spoof Victorian poetry. Carmen squinted through the smoke. 'Perhaps a poet should read it then,' she said carefully. 'Just so we have a second opinion, you know. Here you are then, Andrew darling.' She passed me the manuscript, and also sent a copy to Alan, as well as reading it herself. We published it, and a year later *Possession* won the Booker Prize.

———

I'd heard William Empson read his poems a couple of times, once in Oxford with Alan, when Empson had swayed so wildly in front of the microphone that half of what he said was inaudible and the other half distorted: an Orphic Doppler effect. The second time was in Hull, where Philip introduced the reading, then turned off his hearing aid when he sat back down in the audience – to make sure it didn't suddenly emit any feedback noise, he told me later, although at the time I saw him smile to himself as he settled into forty minutes of silence.

Now Carmen and I were in Empson's home in Hampstead, because Chatto had published Empson on and off since the 1930s and I thought there might be new things he'd like to write for us, or had already written. I sincerely hoped so – his previous books had been shaping spirits for me ever since I began reading them at school – but hesitated to say as much: Empson's distracted air, his shuffling movements and quick bolts of speech were all forms of self-deprecation that made the thought of praising him to his face seem vulgar. Instead, I stood quietly and watched while he and his wife Hetta poured out drinks at a counter in the kitchen, Hetta herding four tall glasses together on the worktop, and Empson shaking a bottle of vodka over them, filling them more or less equally. Did he know how exceptional he was, and how original he looked – no Chinese beard flowing around his neck any longer, but the grey moustache still flamboyant and the eyes twinkly behind their owl-glasses? I had no idea. He seemed to be at once very nervously connected to life, and absent from it. The only thing to do was begin with practicalities.

Was he working on anything new?

But this was too direct; Empson thought we needed to make a subtler and more complicated approach to one another. 'Come outside first,' he said, leading me and Carmen through French doors into the wintry garden, down a flight of stone steps, and halting by a small pond that was murky with leaf mould. 'There are toads in there,' he told us, as if that sentence alone contained the answer to all the riddles in the universe. Carmen and I bowed our heads and stared. If there really were toads, I thought to myself, the cold would probably be too much for them and they'd be hiding under the leaves – a type of ambiguity. But I realised Empson didn't want to hear that, so continued gazing until a decent interval had passed, then pointed to a leaf that was vaguely the right shape. 'Oh yes,' I said. 'Look, there's one.' Empson nodded. 'I told you so.' Then we went back indoors to talk about publishing. He had two books ready to go and another in the works.

Carmen bought Gloria Vanderbilt's autobiography for Chatto, but no one else in the company cared much about Vanderbilt, especially not when we heard that she wanted a publicity campaign costing a small fortune, including a stretch limo to take her to and from her hotel to the one public appearance she'd agreed to make. I was dispatched to escort her and, after hovering in the lobby of her hotel until she eventually appeared, I steered her into the vast lounge of the car waiting outside. An immaculate mask. The scent of roses and rain. We sat for a haughty moment directly outside the place she'd just left, with our front bumper almost touching our destination. Then we edged forward a few feet and I sprang out to open her door; I was not required at the event.

———

Antony Sher had kept a diary while he rehearsed *Richard III* for the RSC in Stratford a few years previously, and Chatto had published it. *The Year of the King*. It did well. But the editor who'd handled that book had now left, and I took over as Tony's contact. I invited him to supper and wondered what he was going to do next; had he ever thought of writing a novel? He had, as it turned out, and his ideas sounded good, so I signed it up. That book did well too, when it came out eighteen months later, and we went to supper again, this time with Tony's friends Neil and Glenys Kinnock. Neil, who at this time was leader of the Labour Party, was talkative from the start but Glenys more guarded. She warmed up, though. 'As the wife of the Leader of the Opposition,' she said over coffee, 'I spend a lot of time standing in the second row – wreath-laying at the Cenotaph, that sort of thing. So I know a good deal about the back of people's necks.' Spoken like a novelist, I thought – perhaps I should sign her up as well? – but she wasn't done yet. 'Nigel Lawson's neck!' she went on, sounding horrified now. 'Blackheads! Mrs Thatcher's neck. Burn marks!' I imagined the hairdresser's space helmet, and the heat rising to a temperature where iron starts to bend.

———

Carmen loved Angela Carter and was proud to publish her, but didn't have time for small-scale fiddly editorial stuff, so when a new Angela manuscript arrived, or a previously published one was reissued, she asked me to deal with it. Angela was suspicious at first, and I could see why – our backgrounds were very unalike, and she assumed my tastes and beliefs could not be similar to her own. But once she'd discovered that we had more in common than she thought, we worked easily together, and she began to trust me. Especially after she discovered that Jan and I had twins: she was writing *Wise Children* by this stage and wanted to observe twins in close-up. At home, though, not in the office.

She arrived for Saturday lunch laden with blankets, bed linen, and the dismantled cot that her own son no longer needed: the blankets and linen were filthy dirty but the thought itself was a kind one. Although in truth I still felt there was something unnerving about Angela, as well as fascinating: the cloud of prophetess grey hair; the floating scarves and rainbow colours; the high insistent voice and head tilting backwards as though she was always looking down her nose. She was paradoxical in everything: warm but chilly, judgemental but inquisitive, self-confident but on edge, bohemian but stern.

The world was a minefield created by stupid men, and she had to walk through it carefully, casting a critical eye. But she also had to speak her mind and right wrongs. She snooped across the room and noticed Raymond Carver's book *Elephant*, which had recently been published and was lying on the table beside my chair. 'What do you think of it?' she wanted to know, then gave her own opinion before I had time to answer. 'Bourgeois sentimentalism.'

———

Jan and I went to Venice for a holiday but took in San Michele as well because I wanted to pay my respects to Joseph Brodsky, who had recently died and was now buried there. (The last time I'd seen Joseph had been on the other side of the lagoon in St Mark's Square, when I'd been visiting Venice with Alan; Joseph had pounced on us through the mist – 'Andrei, Andrei! I am Joseph Brodsky!') Now Jan and I were feeling distracted by the graves of Pound, then Stravinsky, then Diaghilev, but we made our way to Joseph eventually, and stood for a while in the usual vacuity of tomb-visiting. Or did, until we noticed a jam jar beside the headstone that was filled with pens – not expensive Parkers and suchlike, but Bics and biros: the every-day pens that people had actually used. I remembered reading how writer-mourners at Edmund Spenser's funeral in Westminster Abbey in 1599 had thrown their quills into the grave, and thought these donations must prove that the confederacy of poets still existed. Then I looked behind the gravestone and saw a pile of loose-leaf folders. They were the manuscripts of poems – tributes, of course. Or did their authors expect Joseph would get back to them with his opinion, when he had the time? It made me think of my desk at Chatto, almost buried under manuscripts waiting to be read. My own place in the confederacy was closing. I was closing it myself.

———

Carmen encouraged me to publish with Chatto those poems I'd written since joining the company. I should have resisted her, and delayed. My previous collections had all contained poems that were the result of slow writing and severe editing – not just in the sense that I'd worried over them line by line, but also because for every poem I'd decided to keep, four or five had been rejected. It had never bothered me that the failure rate of my writing was as high as this; I'd come to believe that my more successful poems actually depended on the duds, because the duds acted as a kind of provocation or fertiliser. Recently, though, I simply hadn't had the time for this kind of trial and error – which meant that every poem I had managed to produce felt more precious than it was, and also felt less finished than it needed to be. If I'd had an editor, he or she might have helped me to arrive at better final decisions. But at Chatto I was my own editor, so there was no final stringency, and no one to remind me that I needed to follow the same advice that I gave to the authors I worked with – namely, that the processes of revision were as crucial to writing well (if not more so) as the business of getting words down on a page in the first place. Over the years, I'd developed various strategies to intensify these final processes – printing out later drafts of my poems in different typefaces so that they would look like work by someone else, and therefore allow me to approach them with a greater degree of objectivity; asking Alan – the most supportive but also the most rigorous of my early readers – for his opinion; leaving new poems to stand for a while, as if they were a meal I'd made, and then cancelling them or deciding they were fit to go. Now I hurried forward, realising that I couldn't live like this for much longer.

———

Gloria Vanderbilt one day at Chatto and Tiger Stripe the next – Tiger Stripe being a collective of radical writers that included Peter Fuller and John Berger. When Berger finished his new collection of stories, he visited from his home in France and installed himself in Carmen's office, creaturely-sexy and intense, speaking English with a slight French accent, as though to confirm the value he felt in being an outsider. The new book might have been finished, but he didn't have a title for it yet. 'What, no ideas at all?' Carmen asked, with impressive vigour. Berger gave a Gallic shrug and said maybe; he'd recently heard a brass band playing in the market square of the remote village in the Pyrenees where he'd been staying, and been struck by one song in particular. An ancient melody, he thought, that felt in keeping with the spirit of his writing, so maybe the title of the song could become the title of his book? 'Good idea,' said Carmen, with the same fierce momentum. 'What is it?' '"Don't Cry for Me, Argentina",' Berger said. There was a pause, and Carmen deflated. 'Darling,' she said, 'you've lived out of England too long.'

———

Philip rang, which was unusual because of his deafness, so I feared there must be something wrong. There was. He was ill

and due to have some tests: something to do with his oesopha-
gus. It sounded unpleasant but not seriously worrying – he
was often complaining about his health. Although this time he
seemed more bothered than usual, and more than usually tired,
his voice slow and deep, his words dragging. We talked about
Constant Lambert – my book was almost finished by now –
and which jazz players Constant had liked. Duke Ellington
and Louis Armstrong. Well, yes, of course. Philip paused, then
reminded me that he was about to turn sixty-three, the same
age that his father Sidney had been when he died. There was
another silence. If I'd been talking with anyone else, this would
have been the moment to give some cheerful rebuttals: medicine was much better these days than it had been in Sidney's
time; there was no good reason to think a son would die at the
same age as his father. But Philip's death-dread wouldn't stand
for that sort of pap. Any attempt at consolation would have
been taken as silliness, or a kind of insult.

Philip's doctors kept him in the Nuffield Hospital on West-
bourne Avenue in Hull for a few days, and Jan and I went to
visit. It was a quiet part of Hull – a grid of large melancholic-
looking red-brick Victorian houses with a fancy dried-up
ornamental fountain at the centre – and the hospital was small-
scale, like a nursing home. We asked the way to Dr Larkin's
room, then hesitated outside his door, peering through the tight
window with its lattice of wire worked into the glass. Philip
was lying on his bed wearing an open-necked shirt and dark
trousers, watching television. Tennis. It was Wimbledon fortnight. In we went, and when Philip tried to get up to greet

us, we told him to stay put, then sat down beside him. It was difficult for Jan – she hadn't met Philip before and could feel his gloom towering above us – but she gentled him along. She was wonderful: the weather; the food; what was happening in the tennis. Philip brightened for a second – had we seen Boris Becker? Didn't he look just like young Auden?

The sun pounded through the windows and the room got stuffy, so Philip said he'd like a breath of fresh air. We helped him off the bed, waited while he put on his slippers, then I took his arm and we stepped outside through a pair of French doors – there were the remains of an apple orchard in the garden, and we had to keep ducking our heads to miss the branches. Philip leaned on me heavily and dragged me lopsided, even though his arm felt as bony as a boy's.

Now that he couldn't put it off any longer, Philip talked about the will and executing. 'A lot of it is going to be very boring work,' he said, repeating what he'd told me in Oxford three years before. 'You'll be out of pocket.' My instinct was to brush this aside, but I knew better than to do that: Philip wanted to hear things spelled out. Very well, then: what about the bonfire of papers? Philip looked at the ground, the lush uncut grass and shadows of the apple trees. Had he not heard my question? No, he'd heard it all right, but his candour had deserted him suddenly, and he wasn't going to answer.

I led us indoors again and Philip slid back onto his bed. We chatted for a little longer, more desultory now, then Jan and I said goodbye, closed the door behind us, and walked away down the corridor. When we reached the exit to the hospital we turned and looked back. Philip had climbed off his bed and was standing inside the door to his room, his shoulders slumped, his long face framed in the window with its wiry glass. He lifted both hands, holding the palms outwards. He was waving, but it looked more like capitulation.

---

Five months later the phone on my desk rang at 6.30 in the morning; Jan and I were still asleep, so after I'd stumbled downstairs, I took a moment to gather myself, staring out through the window of the sitting room. The house had been a wreck when Jan first bought it, and we still hadn't fixed everything in the garden: the lawn was mossy and the flowerbeds lumpy with builder's rubble, flints, oyster shells from the old days. Then I picked up the receiver. It was Charles Monteith, the chairman of Faber and Philip's editor and friend. Philip was dead.

---

The funeral was set for early in the afternoon, so that people coming from outside Hull had time to make the journey. Jan and I caught the train from King's Cross, recognising several faces on the platform – Charles Monteith; Anthony and Ann Thwaite; Blake Morrison; Kingsley Amis and Hilly, his first wife, getting into First Class. It was early December, and the country was swaddled in thick fog as we made the 'Whitsun Weddings' journey in reverse, everyone sharing stories about Philip but feeling guilty about it, as though his ghost might be sitting nearby and eavesdropping. When we stopped at Doncaster, where the track swerves east, I looked outside and saw that Kingsley and Hilly had already left their carriage and were standing on the platform, gazing into the fog. Kingsley had never been to Hull before, not in the whole thirty years that

Philip lived there, and obviously thought that he'd travelled far enough: this must be the destination.

Blake banged on the glass, beckoning Kingsley and Hilly back onto the train. Then we settled into our seats again and rattled across the dead-flat miles beside the Humber until we reached Ferriby, where Jan and I, the Thwaites, and the Amises got out, because Philip's lawyer Terry Wheldon lived there and he'd asked us all to lunch before the service. Terry was politely anxious and so was his wife: it was obviously a strain for them to have these strangers in their house, especially a stranger as famous as Kingsley. But this only inflamed Kingsley, who looked at everything with bug-eyed astonishment, his lips wet and shining. Then, when Mrs Wheldon took us through to the dining room, where she'd laid out cold ham and potato salad, Kingsley blew up – disdaining the food, contradicting everything, asking for drinks he knew the Wheldons were unlikely to have. Perhaps it was grief.

———

The service was in Cottingham, a pretty village that Hull had swallowed long ago: university people looking suspiciously at London people, and London people feeling out of their element. Kingsley gave the address, which was oddly flat and impersonal – maybe that was grief as well – then we drove in convoy to the cemetery half a mile away. The wreaths were already laid out on the grass beside the grave in a long, loose S-shape, with the one from Philip's library colleagues in the form of an open book. It looked sentimental – the sort of thing that Philip himself would have noticed, inwardly baulked at, then accepted as proof of genuine strong affection – and for a moment it brought everything close. Philip was dead. Philip was dead. Then the brittle, artificial feeling came back. Monica wasn't here, that was part of the reason – apparently, she was too upset to leave the house. But there was something else as well, to do with visitors distracting the people who'd seen Philip every day and wanted to grieve for him as one of their own. This was their last chance to share the existence he'd chosen with them, and already he was being translated.

---

Because Ted Hughes was poet laureate, he'd been booked to read one of the lessons at Philip's memorial service in Westminster Abbey: 'Let us now praise famous men.' Ted had mixed feelings about Philip: he thought that he'd closed down on life too early, and he didn't believe that negative feelings were an efficient fuel for poetry. He also knew that Philip hadn't rated him much ('Ted Huge'; 'The Incredible Hulk'), thought his poems were formless, and the whole pike-catching, pig-scouring, wodwo-quizzing persona a bit ridiculous. What he didn't know was that Philip had hung a photograph of him – leather-jacketed, one hand pointing to heaven – on the wall above the cistern in his downstairs lavatory, for regular satiric surveillance.

But all this was set aside during the service, and Ted's thrilling voice did the job. Then, when the service was over and the congregation began streaming outside, there were trumpeters in the high crossing beside the organ, scattering down jazz. I knew it was coming, that melancholy blast, but it still caught me by the throat. I halted in the nave on my way to the West Door, the congregation jostling past me, and for a moment saw Philip's life shimmering back down the Humber to Hull, then across the Irish Sea to Belfast, then around the Wrekin in Shropshire, then through the colleges in Oxford, then past the ruined cathedral in Coventry, and finally settling into the house of his parents, where he sat down as a child and bashed away on his drum kit.

When the music stopped, I walked out into Parliament Square. In the days leading up to the service, Monica had delegated to my co-executor Anthony Thwaite the work of first editing the poems, then gathering a selection of Philip's letters, and had asked me to write his Life. I looked around me, as Philip's friends and admirers dispersed through the sunlight. It was my job now to pull their stories into his story. To find words at once true and kind, or not untrue and not unkind.

———

I talked with Anthony about Philip's will, and told him what I'd said to Philip when we were sitting round my dining table in Oxford: how if Philip wanted to destroy any unpublished papers, he'd have to do it himself. Word now reached us from the lawyer Terry Wheldon that the bonfire Philip had promised to make had never in fact been lit, but that when he was carried out of his house in Newland Park in Hull for the last time, on his way to the hospital where he died, he'd looked up from the stretcher with terror in his face and implored Monica to destroy his diary. She'd promised to do as he asked, but wasn't well enough to tackle the job herself, so had asked Betty the loaf-haired secretary to take charge instead. Betty was efficient, that was one of the things Philip always liked about her. Now she collected the diary from Monica – twenty-something volumes

– stacked it on what used to be Philip's desk in the university library, and spent an afternoon tearing out the pages, before feeding them through the jaws of a shredding machine. After that, remembering stories she'd recently read in newspapers about how Iranian protesters who'd taken over the American embassy in Tehran had glued back together the ribbons of shredded confidential documents, she burned the remains.

A few of the diary's hard covers survived – Betty gave them back to Monica as proof that she'd done what was asked of her – and when I later saw these, and found their insides were sprinkled with jottings, I got some idea of what had been destroyed. Philip had been writing the diary with only a few pauses since his schooldays in the 1930s, recording mundane daily events and 'celestial recurrences' ('the day the flowers come,/ And when the birds go'), while at the same time unburdening himself of his most unvarnished thoughts. Thoughts about other people, about himself, about politics, about death, about fear, about loathing, and about sex. No doubt some passages would have upset people if they'd been published immediately, and in that sense it was easy to see why he'd wanted the diary destroyed. But why not keep the whole thing under wraps until all the upsettable people were no longer around? That's certainly what I'd have recommended, if the diary had still existed. As it was, I felt convinced that the destruction was a dreadful loss – and not only because it denied the world a uniquely close insight into the mind of a great poet. The diary was also a mind-dump and heart-record written with no regard for questions of tact, or discretion, or the feelings of others. If it had survived, it would certainly have increased the number of Philip's detractors, because it would undoubtedly have multiplied the ways in which he gave offence. But it would also have been a matchless record of the way tolerance combines with intolerance, and light with dark, in the deepest wells of self that most people prefer not to investigate or even acknowledge.

So no diary. And no pornography either, or very little. When Terry the lawyer visited 105 Newland Park the day after Philip's death, he'd scooped Philip's girlie mags into a cardboard box and incinerated them: he thought they would 'damage his client's posthumous reputation'. Monica told me this when I visited her alone for the first time, and gave her reckless laugh, but as I went through the house, I did find a few examples still lying around: copies of *Swish*, mostly, filled with pictures of undressed girls sitting on desks and windowsills. A lot of them, I thought, looked like either Christine Keeler or Mandy Rice-Davies.

I put the magazines in a cardboard box and imagined they'd be part of a Larkin Archive one day. Which brought me back to the other question: what to do about the unpublished poems, if there were any, and the notebooks Philip had used to draft his work? My own thoughts were clear, as I'd told Philip myself: they should be preserved. But now the will had been read, Anthony and I had found that one clause said everything unpublished at the time of death had to be destroyed, while another clause said that any money realised from the sale of material unpublished at the time of death should be given to such-and-such a charity.

Monica and Anthony and I referred the will to a QC, who declared the will 'repugnant' – which in plain English meant that it contained a contradiction. As we thought. But this muddle turned out to be a blessing for us as preservationists, since it left us free to interpret the terms of the will as we saw fit.

And we were all of one mind: the unpublished material should remain where it was, a good deal of it should be edited and brought into the light of day, and the whole lot should eventually be passed to the university in Hull for safe keeping. Hull, not Oxford, which was the other possibility, because Hull is where Philip had made his life.

———————

Although the biography was due to be published after Anthony had done his editorial work on the poems and the letters, I decided there was no time to lose in interviewing people who had known Philip, and began with Monica. But she was still in a bad way; she'd been recovering from shingles while she nursed Philip through his last six months, his final illness had worn her out, and now that he was gone, she had collapsed. She sat all day and slept all night in his chair, the G-plan chair with its back to the garden window, where he'd written his poems on a board set across the wooden arms. She no longer changed out of her nightdress and dressing gown. Her hair was matted into a thick grey tangle. She was incontinent and leaked into the cushion of the chair, making the house reek. An alcoholic Miss Haversham, drinking gin out of a glass beer-mug. Chain-smoking and dropping ash on the letters and other manuscripts scattered at her feet. I sat on the tight little sofa across the room, breathing through my mouth as I asked my questions. When and why and how. She struggled to remember, even though scenes from her life with Philip were evidently replaying inside her head on an endless loop. As we came to the end of our first long conversation-interview, I asked who else she thought I should talk to. Monica pouted and groaned and tipped forward to rootle among the papers at her feet. She was looking for Philip's address book, and when she found it, she tossed it towards me. Loose pages fluttered onto the carpet, and I scrabbled them together. 'Everyone you need is in here,' she said in her scratchy voice, old-fashioned smart. 'Go and see them all. But first go upstairs to the book-room.'

The book-room? I had no idea what Monica meant; I'd never been upstairs in Philip's house before; there'd been no occasion. But once I'd climbed past the plate that warned me to prepare to meet my God, and peeked into the bedroom where Philip used to sleep (the wide cold bed still made-up, with a child's rabbit-toy propped against the pillows), and stood for a moment in the bathroom where Philip had set up the lectern and Bible that he'd bought from a decommissioned church nearby, so that he could read the Bible while shaving in the morning, I found it. A small wooden door opening into a narrow space under the eaves, with no books but dozens of cardboard shoeboxes inside it, all initialled in Philip's handwriting. This was the beginning of the written evidence trail, and it looked so richly detailed, so like a librarian's archive of his own life, I thought that a publishing scoundrel such as myself should feel nothing but grateful. But as I turned back down the stairs, I began to wonder. Was the abundance a kind of decoy? Had Philip kept this material and made it so obvious and accessible because there were other things in his correspondence – in his life – that he wanted to hide? I sat down again in Monica's stinking sitting room, breathing through my mouth in little sips. 'Where are his letters to you?' I asked.

In the 1960s, when Philip began his affair with Maeve Brennan, who worked with him in the university library, Monica had bought a cottage in Haydon Bridge in Northumberland. It was a bolthole – a refuge from the difficulties of her life with Philip, and also from her work in Leicester, where she'd worked in the English Department since the late 1940s. Once Philip's relationship with Maeve had cooled into friendship again, Monica let him know that he was welcome to come and stay there too; it could be their home away from home.

Now Monica told me that Philip hadn't expected to like it: the cottage was near a busy road, it was pokily cramped, and the journey from Hull was a slog. But the remoteness appealed to him, and the small yard behind the house overlooked the Tyne; he enjoyed watching the river swirl down towards Newcastle. Still, she was often there by herself, and that was the answer to my question. A lot of Philip's letters to Monica were in the cottage in Haydon Bridge. She asked me whether we could drive up together and collect them, straightening her glasses and staring at me through the murk of their lenses, daring me to say yes.

But she wasn't well enough, she reluctantly accepted that, and I asked Marion to come with me instead: she knew that part of the world, and she'd be good company. We left early and drove all morning, the country yellow with rain and a strong side-wind blowing in off the North Sea. When we reached Haydon Bridge I overshot the house – I remembered Monica saying it was close to a road, but surely not this close and not this road, the main road to Newcastle? I turned back to park outside the front door, the car shaking as traffic sizzled past. The bolthole was a shabby little box: the sort of place I'd normally give half a glance, feeling sorry for whoever lived there.

We collected the key from a neighbour, but the front door was warped by rain and jammed by junk mail. I heaved with my shoulder and we squeezed through. Damp-smell – mouldy wood and rotting carpets. Mouse shit and wet dust. Bare boards in the hall and the stairs also stripped, but tins of food piled at the side of each step, and one of these tins, treacle, had leaked a small gold glacier. Why all this hoarding, that was the first question. It made the place seem less like a refuge than a bunker, somewhere Philip and Monica could shelter during a disaster. But something else was bothering me now, something much more perplexing. The door into the sitting room was gaping open, and the carpet in there – dark purple, ecclesiastical – seemed to be rucked up beneath a desk that had been dragged into the centre of the room. So that was it. The house had been burgled, a while ago apparently, and the neighbours hadn't heard; Marion and I were first on the scene.

When we left the hall and turned into the sitting room, the invasion was even more obvious. The back window had been smashed – there was a starburst in the glass where someone had reached through and flipped the catch, and mud on the sill. And other kinds of wreckage, too – drawers and cupboards lolling open in the kitchen, pictures cock-eyed on the walls, heavy boot-prints up the stairs, one of them clipping the sticky edge of the treacle-trail and trampling it onwards. The thieves must have been disappointed, though. There was nothing here worth more than a few pounds, and obviously never had been.

Except there were valuable things: irreplaceable things. I opened the back door and stood in the yard as Philip must have done, watching the river growl past. The wide, dark brown, angry river swollen by recent rain, dragging a whole tree through the central arch of the bridge to my left, noisily grinding its branches, then tearing them free. There were letters. Even here, in the puddles and corners – they must have blown out through the smashed window. I gathered them up, then turned inside again, and Marion and I began working methodically through the house. The letters were everywhere: in the kitchen on countertops and in drawers; underneath the desk in the sitting room and crammed into every drawer; on the seats of the two large armchairs and stuffed down the side of cushions; in the grate of the fire, mizzled over by soot; pressed between the pages of books in the downstairs lavatory. I found a plastic bag and put them inside, dozens of them, then headed upstairs.

I paused on the threshold of the bedroom. This was where Philip and Monica had played together, traffic rattling the window that overlooked the road, and the river roaring out of sight. I remembered the pictures I'd seen in Philip's photograph albums in Newland Park – Monica posing on top of a cabinet in the library, when the building was closed to other visitors. Monica in her stripy tights, with one knee drawn up and a faraway look in her eyes. Monica on holiday on the island of Sark, dangling her legs in a rockpool, with the ripples untying the contours of her thighs. Monica face down in the sand of a lonely beach, also on Sark, with the V of her bathing costume tugged into the crease of her arse. She may have been disparaged by some of Philip's friends, by Kingsley in particular, but it was obvious that she and Philip knew how to enjoy each other. Couldn't do without each other, in fact. When Philip went off with Maeve, or with Betty in the last part of his life, Monica had always eventually swallowed her anger and taken him back when he wanted her. 'He was a bugger,' she half shouted at me one day in the reeking fug of Newland Park, droplets of gin spinning from her mouth. 'He was a bugger, but I loved him.'

I stepped into the room, edging past an ironing board with a cream silk blouse draped across it and the iron still standing in place: Philip and Monica must have abandoned the place in a rush. On the nightstand they'd even left behind their copy of Iris Murdoch's *The Flight from the Enchanter*, which Monica had told me they used to deface while lying in bed together. I opened it and looked inside: it was like Tom Phillips's *Humament*, only sillier and filthier; everything including the chapter numbers had been given a makeover – TEN was now elaborated into 'I fuck my sTENographer'. The effect was so vivid, so redolent of secret life, that I thought the past and present might suddenly fuse, and any minute now I'd hear Philip's car arriving outside, and the doors slamming, and the scratch of a key in the lock. I liked that sense of proximity, but it made me hurry up as well, peeling back the bed covers and finding more letters there, and more in the clothes basket, and more on the shelf in the bathroom, and more on the cistern of the lavatory. What about the wardrobe in the bedroom? I opened the door and ran my hand across Monica's dresses and coats. The dampness was so bad, one of the dresses ripped as I touched it, and letters slipped out of the pockets into my hands – and when I'd collected them, I shunted the clothes aside and found at the back of the cupboard, shielded by a heavy winter coat, another plastic bag. This one had already been packed by Monica herself and was overflowing with letters.

Marion and I tramped back downstairs. We'd only done what we came to do, which was what Monica herself had wanted, but when I had counted the letters and bagged them up – there were more than a hundred – I felt like a thief. And when I took the key back to the neighbour, I found myself apologising for the burglary, as though I was responsible for that as well.

A fortnight later these same neighbours rang Monica, saying they were sorry to give her bad news, but there'd been another break-in at the cottage, and this time the thieves had been better organised. They'd brought a van and stolen everything moveable – the desk, the bed, the ironing board, the chairs, the clothes, the wardrobe, everything. It was a disaster for Monica; she felt that a part of her life with Philip had been ripped away from her, and her misery deepened. But she could see there was a silver lining as well – just as I could see that the story of the burglary gave a convincing reply to people who thought all biographers really were just 'publishing scoundrels' and nothing more. If Marion and I hadn't taken the letters when we did, those would have been stolen too, and no doubt tossed aside. Scribbles from the gloomy old sod who sometimes came here for a holiday, but never liked it enough to stay for long.

---

As I had resigned from Chatto to concentrate on writing about Philip, Jan and I sold our house in Hackney and moved half a mile west, to a place better suited to our three children and our own lives. There was a room in the basement I could use as a study. It was low-ceilinged and dark, despite the French doors into the garden, and this gave a battened-down and semi-secretive feeling that appealed to me. I thought that if I'd been writing at the top of the house, I'd have been living too much in my head: an egotist. Down here I was half submerged in the materials of the unconscious: an id-man. This might not have been ideal for writing biography, where I needed to be continually vigilant about my own intentions, but it certainly suited poems. And especially the poems that I now wanted to write.

Having three young children to care for meant that Jan and I were often exhausted in ways familiar to every parent, and in my own case, this soon fed into a deeper depression than any I'd known before. Like my father before me, I found myself withdrawing from the family life I'd so much wanted to help create in the first place. A part of me felt that I needed to steer clear of this in my poems, so as not to add insult to injury. Another part of me remembered Graham Greene's judgement that all writers worth the name have a sliver of ice in their heart; I wanted to record everything that was in my mind, no matter how miserable or selfish it might be.

This latter part, the cold-hearted part, turned out to be the more forceful of the two, and in the shadows of my subterranean study I gave it free rein. It meant that for the first time in my life as a poet, the balance I'd always tried to maintain between conscious and unconscious forces was tilted decisively in favour of the latter – to the extent that I often stared down at what I'd put on the page and wondered whether I'd written it myself. Dream visions. Nightmares of dissociation and betrayal. Queasy violence. My mother's bruised face, Jan's face, and Joanna's face twirling in a kaleidoscope of fragments. Death fantasies and death wishes. And all of them coming to me in forms I hadn't used before, as though these dangerous subjects insisted on speaking in a voice that was new to me. Short lines, broken rhythms, oblique allusions. When the fit passed – and it felt like a fit, a period of illness – I collected the poems and gave them a title that Browning had also used for one of his enigmatic poems of loss – *Love in a Life* – and sent it to Faber, who would remain my publishers from this point on. In that sense I had found a home at one remove. As far as the contents of the book were concerned, I knew that I'd shaken the foundations of my actual home.

I opened the address book that Monica had given me and looked for the names that would help me to map Philip's story, then went to see them – the childhood friends, the Oxford friends, the girlfriends:

Ruth Bowman, who was Philip's fiancée in the early 1940s; now she'd retired from her job as a schoolteacher and was living in Kent. Shy, dignified, and proud of her connection with Philip, but suspicious of bright lights.

Winifred, the 'sweet girl graduate' that Philip had fallen for in Belfast, and whose photograph album he'd written about; when I visited her in Winchester, where she went to live after leaving Northern Ireland, she opened the thick black pages – and there she was, innocent and flirtatious as she swam through dark water towards the camera lens.

Maeve, who spent all her adult life in Hull working in the library while also looking after her retired dentist father; a strict Catholic who tormented herself when she agreed to sleep with Philip, then was dumped by him as a lover, if not a friend.

Betty the loaf-haired secretary, who never thought of wedding bells when she began sleeping with Philip towards the end of his life, but didn't want to talk about that. Except to say that Philip had once told her Eliot also had an affair with his secretary – 'Only he *did* marry her, you know.'

Monica. Monica time and again because she had loved Philip best and knew him better than anyone, and because all Philip's possessions were still with her in the house in Newland Park. Once when Jan and I were visiting, she said I could take some of the manuscripts home, because it would be easier for me to work with them there. Jan and I were staying overnight in a hotel around the corner, in a room at the end of a long bunga-low extension overlooking the car park at the back of the main building. I piled the manuscripts on a chair beside the bed, and stayed up late watching a World Cup match on the television, the sound turned down low because Jan was asleep – she was pregnant with the twins.

There was no light in our room except the iceberg glow of the TV screen, and no commentary but a murmur. Then the metal curtain hooks started scraping along their runners, and a hand poked through, curving downwards to twist the latch and open the window. More thieves! I leaped out of bed, roaring at the top of my voice, and ripped the curtains apart to reveal a pyramid of pissed boys who were amazed to find anyone in the room, let alone a man naked and bellowing. I kept at it, trying to blow down the pyramid with my voice – and amazingly it worked: the boys landed in a heap, then disentangled and scattered across the car park. First the robbery at Monica's cottage, and now this. The boys must not have known the room was occupied, and thought they could steal a television – but why were so many of Philip's manuscripts only narrowly escaping destruction? Was he trying to organise, from beyond the grave, a version of the final bonfire he'd promised and failed to light in life?

And Kingsley, whom I'd never met while Philip was alive, only read or heard spoken about by Philip himself and by mutual friends, and by Kingsley's son Martin. Now the funeral was over, I asked whether we might talk, and Kingsley said come to his flat in Regent's Park Road at the foot of Primrose Hill, where he lived on the floor beneath his first wife Hilly and her second husband.

Kingsley had the reputation of playing himself: funny, particular, rude, boozy. The man who showed me into the downstairs flat for our first meeting (Hilly invisible on the floor above, her disembodied voice calling out from the top of the stairs, 'Everything all right?') was deflated and melancholy; he said that ever since he and Philip had first met as undergraduates in Oxford forty-odd years earlier, Philip had always been the person he relied on to tell him the truth about his writing – what worked and what didn't. 'Now that he's not here,' he said, 'I won't know what's any good any more.' He stared into the fire, his face congested. But we talked easily enough – Kingsley holding nothing back, accepting that the biography needed to be thorough, giving every appearance of helpfulness but at the same time flicking out little hints of surprise and sourness. Was that his way of admitting his friendship with Philip had become more partial towards the end? Or did he resent having to download his memoirs for me – this whippersnapper who'd known Philip for much less time than he'd done, and whose opinions, vocabulary, attitudes, everything, were so obviously at odds with his own? The longer we talked, the more Kingsley's conversation seemed like embers, smouldering and ready to burst into flames whenever a fresh gust of annoyance blew across them.

We kept going until one o'clock, then Kingsley wiped his palms on his knees and began putting on his coat, saying we'd now have lunch in the pub over the road. Once we'd navigated the throng, and found the corner table that Kingsley had previously booked, he ordered what he was careful to specify would be our *first* bottle of wine. I wanted to think this was a sign that we were becoming friends – but it wasn't. It was Kingsley's way of making sure that he felt rewarded for his trouble and his memories.

Next time we met, for another interview, Kingsley finished what he had to say a little sooner than I'd expected, so we could catch a taxi into the centre of town: he'd booked a table for one o'clock at Simpson's on the Strand. Once we got there, Kingsley ordered roast beef, which was carved on the trolley beside our table, and over the next couple of hours we drank three bottles of expensive claret. There was no question of us splitting this bill: this was on me. The whole performance reminded me of an evening when Philip and I went to supper at an Indian restaurant in Hull, and Philip gleefully pushed through the door, slapping the breast pocket of his jacket. 'I hope you've brought your wallet,' he'd said; 'I seem to have forgotten mine.'

At Chatto I'd always dictated my letters, talking into a hand-held recorder, then sending the tapes to a professional typist, who returned the hard copies a day later for checking and signature. Sonia, the typist was called – we'd never actually met, and I knew nothing about her except that she lived in Sittingbourne, in Kent. Sonia of Sittingbourne. Now that I'd finished the first draft of the book about Philip, which I'd written in longhand, I got in touch with her again and asked whether she'd be willing to type that for me, if I dictated it to her. My plan wasn't just to find a way to speed things up; I thought dictation would help me revise my first draft because I could edit as I went along, and make sure my sentences sounded like natural speech. However intense its subjects might be, I wanted the book to have a clear surface, just as I'd always wanted my poems to have a clear surface. The idea all along had been to make my writing look like water but turn out to be gin.

Ruth and Winifred and Monica and Maeve and Betty and Kingsley: I'd promised to send them the book about Philip in typescript, so they could change facts I'd got wrong, and object to things they found hurtful or embarrassing. Maeve was the one I felt most worried about, even though she was also the one who'd told me least. She was prim and proper, which was partly what Philip had loved about her – her reserve, and the sexiness of persuading her to set her reservations aside. But when Maeve had read my draft, she told me that she felt she had held back too much during our interviews. Now she'd written a reminiscence of her life with Philip, sat up all night to get it done, and here it was, thirty pages or so: I was welcome to quote whatever I liked.

---

I finished dictating my revisions, sent the last tape to Sonia, and a week later had a legible manuscript of the whole book: six hundred and some pages. A Jiffy bag arrived in the same post as the final chapters, with a cassette inside it which was the same small size that I'd been using in my own tape recorder, and a letter signed 'Raymond Cass', which was not a name I recognised. Cass introduced himself as the hearing specialist who used to fit Philip's hearing aid, and added ('if I may use a figure of speech to a literary man') that with his 'left hand' he was a spiritualist who had 'made contact with Dr Larkin' in his afterlife. The letter went on to say that the cassette contained a recording of their conversations 'thus far' and explained that they'd been conducted through the medium of a high-frequency radio.

I'd sometimes played planchette at school to give myself the shivers. I once pretended to see a ghost when staying in the remote countryside with a girl I fancied, thinking this might hurry things in the direction I wanted them to go. I'd had my palm read by pretend gypsies at village fetes. But I had no belief in the spirit world, just as I also had no belief in the afterlife. All the same, I was curious to know what was on the Cass cassette, so slotted it into my recorder and pressed 'play'.

There were three 'conversations' – except they weren't really conversations, they were just very brief verbal encounters. In the first, a soft nasal northern accent (Cass himself, although the voice reminded me of Peter Cook's character the Misty Mr Wisty) asked, 'Are you there, Philip Larkin?' and was answered by a long crackling silence and then, at the edge of hearing, a noise that sounded like a bat flying in rings round the house, cheeping 'Philipphilipphilipphilip'. It wasn't convincing, but Cass wasn't deterred. 'Do you miss your friends?' he continued, speaking more boldly now. 'Only one friend,' the other voice shot back, itself sounding more confident and also a great deal more like Philip – it had the authentic Eeyoreish dying fall. Who might that friend be?, I wondered. Monica? She'd outlasted all Philip's other loves, and was now half demented with missing him, living in what used to be his house and leaking into his chair. Yes, surely Monica – not that the ether would confirm or deny it. Then Cass lobbed his final question: 'Dr Larkin, what are you doing in the afterlife?' There was another pause, another burst of static, and the same Eeyoreish voice. 'Tramping,' it said. Tramping, I repeated to myself: a Hardyesque word ('A Trampwoman's Tragedy'), so that fitted. Or possibly a cosmic typo, a mangling of what should have been 'Wanking'. But I kept that thought to myself when I wrote back to Cass and encouraged him to get back in touch if he had any more contact.

It wasn't that I believed Cass really had communicated with 'the spirit of Dr Larkin': I thought Cass was probably a harmless crank who'd somehow (and maybe unconsciously) ventriloquised a voice that sounded remarkably like Philip's. But when Cass sent me a second Jiffy bag nine months later, I wasn't slow to open it. There was another letter inside, and another cassette. 'Dear Andrew (may I?)' the letter began, with a courtesy that already felt old-fashioned in the dawning age of internet informality, before going on to explain that since the biography was about to be published, Cass thought it only reasonable to assume that Philip had already read it, and he'd therefore 'taken the liberty' of asking him what he thought of it.

'Do not be surprised', the letter continued, with a much deeper note of comedy than any I thought Cass could have intended, 'if you feel the voice of Dr Larkin sounds distressed. It is usually the case that the spirits of the recently departed sound distressed, especially if, as I believe was the case with Dr Larkin, there was no expectation of there being an afterlife.'

I slid the tape into the recorder and once again pressed 'play'. There was another burst of crackling and static, then Cass put his question: was Philip happy with my book? 'Very satisfactory,' came the reply, in what for a moment at least I felt certain must be Philip's own voice.

---

In a recurring dream I was talking about Philip to a room full of strangers, the seats raked like a lecture theatre (or a gladiatorial arena), telling them some of the things I'd unearthed. They were all anecdotes and details I'd never have considered talking about in public when Philip was alive. But now, in Philip's afterlife, I'd decided candour was the best policy, partly because Philip himself always spoke frankly about things he thought were important. Hence the lecture and the revelations and the steeply raked auditorium. Hence, too, as the dream continued, my dismay when I noticed that Philip himself was sitting in the audience – at which point I usually woke up, horrified by myself.

But not today. Today I remained asleep, went on spilling the beans, eventually faltered to a conclusion, then realised as I packed up my notes that the only way I could leave the room was by climbing the stairs, which would take me past the end of the row where Philip was sitting. As I came alongside him, expecting some kind of rumpus, he stood up and produced from nowhere a collar made of plaited hay, which he draped around my neck. At which point I came to my senses and lay in the dark wondering why I didn't feel more upset. Because the hay wasn't a collar, I realised, it was a kind of garland. And because it wasn't made of hay, either, but cut grass – cut grass as in Philip's beautiful poem of the same name:

> Cut grass lies frail:
> Brief is the breath
> Mown stalks exhale.
> Long, long the death
>
> It dies in the white hours
> Of young-leafed June
> With chestnut flowers,
> With hedges snowlike strewn,

White lilac bowed,
Lost lanes of Queen Anne's lace,
And that high-builded cloud
Moving at summer's pace.

———

In the same week that I published my Life of Philip, Andrew Morton brought out his biography of Princess Diana. *The Scotsman* interviewed me about my book before I flew to Edinburgh to give a talk about it and, when I arrived at the airport, I picked up a copy of the paper to see what the journalist had written. The headline above the piece said: 'Andrew Motion Already a Millionaire'.

# Part Five

---

## 1993–1996

My Larkin book was making its way in the world, and Faber asked me what I was going to write next. I wanted to say, 'My own poems,' because they'd been starved of oxygen during the seven years that I'd been working on the biography, and I needed to revive them. But I found myself returning to a question that had first confronted me in Hull: might I have become so saturated in Philip that I wouldn't be able to avoid sounding like him? It seemed possible. The more deeply I'd thought about his poems, the more intensely I enjoyed reading them – not least because they transcended aspects of his personality that might have acted as inhibitors. His quarrel with others – in his correspondence and elsewhere – had sometimes produced disagreeable rhetoric; his poetry arose from the quarrel with himself. Why wouldn't I want to follow the example of such a master?

The answer was the same one that I'd been giving myself for a while: writing about Philip had showed me the ways in which we were like each other, but also and mostly how different we were. Henceforth, I didn't in the least mind doing whatever was necessary as an executor of the estate, and I certainly didn't want to disavow Philip in any way: we'd been fond of each other, and I felt fond of him still. But at the same time, I didn't want my life to be swallowed by his posthumous existence, or to think that I had no future except as his wingman.

I scanned the horizon and immediately saw Keats. I'd loved Keats's poems since my first brushes with poetry itself, and that seemed reason enough to write about him. Then there were his letters, which had influenced my own thoughts about poetry more decisively than anything else I'd read. Then there was the fact that no new Life of Keats had been published for a generation, and all the existing ones falsely (as I thought) made him out to be a kind of history-dodger who lay panting on a bed of lilies while the other Romantic poets leaped onto the barricades. And finally, overwhelmingly, there was the marvel of Keats's writing and character, and the pathos of his shooting-star existence: the pugnacity, the passion, the precocious brilliance, the genius for friendship, the comic instinct, the heroic perseverance. Philip had created most of his poems by saying 'no' to life, or 'maybe'. Keats had almost always said 'yes' – despite the fact that he'd lived in much closer proximity to tragedy than Philip had ever done. I thought that by choosing Keats, I'd allow more yes in my life; more yes in myself. Where Philip had crouched fearfully in the shade of 'extinction's alp', Keats had struck a balance in his thoughts about mortality: 'for many a time/ I have been half in love with easeful Death,/ Call'd him soft names in many a mused rhyme,/ To take into the air my quiet breath'. *Half* in love with death: that was much closer to my own feelings. Half in love with death, and half with life.

---

There were various other kinds of business to deal with before I could start: different structures for different times. First Jan and I moved house again – staying in north London, but shifting further west into Tufnell Park. Then, soon after we'd settled in, I applied to run the Creative Writing MA programme at the University of East Anglia (the founder, Malcolm Bradbury, was retiring after twenty-five years in the job). It was partly to earn money, and partly because I missed teaching and believed in the value of courses like this one. I knew there was a sense among the generation older than me that fostering young writers inside universities was a kind of scam, like giving steroids to athletes. And if not that (or as well as that), it was a contemptibly American idea – a form of creative narcissism that had no place on English soil. But these prejudices had always seemed ridiculous to me. Even though I'd never taken a creative writing course myself (because they didn't exist at the time when I might have signed up for one), I felt that I might as well have done, given the kind of manuscript-swapping I'd done with Alan ever since our graduate days. It had convinced me that writing courses for young writers are quite simply as valuable as ballet school is for young dancers, or drama school for young actors, or art school for young artists. In any case, UEA was host to the most famous writing course in the country: Ian McEwan and Kazuo Ishiguro had both been students there in the early days; Angela Carter and Rose Tremain had sometimes worked there alongside Malcolm.

I began work in the autumn, commuting for two days' teaching a week, and staying overnight in a b. & b. near the university campus. I loved it: the quick immersion in a community, the clever and talented students – then the slow journey down through the flatlands of East Anglia, with its glimpses of childhood scenes that I knew by heart, and back into London again. It was an in-between life, but that suited me in all sorts of ways. It made room for both halves of myself, and added to my sense that a part of me preferred to live like a ghost, belonging nowhere definite.

'Show not tell': that's the maypole-phrase most creative-writing teachers dance around, and it's easy to see why. Young writers quite rightly want to tackle large subjects, and easily fall into bad habits of abstraction: urging them to stick to things-in-themselves helps them to stay grounded. Keats said so, several times: 'O for a Life of Sensations rather than Thoughts'; 'We hate poetry that has a palpable design upon us'; 'Axioms in philosophy are not axioms until they are proved upon our pulses'; Ezra Pound had said so, and made it one of the founding principles of Imagism; William Carlos Williams said so: 'No ideas but in things'. The most powerful (or anyway the most widely praised) currents in contemporary British and Irish poetry demonstrated the same principle: Ted Hughes slicing the horns off cattle or marvelling over salmon in a river; Seamus Heaney picking blackberries or excavating sacrificial bodies from a Danish bog.

But what about the opposite point of view? What about Hannah Arendt: 'Poetry, whose material is language, is perhaps the most human and least worldly of the arts, the one in which the end product remains closest to the thought that inspired it'? What about Auden, who had first encouraged me to read Arendt and whose own poems often philosophise or play tricky mind games? What about John Donne, for whom thought, according to Eliot, was 'an experience; it modified his sensibility', and whose ways of proceeding became a guiding light for the New Critics of the 1930s? (Allen Tate in 1932 compared Emily Dickinson to Donne and said that she *'perceives abstraction* and *thinks sensation'*.) What about the flock of contemporary Americans who used poems to cogitate and opine, and made a lot of their British and Irish counterparts look like chatty anecdotalists? Didn't they prove in their various ways that telling and not showing could be just fine?

My students at UEA looked at me as though I was about to choose one side or the other. But that's not what I wanted to do. I wanted to bring showing and telling together. To say that Keats never meant that 'feeling beats thinking as a way of understanding the universe', but instead meant 'think with the senses'. To convince them that 'show not tell' is too neatly binary. And at the same time to remind them to stay vigilant about real things in real places – to convince them that the road to the stars begins under their noses, and that writing in humility has the furthest reach.

On my London days and during the vacations I made a start on my Keats book, catching the Overground every morning to the house in Hampstead (long since a museum) where Keats spent the last few years of his life, settling into the library-room above the front door, and reading until closing time. When it rained, damp seeped through the walls and darkened them – the house was beautiful but jerry-built, the walls only one brick thick. When the skies cleared, tourists paused at the front gate beyond the library window, gazed admiringly, then advanced up the wide flagged path as if they were approaching an altar.

Coming to worship, not to sacrifice – Keats is a beloved person, and this is a beloved place. But the longer I sat there watching the pilgrims, inching my way deeper into Keats's mind and life, the more clearly I saw that the house wasn't only what it seemed to be. It was a palace of poetry but also saturated in sadness. The place where Keats had written some of his best poems, but also the sickbay where he heard Fanny Brawne rustling through her days and nights in the adjacent half of the house, knowing that he would never be well enough to marry her. Where he said goodbye to her when he left for Italy, hoping to recover his health but expecting that he would never return. Where Fanny's mother, a few years after Keats's death, saw off some guests after dinner one evening, accidentally set fire to her dress with the candle she was using to light them to the front gate, and burned herself to death.

———

I wanted to go wherever Keats went; it was my version of the foot-stepping that Richard Holmes recommends. But I wondered: why stop in England and Scotland? Why not sail from London to Naples as Keats did in 1820? It was a crazy idea: I'd never previously done anything more nautical than sail a sponge around my bath. But it was also a glamorous idea – a flirtation with danger and difference – and that made it hard to resist. I asked around and heard about *Excelsior*: the name put me off, but the description of the boat was right. A fishing smack built a hundred years ago, 120 feet long, twin-masted, liver-coloured sails, with an engine for emergencies. She was registered in Lowestoft on the Suffolk coast, and had a crew of six who used her for Outward Bound programmes: they were used to sailing long distances.

How to pay for it, though, that was the question – and the answer dropped out of the blue. While I was at the Cheltenham Literature Festival, about to go on stage and read my poems, I met the novelist Nigel Williams, who was then running the

BBC's arts series *Arena*; I mentioned to him that the bicentenary of Keats's birth was coming up, and suggested the BBC might like to make a film centred on the voyage to Italy. He jumped at the idea and hired James Runcie as the director.

---

One day I felt perfectly fit and healthy, the next I had pins and needles in my feet, and a week later I couldn't tell whether the water was too hot or too cold when I stepped into the bath. I washed myself, dried off, and lay down in the bedroom. Spring had started early, and buds were already opening on the lime tree outside my window, quick leaves flickering over the black trunk with its white mould-spots. Was there really something wrong with me, or was this just a fantasy of departure, provoked by thinking about Keats and early death? I should go to the doctor and find out. But supposing the doctor found something serious? That might mean no voyage to Italy. I decided to say nothing.

---

Stewart was the skipper of *Excelsior*: six foot three, barrel-chested, white-bearded, wind-slapped cheeks, shy but definite, a Lowestoft local. He and the rest of the crew-crew sailed round from East Anglia and tied up in Tower Dock by Tower Bridge, where I went aboard and the film-crew joined us – James the director, his assistant (whose face turned milky with seasickness the instant she left dry land), a sound man, and a camera man. I said goodbye to Jan and the children on the quayside and tried not to notice how aggrieved they looked, and how anxious. Then the dock-gates opened and we chugged into the Thames, sails still furled, catching the outgoing evening tide. As the spires and domes of the city shrank behind us, and the flashy geometries of Canary Wharf, my ideal vision of the journey blended with things as they actually appeared, bathing them in pearly dream-light. The ruins of ancient wharves, the flat skyline where buildings gave way to marshland beyond Greenwich, the scuzzy mud-lumps and gluey channels, and then – as the sun finally vanished – turbulence in the river-mouth and the sailing centuries rushing towards me. Raiders and pirates, warriors and adventurers, traders and idlers.

First thing after coming back from Italy I went to see my GP Dr Sills and explained: six weeks ago I couldn't feel my feet, now I couldn't feel anything below my knees – I was rotting from the toes up. The doctor reached towards a saucer on his desk, chose a paperclip, unbent it, then stuck the sharp point into my ankle. Nothing. He tried again. Still nothing. Dr Sills picked up his phone, made an appointment with someone whose name I didn't catch, and a couple of hours later I was travelling through the guts of University College Hospital to meet what turned out to be a lemon-sucking Scotsman. More prodding and poking. Could this man see what the problem was? Not clearly – there would have to be an MRI – but he thought there might be a tumour on my spine, which was interfering with the messages that my brain sent to the rest of my body. Was it malignant? The Scotsman shrugged. Too early to say; the MRI would tell us. Meanwhile, I should go home and rest; someone would be in touch.

It was early summer, tall blue sky and mild English heat. I walked slowly towards Goodge Street Tube station, paying more attention than usual to the traffic-glitter, shop windows, clothes, hair, gestures, expressions, speech-snatches. 'Look thy last on all things lovely,' I said under my breath: Joanna was always quoting that de la Mare poem; I had learned it from her. Would I see her again? Would I see any of this again? I was forty-three, almost the same age that my mother had been when she had her accident; if I'd been Philip, I'd have thought that meant my chances of surviving were slim.

> Look thy last on all things lovely,
> Every hour. Let no night
> Seal thy sense in deathly slumber
>    Till to delight
> Thou have paid thy utmost blessing:
> Since that all things thou wouldst praise
> Beauty took from those who loved them
>    In other days.

A DHL van bounced onto the pavement ahead of me and blocked the way. As the driver swung out of his cab, gripping a package under one arm, people started shouting at him. 'You can't do that! You can't stop there!' The driver scuttled towards a doorway and the voices got angrier. 'Oi! This is a pavement, not a parking lot – fuck off.' A fist banged on the side of the van – a hollow metallic boom – then the driver threw his package through an open door, dodged back into his cab, slammed into gear, bumped off the pavement into the street, and revved away with a snarl on his horn.

Energy! Gusto! Life! I wanted more of it.

———

The May sun in the Solent was as hot as July and the breeze idle – all the sails set, but *Excelsior* hardly moving: canvas slack, a trickling sound under the bows, the crew-crew occasionally cocking an eye to the heavens and shaking their heads, the film-crew and me drowsily switching our half-minds between the busy English coast on the starboard side, with its trippers and funfairs, and the quiet green shore of the Isle of Wight. Then there was a sudden swirl in the surface on the port side, as though a gigantic plug had been pulled from the seabed, and the water twisted into a tornado shape fifty feet across. What was that? I looked to Stewart, but Stewart only blinked. Nothing special; not a portent or a problem. Just a thing that sometimes happens out here. We sailed slowly on towards Start Point in Devon, where we would turn south, and voices from either side of us continued to drift across the water: children playing and pointing. Look at that! A sailing ship!

———

I came home from hospital and the sour Scotsman, then lay on my bed staring into the lime tree again – the smart leaves and permanently damp-looking trunk – telling myself that I should ring my father and tell him about the tumour: I couldn't not, even though I knew it would make him worry. Then, as I rolled onto my side and reached for the phone, I heard the sound of whistling, sat upright, and saw through the window a man at the top of a ladder propped against the house next door. Sixty-ish, a sprightly grandfather type, tweed cap and blue overalls, with a bucket of water slung from the hook beside him and a bright yellow chamois leather in his right hand. A window cleaner. It felt like years since I'd seen one; had window cleaners died out like rag-and-bone men or knife-grinders? Maybe I wasn't living at the end of an era after all. Or maybe I was, and the end was arriving more slowly than I'd thought.

I leaned back against the pillows, dialled my father's number, and heard the ring tone. There must be a million phones in the world that made exactly the same sound, but I'd have recognised this one anywhere. Which meant that while I listened to it, I also saw everything that lay nearby: my father's desk, the cream-coloured blotting pad with back-to-front writing on it, the cramped study with pictures of myself and my brother, and my mother as a young woman, the logs and scrunched-up newspaper ready to light in the fireplace, and the door into the kitchen ajar, giving a glimpse of his wife Susan as she lounged against the rail of the Aga and smoked a cigarette. 'Ooouw' – that irritated whine she often made, as though she'd been interrupted while trying to solve some immensely difficult problem. 'Oooouw, who can that be?' And my father's reluctance to pick up – the fingertip grip, the receiver three inches from his face, the cautious frog-in-the-throat quavering 'Hello?'

Just as I was about to say, 'Hi, Dad, it's me,' there was an interruption. A slow, gritty scraping noise that could mean only one thing. The window cleaner's ladder was dragging across the bricks of the house next door. Dragging because the window cleaner had lost his balance and was about to fall. Was already falling, in fact.

I gabbled to my father, 'Something's happened and I'll have to call you back,' then hung up while my father's mystified face flashed across my mind – the frown, the head shake, the mumbled answer to Susan's question through the half-open door, the return of the receiver to its cradle – then slid off the bed and looked outside. Somehow the window cleaner had delayed his fall for a few seconds and his boots were still dancing on the ladder-rung, the water was still slopping in his bucket, and both his hands were still squeezing the side-struts of the ladder as he tried to pin them against the wall. But the chamois leather had already dropped onto the paving slabs in the front garden twenty feet below. I could see it there, among the violets and celandines. A thing that had already fallen.

Then the rest of the world accelerated and broke into smithereens: the bucket arching away, the tuft of water flinging out sideways, the clatter and splosh as they hit the ground, the water-stain spreading. A black pool. And the window cleaner following. His quick gasp. His cap tipping off to show the sickly-white top of his head. The baggy thump as his body flumped onto the slabs beside his bucket. The bucket still rolling with a hollow circling sound. The window cleaner not moving. His right leg twisted underneath him, and the worm of blood crawling out of his ear.

I rang 999, and the ambulance came so quickly, it was already pulling into the street when I opened the front door. I wanted to help, I felt responsible, and began to say as much to the ambulance man who was running through the gateway to kneel beside the body. 'Oh yeah?' said the man, fiddling with the window cleaner's boiler suit, checking for signs of life. 'How's that, then?' 'Nothing,' I said, 'I didn't mean it like that,' and stood back. When the police arrived a few moments later I kept it simple, saying nothing except what I'd seen. 'Is he going to be all right?' I asked, before faltering to a stop. The policeman shook his head.

I went back into the house and shut the door, leaning against the cold wood while the others finished their work outside; I heard them lift the body onto a stretcher, stow it in the ambulance, then drive away. Long before their siren faded, and the police knocked on my door and took my statement, I knew that my tumour wouldn't kill me. Zeus had fired a death-bolt, but it had missed me and hit the window cleaner instead. Which made me a murderer, didn't it? Or did I mean survivor? I picked up the phone and dialled my father's number again.

———

The film-crew went ashore at Teignmouth – the BBC couldn't afford for them to come all the way to Italy, so they were going to meet me in Naples in a fortnight and we'd pick up the filming there. I stood on deck to wave them off, but Stewart told me to step aside: there was a tricky sandbar in the mouth of Teignmouth harbour, and if I wanted to behave like a poet and watch the red cliffs fading into the mist, I should move to the stern. I did as I was told, and saw England disappearing piece by piece: trees and fields becoming a single smear of green, then green becoming blue. Plain sailing should mean *Excelsior* would arrive in Italy on time, and if we were running late, Stewart could always switch on the engine. There was a deadline, after all. There was a budget.

———

The doctor found a place for me in the National Hospital for Neurology and Neurosurgery in Queen Square – a corner bed with a window on my left where I could stare at a world with no sickness in it: slates, moss, a chimney stack with two ochre chimney pots, and the sky above, the endless, open, empty sky.

No obvious memories of my mother there. The ward to my right, though – that was another matter. Curtains drawn round a bed where someone was groaning to death. In another bed, a confused old man muttering, 'Naughty, naughty, naughty.' Was he talking about himself? Whenever a nurse came near, his voice got louder – 'NAUGHTY, NAUGHTY, NAUGHTY' – and that sounded more like imploring. He wanted someone to be naughty with him. He craved it.

———

The mood on board was more concentrated now, the crew quietly going about their business while I fished for supper with two lines trailing off the stern, one for mackerel and the other a steel wire with a small plastic octopus tied on the end, a lure for I wasn't sure what. Something in myself, I sometimes thought, a feeling of separation from my own life in general, and from my dear ones in particular, that I wanted to heal. Or was that because my mind was beginning to slide? Slop-slop of waves under the bow. Hot sun. Sails sometimes shrugging and smacking, but mostly hanging slack. Stewart disappearing into his cabin, then reappearing with a small squeezebox and play-ing a tune or two, singing shyly under his breath, not making a performance of it, the engine puttering, driving us down the long curve of the world.

There was a bang and a clank below decks, and Stewart made a face, then swung through the hatch into the engine room: what the hell was that? He was gone for longer than anyone wanted, and reappeared looking crestfallen, wiping his hands on an oily rag: the engine was broken, he said, and he couldn't fix it. He admitted this so calmly, it took a moment to understand. And another minute to realise that now we had to make a decision. Should we turn back to England or press on towards Naples? I imagined Jan and the children at home, and their disappointment as well as my own; there'd been so much build-up to this journey, it was bound to look like a failure if I returned before they expected me. Then I thought of Keats facing the end of his life, realising that he had no choice about whether to continue. I made up my mind. We'd keep going. Stewart radioed the film-crew and told them we might be late arriving in Naples.

———

A dribble of sea-miles, infinitely slow. I lay every night in my wedge-shaped cabin near the bow with my head pressed against the wall of the hull, and listened to the sea beyond it: a continuous low roar, as though we were travelling at speed. But that was only the sound of the world turning, there was no speed for the boat, no movement at all, and when I went back on deck in the morning, and then the next morning, and then the next, the prospect was always the same. A painted ocean with theatrical little water-spirits sometimes twitching across the surface. Shadow-play. A pigeon resting on its journey between here and there, pacing around the deck until one of the crew caught it and wrung its neck: that was supper for one, and mackerel again for the rest of us. And boredom. Boredom hardening across my skin like cement. Infinite boredom filtering into my foundations, blocking my connection to things, unbalancing me. No alcohol, no cigarettes left, nothing to read, no distractions to stop my mind collapsing on itself. Surely when we reached Biscay the wind would come back: Biscay was where storms happened, everyone knew that. But *Excelsior* slid into the bay

as slowly as a water-drop creeps down dusty glass, then stopped
dead still. Ropes creaked, voices mumbled, someone threw a
coin overboard to bribe Neptune, and Neptune ignored it.

> The very deeps did rot: O Christ!
>     That ever this should be!
> Yea, slimy things did crawl with legs
>     Upon the slimy sea.
>
> About, about, in reel and rout
>     The death-fires danced at night;
> The water, like a witch's oils,
>     Burnt green, and blue and white.
>
> And some in dreams assured were
>     Of the spirit that plagued us so:
> Nine fathoms deep he had followed us
>     From the land of mist and snow.

———

A nurse brought me an article from the newspaper. The surgeon who was due to remove my tumour had made headlines a
few weeks earlier by saving the life of a boy who'd been stabbed
in the head in a gang fight: here was a photograph – an X-ray of
the boy's skull, which showed the knife-blade actually touching
the brain. It looked like the hull of a small sunken boat, ship-
wrecked on a silvery coast. If the surgeon could do that kind
of magic, pulling out the blade with no harm done, surely he
could perform the delicate manoeuvre of poking behind a spine
to remove a tumour.

The surgeon himself obviously thought so, when he came to talk to me before the operation. Compact, well fed, dapper, rich-looking, with a small gull-cloud of nurses and juniors fluttering behind him. Unsmiling. 'Are you the man that wrote the book about Philip Larkin?' he wanted to know. 'Yes,' I told him, expecting a spark of sympathy. 'I don't approve,' the surgeon said. 'I don't think people should pry into the lives of poets. The work is the thing.' Then he turned on his polished heel and disappeared, his cloud trailing behind him, and later that day I was wheeled downstairs towards the operating theatre.

———

It had been a while since I'd had an anaesthetic, but once I heard the voice above me beginning to count down from ten, and felt myself enter the strangely passive state familiar to most hospital patients, I also remembered the equally strange flicker of doubt that came with it. The half-panicky, half-triumphant feeling that my system would turn out to be an exception proving the rule, and the drug would have no effect. That I'd be fully conscious when the surgeon turned to his trolley to select a knife, but unable to protest I was still awake. Had it been like this for my mother, during her years of unconsciousness? Had she known more than she could tell about what was happening around her? Had she . . . ten, nine, eight, seven . . . but I couldn't hold on, not to her, not to anything, and slipped below the surface.

———

One of my fishing lines sliced savagely down through the water like a cheese-wire. Not the mackerel line, but the metal wire with a plastic octopus attached and a hook inside the octopus. It was tied to a small electric winch, so I flicked the switch, and five minutes later there was a shark on deck – a young one, six feet long maybe, but big enough. Snapping and lashing and reeking of ammonia: that fear smell. A moment later, Stewart was kneeling astride it, wearing thick rubber gloves and jerking out the hook. Was he going to kill it? The shark suddenly stopped thrashing, and Stewart lifted the limp body in both arms like an unconscious human, then carried it to the side of the boat and dropped it overboard. The rest of us crowded round to watch. As the body wavered down through the first few feet of clear water it stayed motionless, a miniature grey submarine resetting its machinery. Then it snapped back to life, at exactly the same moment as a much larger shark, the mother perhaps, cruised up to inspect. And a whale breached further off, near the horizon – as though every creature in this acre of sea was suddenly rousing. A stink of rotting fish floated from the whale's plume and crossed the boat. Then the bay was silent again, the dream over.

———

The miracle of coming round, and the shock of realising that I was returning from a state in which time didn't exist, and the confusion of finding myself in a room I'd never seen before, knowing that something had happened, something important and intimate that I couldn't remember and never would. Or had they suddenly cancelled the operation after I'd lost consciousness, and I'd have to go through the whole thing again on another day? I asked the nurse, but she interrupted me before I finished my question. It was all done, and the tumour had been benign. A wee thing the size of a pea, she said, but enough to ruin my wiring. And gone now. Just a few days in hospital, then rest at home before going back to work – the wound had to heal.

——

As I climbed into my bunk every night on *Excelsior* I realised that when Keats had done this, he must have felt it was like climbing into a coffin. Keats had already imagined his own vanishing in the 'Ode to a Nightingale', and rehearsed his half-wish to 'Fade far away, dissolve, and quite forget/ What thou among the leaves hast never known,/ The weariness, the fever, and the fret/ Here, where men sit and hear each other groan'. But what did Keats think about the words he'd written, when he knew that his actual death was only weeks away? When he felt the wooden walls of his berth tightening around him, and saw the ceiling an inch from his face?

I shut my eyes, folded my arms across my chest, and listened again to the Atlantic seething beyond the planks of the hull. I'd remembered at last what it reminded me of, that vast monotonous sound, and it wasn't Keats. It was George Eliot. I was listening to the roar on the other side of silence.

——

My wound refused to heal. I lay in my corner of the ward watching clouds trail their shadows across the ochre chimneys, and my wound wept. When the nurses realised, they called for a doctor, who gave me a lumbar puncture to drain the fluid from my spine: that should fix it. My brain clunked onto the floor of my skull with a thud like a log falling onto concrete, and the morphine kicked in, triggering a dream-vision. I was watching the sea at sunset, marvelling at small waves that were streaked with orange and red, but inky in the hollows. From one of these hollows a man rose up, a naked body fitted with the head of a wolf, striding towards me through the water. 'I know you,' I wanted to say, meaning that I'd met him in my reading, but my voice wouldn't work. The wolf-man came closer, dripping and grinning, then stepped straight into my body: he fitted exactly.

———

Confinement. The wolf-man and my own mind locked in the same skull-dungeon, comparing savageries and exchanging confidences. The words were untranslatable, roiling in black shadow, distorted by echoes, yet their meaning was clear in outline. Something to do with self-disgust; something to do with shame; something to do with sins confronted and absolution denied. Was madness like this? Was I glimpsing what had previously always stayed just out of sight – the fixed form of depression? If so, there was no clue about how I might control it in the future, or expunge the sense that at some deep and primitive level I was half in love with disaster. For the moment at least, the wolf-man was the one in charge, relishing his moment off the leash, feasting on my flaws and weaknesses. Then, as suddenly as he'd arrived, he shrank away again. Clawed open my scalp, dragged his foul body into the daylight, and sealed my skin shut behind him. I rolled my head from side to side on the pillow, trying to rinse myself clean. There were pigeons and vapour trails in the sky outside; then little buffets of sickly sleep; then visitors at my bedside. Jan. The children. My father, briefly, standing at the end of the bed and crying as he smiled. Sandy. And Alan, sitting in the chair under the window while these others came and went, sometimes talking but mostly reading. Alan, who was there before anyone else arrived, and was still there when they left, as he had always been.

———

We were through Biscay and in Trafalgar now, the coast of Portugal simmering on the port horizon, and Stewart said our becalming was over, there was a storm coming: he'd been listening to the forecast on his radio. A bad storm, too. He sounded anxious and ordered everyone to get below decks or put on their gear and tie themselves to something fixed and solid – one of the deck-hatches, a mast. I chose the rail beside the tiller and asked Stewart whether, in all his life at sea, he'd ever thought he was going to drown. Only once, Stewart said. He'd caught his foot in a fishing net, and when the net went overboard, he fell with it. What was frightening, he said, is how fast boats move, even when they seem to be standing still. Water never stops flowing. One minute he was floundering under the stern, freeing himself from the ropes; the next, his boat was a little black trapdoor on the horizon.

———

The sea deepened and the sky boiled over, slate and charcoal avalanching as *Excelsior* galloped forward at last. Storm force six, storm force seven, with Stewart's anemometer, which he'd strapped to one of the masts, hurtling into a blur. And waves rioting over the guard rails, then writhing back through the bilges. And then more than just waves – huge monsters of water that ran riot over the entire boat and knocked the breath from my lungs, skinning and shining me. I was safe, I was tied to a stanchion by the tiller and I was safe, but I wondered again: is this what I'd wanted all along? An end to the complications of life, and the failings in myself that had created them? Fulfilment and absolution and nothing in the same instant?

Stewart bellowed through the clamour – 'Check your rope' – and as I retied myself, I looked off the stern. There was no sky there now, but a grey water-wall that arched into a gigantic claw-shape poised to strike and annihilate. 'Is that going to sink us?' I shouted back. Stewart shook his head – 'No' – and right on cue *Excelsior* hitched up her stern, dipped her bow into the trough that opened ahead, and the huge mass of water wriggled smoothly beneath us. Then Stewart faced forward again, and his face fell. 'That might, though,' he said.

I shielded my eyes and peered ahead but could see nothing except blizzarding rain and spray. Foam ribbons and rivery banners. Waves like glittering knives, like scythes, like serrated blades. Then something began to take shape – a black prow, a high deck loaded with steel containers, and at the far end – so far, it might have belonged to some other ship entirely – a wheelhouse with a single windscreen wiper smearing the glass, and the blur of a wheelman. A wheelman who would never be able to see something so small and smashable as ourselves, as we charged towards him in the midst of this fury.

Never once, in all the times that I'd thought about death, had I reached the moment where I thought it might be about to happen: not when I'd been ill as a child, not in the grip of any depression, not when I first began to feel the effects of my tumour. Now, as the tanker reared above us, seeming as long as the bay itself and feeling millions of tonnes heavy, I saw my right to life vanish, and waited to feel the plunge of terror. But there was nothing like that. Despite the roar and rage of the storm, despite the waves thrashing and the sky collapsing, I felt entirely blank. As though I'd finally reached the centre of myself and found nothing there except my own ghost.

Stewart heaved on the wheel, shoving with the whole weight of his body, and called for me to come and help. I broke out of my trance and slithered forward, thinking that my rope wouldn't stretch far enough to let me reach – but it did, and I leaned into the wheel as well. The end of my tether! A moment ago it had felt as though I'd lost all sense of connection with myself. Now every atom of flesh and blood felt the current of the sea pouring through me. Streaming through the wood of the tiller as well, as it quivered and refused our pressure, then miserably gave an inch, and then another inch, until gradually, very gradually, we were no longer facing the tanker but gliding alongside it. I could have reached out sideways and run my fingers along the hull. I could have done, but the metal was disgusting, a man-made contagion, a colossal mess of rust-freckles.

Then the tanker was gone – just like that. And when I glanced behind me, the retreating silhouette seemed so harmless, so absolutely a thing that belonged in the past and would never return, that my revulsion immediately turned into a kind of embarrassment. The prospect of death had turned into another story about life. What sort of story, though, and what sort of life? Despite knowing that I'd been spared – had in a sense been restored to life – I also felt that some part of my connection to the world had been broken, leaving me to live more like a spectre than ever. And as if to confirm this, everything I could now see seemed not so much proof of continuing life as a peculiar sort of apology. The squared-off stern of the tanker looked as shifty as an unpopular guest leaving a party early, and the colossal engines produced only the mildest swirl in the water above the toiling propellers.

# Part Six

---

## 1996–2002

My back still hadn't entirely healed but I was well enough to feel restless again: I needed to get back to work. There was a problem, though. While writing at home was easy – I could take a break whenever I needed – the commute to Norwich was arduous, and so was teaching. I took to lying on the floor of my office when I was alone, nursing my spine, and otherwise took a cue from my father and adopted a variety of brave faces. I hoped they fooled other people better than they did me: I shouldn't be doing any of this yet; I wasn't ready.

Then I bumped into Max Sebald – W. G. Sebald – in the corridor outside his basement office in the same building as my own. He'd taught German at UEA for the past thirty years and more, but now he'd been told that the university was about to shrink his department; students didn't want to study foreign languages in the numbers they once had. That was disappointing, I said, but if it meant that he now had some time on his hands, would he be interested in teaching creative writing? It felt almost impertinent to ask. We'd smiled and nodded to one another often enough in the six years that I'd been working at UEA, but we'd never had a proper conversation before. Max had always seemed too withdrawn for that, too courteously inclined to keep himself to himself, wearing the distracted look of someone about to set off on a long journey. Now he fingered his moustache – the gentle, melancholy face, the old-school tweed jacket and corduroy trousers: it looked as though he might think creative writing was a waste of time. But two of his books had recently been published in English for the first time and done well at home, then spectacularly well in America – so maybe it would appeal after all? Max sighed, took a peppermint from his pocket, laid it carefully on his tongue, and said we should have supper and talk about it some more. In fact, why didn't we meet later this evening in the Pizza Express in the centre of Norwich?

We found a window seat looking up the slope towards the big market square. By day it was crowded with shoppers and tourists. Now the pavements were rapidly emptying as the sun set – a fireball, blazing behind the dark silhouette of the castle. 'Hey! Hey!' A young woman ran past in bare feet, clutching a white Scottie dog to her chest while coins spilled onto the pavement from the pocket of her jacket. Another woman followed behind, picking up the money, slipping it into her own pocket, and smiling through our window to reassure us that she wasn't a thief, she was just helping her friend. It made me smile too. I'd been sitting with Max for no more than a few minutes and already I was seeing the world through his eyes: history and its ambiguities; human folly and human reparation; the sadness of the creatures. The sunset behind the castle turned into crimson lava, bulged against the horizon, then suddenly quivered and disappeared. Max said he wanted to start teaching the fiction graduates next term.

Ever since my conversations with Anne Stevenson in Oxford twenty years previously, I'd thought of writing as a peculiarly

physical business – riding the body as well as the mind. Now I
passed on my own version of the same idea to my students. No
matter how sophisticated our conversations about poetry might
become, I often told them, we must never forget the very primitive relationship between the rhythm of a line and the rhythm
of our pulses, our heartbeats, the coursing of blood through our
veins. But as I did so, a question bobbed in my mind. What
effect would my illness have had – or still be having – on my
own writing? I'd kept a prose diary during my time on *Excelsior*
but said nothing in it about my tumour, which anyway wasn't
diagnosed until I got home again, and since then I'd shied away
from writing about my operation and its after-effects. Was
it because I couldn't stand the idea of concentrating on such
things after writing so much about my mother? All I knew
for certain was that the poems I was writing now – and would
shortly publish in a book called *Salt Water* – contained no obvious references to surgeons' knives and hospital wards. Without
any conscious planning on my part, but no doubt because I'd
recently spent weeks at sea, they recast my thoughts about
death as a set of meditations that were almost entirely set on
shorelines, or in estuaries, or along riverbanks. Liminal places,
suitable for thinking about living betwixt and between. My
original sense that all poems were a form of elegy was turning
out to be like Adam's dream: I had reawoken from my illness
and found it true.

---

I invited Ted Hughes to give a reading at the university. Since
that first encounter in London when I was still a schoolboy, our
paths had crossed a few times – first in the mid-eighties, when

he'd rung out of the blue and asked me to be one of the judges in a poetry competition he was organising. In those days I was still comparatively new to the wild places of his poems, and supposed that he must live in a Neolithic time capsule where telephones didn't exist; for a moment I thought the call might be a hoax.

'Of course,' I'd said cautiously, expecting that any minute now one of my real friends would reveal themselves with a sarcastic guffaw. But there was a pause, then a second question, and this time there was no doubt about it: only Ted had a voice like that.

'Of course?' he said, sounding incredulous. 'Are you sure?'

'Of course. No problem.'

Ted grunted. 'All right then,' he said. 'But you remember J. B. Priestley's advice to a young writer, don't you?'

'No – what's that?'

'Never do anything for anybody.'

Since then, we'd met at a few public events, such as Philip's memorial service, and sometimes more privately. Once Craig and I had driven over for tea in Court Green, Ted's house in Devon, when we were teaching nearby: Ted's daughter Frieda had burst in, looking to my eyes so much like the photographs of her mother Sylvia Plath that I thought I must be hallucinating. Another time Ted had invited me and Jan and the children to supper, also in Court Green, and we ate a salmon that Ted had caught himself. 'A feast,' Ted called it, making the word sound like a sizzle of gunpowder.

On the face of it, these encounters made us friends – but still a little warily, for reasons that had something to do with my connection to Philip. After all, Ted and Philip had for a long time been identified as the two tallest trees in the English poetry-forest of the last fifty years, and they represented two very different kinds of writing: Philip formal, insular, ironical, suburban, tidy; and Ted experimental, cosmopolitan, emotional, rural, and shaggy. No reader could like them equally – could they? – however much they might value their differences. On the other hand, Ted had just written me a wonderful letter about my Keats book, a letter I treasured, which said among other things that he'd always shared Keats's sense of living as an outsider, and wished he'd left for Australia as a young man like his brother Gerald; he'd have gone to ground there, he insisted, 'like a wombat'.

I'd taken this letter as my excuse to invite Ted to give the reading at UEA, and when he accepted, he said that he had friends who lived near Norwich and wanted to see them again, so he could kill two birds with one stone. The image was a cliché, but the words came back to life when Ted used them, and the reading was like that too: the spellbinding voice making everything marvellous, the fierce shy face brooding over the lectern like a hawk over its kill.

Jan came up from London to listen, bringing a friend with her, and they sat either side of Ted at the dinner afterwards, in the upstairs room of a restaurant near the cathedral. Low lights and full glasses. Black beams and bulging yellow walls. Expansiveness after the tensions of the reading. Jan's companion was used to celebrity, but even she became skittish in Ted's force field, and Jan was lit up by him as well – teasing and glinting, tucking her hair behind her ears. I thought back to the Wordsworth reading thirty-some years previously: Ted still had the same crackle and creaturely stealth-force, the dangerous allure of his fascinating ghost-companions. But it dimmed when I introduced him to Max, whom I'd also asked to the dinner. Ted seemed not to know who Max was, and Max was too self-deprecating to start a conversation. I thought of Joyce and Proust meeting in Paris in 1922 – their awkwardness and lack of connection. In one of several subsequent versions of the encounter, Joyce told his friend Frank Budgen, 'Our talk consisted solely of the word "No".' Ted and Max didn't manage much more than 'How do you do?'

Next morning, as Ted and I said goodbye beside the bunker-ish university lodge, nursing our hangovers, I told him the story about Philip and Raymond Cass the spiritualist. Ted listened in silence, his face stern, then told his own story about an aunt who had sometimes had visions of family members wreathed in flames: when that happened, it meant they would soon be meeting their Maker.

'Really?' I wondered.

'Really,' Ted said, stretching the elastic in the word, then releasing the *-ly* with a sharp little snap. 'It's as well to keep an open mind.'

———

Now Jan and I were on our way to Dartington in Devon to do some work at a literary festival, and Ted had invited us to stop on the way for lunch with him and his wife Carol in a pub called the Star, beside the River Exe; the pub would suit him better than home, he told me as we finalised the plan, because the pub was within easy reach of the hospital. Hospital? I didn't know that Ted was ill. Although perhaps I'd misunderstood. Perhaps he wasn't ill himself but visiting a sick friend. I put the question aside. Ted often had an air of mystery about him. A lifetime of press-grief meant there was a permanent need for cover.

Ted and Carol were waiting in the garden of the Star, and the moment Jan and I came in from the car park, I could see that Ted had lost a lot of weight, so knew he must be a patient after all. Not that he said anything about it. As we sat down at their table and settled ourselves, trying to ignore the looks thrown by others sitting nearby – isn't that the poet laureate? – Ted was his usual mixture of shyness and decisiveness: there was the same granite voice, the same flicker of astonishment and relish, the same kindness and curiosity.

We talked about Keats for a while – Ted enthusing and excited – then switched briefly to Philip, and Ted became cagier, muttering about the complexities of Philip's 'difficulties with girls', prodding the subject carefully, as if he were tending a fire that might spit out sparks and burn him. Then I changed the subject back to fishing, and he revived again – but only briefly. Suddenly he was tired, and it was time to go. I looked round the cramped little garden: faces busily ignoring us, empty crisp packets blowing across the grass, cloudy glasses on wooden tables, shining mudflats in the estuary beyond, and the sound of metal ropes ticking against the masts of boats. It was obvious that something was wrong with Ted, but surely it couldn't be serious. Despite everything, he was still too much himself for that to be possible – too burly and weathered and fit. Given time, he was bound to recover. We'd see each other again soon.

---

I was back at UEA, about to start my morning class, when the phone rang in my office. It was *The Times* telling me that Ted had died. Did I have anything to say? I gave my answer, hung up, then the phone rang again. A different newspaper. And

then again and another paper. And then again. And then again
– people I'd never met or heard of, all asking the same questions. What was Ted like (sorry, I know he was your friend,
but can you keep it short)? Now that he's dead, who's going to
be the next poet laureate (sorry again, but we have to ask)? I
said something and nothing, then walked to my classroom and
began teaching; for the next three hours I could hear the phone
screaming along the corridor.

And screaming again when I got back to London that evening
– although I still found it hard to accept what had happened.
Auden's death had been a shock, but not exactly a surprise –
his poor state of health guaranteed that. Philip's death had produced a much more intimate sense of loss – but again, given his
final illness, and the evidence of his frailty that Jan and I had
seen first-hand when we visited him in Hull, not entirely unexpected. But Ted was a different matter: the force of his writing
and the scale of his living had made his death seem outrageous.
I recoiled from it and switched on the answerphone. I needed
to grieve for him in silence. We hadn't known each other all
that well, and we were certainly very different sorts of creature,
but I'd been reading him since I was a teenager, and the rapt
attention that he'd given to the world had helped to open my
eyes. I wanted to brood on that. I wanted to follow his poems as
they swam downriver into the world without him, steered like
salmon by their own shifting weight.

He was probably hatched in this very pool.

And this was the only mother he ever had, this uneasy
    channel of minnows
Under the mill-wall, with bicycle wheels, car-tyres, bottles

And sunk sheets of corrugated iron.
People walking their dogs trail their evening shadows
    across him.
If boys see him they will try to kill him.

All this, too, is stitched into the torn richness,
The epic poise
That holds him so steady in his wounds, so loyal in his
    doom, so patient
In the machinery of heaven.

---

I had to think about the laureateship, whether I liked it or not.
The phone never stopped ringing and people never stopped
asking about it, even though Ted's ashes were hardly cold in
the ground. It was journalists, mostly, wanting to know: was I
interested in taking it on myself? There was a simple answer to
that: I'd never thought about it, mostly because it didn't seem
like the sort of thing that any reasonable person should have in
the forefront of their minds, and partly because there was no
need: big healthy Ted, with his animal survival instincts, would
outlast us all.

Although now things were as they were, and a part of me
was at least curious to know how the selection process operated.
Eventually I asked a friend who worked at the Arts Council,
and he explained. The secretary of state at the Department for
Culture, Media and Sport was in charge – Chris Smith. Chris
was going to canvass opinion from interested parties – poets,
other writers, organisations like the Royal Society of Literature
and the Arts Council itself – then send a shortlist of names to

the prime minister, Tony Blair, who would make a recommendation to the Queen, who would rubber-stamp it. Chris had
already suggested the new appointment should be for ten years,
not life, and that seemed to me like a very good idea. The position obviously needed overhauling in a respectful sort of way,
and if the term was limited, it was likely to increase the chance
of someone interpreting it as a job, and not just as a peculiar sort
of honour.

———

I tried again to banish the subject from my mind, and again
failed: the newspapers were all over it now; the succession had
become hot gossip. Why so hot was hard to tell. Something to
do with Ted being a controversial figure, perhaps. Something
to do with the recently created internet and everyone being able
to share their opinion. Something to do with the long overdue
fracturing of an 'establishment' idea of poetry. Something to
do with Blair's new government (he'd been prime minister
for only eighteen months), and the idea that poetry might be
a part of Cool Britannia. Something to do with the death of
Princess Diana and the strange, febrile mood that still lingered
in the country. It meant, among other things, that there weren't
many serious think-pieces written about what being laureate
might involve, just lots of light entertainment. The poets that
journalists thought might be in the frame (but what did they
know?) were either exciting firebrands or boringly safe hands,
they were populists or elitists, they were Radio 1 or they were
Radio 3, they were Jaguars or they were Volvos. The more time
passed, the sillier it became – and now word leaked out that
there wouldn't be an announcement until after Ted's memorial

service, which was due to be held in Westminster Abbey in May 1999, six months after his death. Shortly before that, the *New York Times* ran a story describing the laureateship as 'a double-edged chalice'. In my own view, that seemed about right.

About right, and a good reason to steer well clear, especially since there were so many candidates who would suit the role very well: Grace Nichols, Wendy Cope, Carol Ann Duffy – there'd never been a female laureate, and it was high time. But in the small hours of early morning, when I couldn't prevent my mind from thinking about what would happen if my own name were to be put forward, I realised that I'd say yes. Yes, despite the mockery which had routinely been aimed at laureates in the past and would certainly now be directed at me. Yes, despite the likely invasion of my personal life, which was vulnerable to gossipmongers. Yes, despite the disruption to my writing routines. And yes, despite an even larger problem. I'd published eight collections by now, and won some prizes, and written a good deal about other people's poems, and given readings in the UK and elsewhere, but it was obvious that my career – if 'career' was quite the word for it – depended to a great extent on my concentrating on personal themes: my mother's accident, my feelings about my father, my life with Jan and the children. Depended too on my thinking of poetry as something that defined the one area of my life where I didn't have to take orders from anyone except myself. What would it be like to have to field requests – perhaps even commands? – to write about subjects which in the most fundamental way were not my own idea? Specifically, what would it be like to take on more public subjects, and royal subjects in particular? Would I simply not be able to rise to the challenge of writing about them, because I might not be able to summon the necessary strong feelings to give me lift-off? Or would it be good for me to broaden the horizons of my writing? As the questions piled up, a ripple of helpless optimism ran through me. Most definitely it would be good for me. Good to tackle difficult subjects I might otherwise avoid, and good to turn my face more openly to the world. As I fell back to sleep, it all seemed possible – although I knew very well how deceptive these kinds of late-night speculations could be.

———

Early April. Late-spring sunlight on the garden, and the children bathed and ready for bed. I'd been out giving a reading somewhere, and when I got home my younger son Lucas ran up to me in his pyjamas, saying that an important-sounding person had rung earlier in the evening, and wanted me to call back: this was the number, written on his palm. I sat down, he held out his hand, I dialled the number, and a moment later I was listening to a voice that I didn't recognise. An amused, grandee, chin-tucked-in, stifled-chortle sort of voice. Hayden Phillips, he said, although the name meant nothing to me. Hayden Phillips who explained that he was speaking from his office in 10 Downing Street, and then delivered a message of such complex formality it took me a while to understand what he meant: 'The prime minister is of a mind to recommend to the Queen that you be appointed the next poet laureate, but before he does so, perhaps you'd be good enough to say whether you'd be of a mind to accept the position, were it to be offered?' I leaned back in the sofa, astonished. By the terms of the message – did people really still talk like that? – and also by realising that in the six months since Ted had died, through all the press nonsense, I still hadn't properly asked myself whether

I wanted the job. Not during daylight hours, anyway.

I told Hayden that I'd almost certainly say yes, but would like to have the weekend to think about it, then spent the next two days deliberating. If I turned it down, life would be simple. No one else need know that I'd been offered the position, and although a few people might tease me for being passed over, I could always say that I felt well out of it. And a large part of me would indeed feel very well out of it; my late-night deliberations had already shown me that. No wonder Philip had let it be known that he would have turned it down if anyone had offered it to him when Betjeman died – Betjeman who had ended his life hating being laureate so much, he'd contemplated resigning. On the other hand, accepting the appointment would be a kind of accolade – wouldn't it? My father would be proud of me, my mother would smile from her grave, and the writing effort of my life would seem to be rewarded at least in one short-term way. And not only that. I'd always wanted to align my sedentary life as a poet with action in the world on behalf of poetry itself. Up to now, I'd relied on my work as an editor and a teacher to do that. But being poet laureate would allow a much larger repertoire of ways and means. I thought of Keats saying that he wanted to 'do good in the world'. I thought of Pope saying, 'A mutual commerce makes poetry flourish; but then Poets like Merchants, shou'd repay with something of their own what they take from others.' I rang Hayden on Monday morning and accepted – half the voices in my head telling me that I was doing the right thing; the other half howling that I was making the worst mistake of my life. But there was a snag, I told Hayden. I was about to fly to Adelaide in Australia to read my poems at the Festival there, so could the announcement of my appointment be delayed until I got back?

No problem, Hayden said. Although why not come into the office in Downing Street before I left, and talk things over?

———

When I knocked on the front door of Number 10, I was led upstairs to the top floor. Hayden turned out to be clever and charming, like his voice, crouched in a desk-redoubt that was heavily defended by telephones. He reminded me that I'd hold the position for ten years, not life, and assured me that there was no formal job description. But he added that every-one expected me to write poems about significant events in the royal and national calendar, and also hoped that I'd 'take up the cudgels' for poetry. Something in schools, perhaps? Poetry is usually a difficult sell in schools, isn't it? I told Hayden that taking up cudgels was exactly what I had in mind; in fact, while I'd been thinking about the position during the weekend, I'd effectively split it in my mind's eye into a writing half (those poems about royal events) and a work half (poetry in schools, poetry on the radio, poetry as a part of everyday conversation – generally defending and diversifying it in ways that had never seemed necessary to previous laureates but did now). It would be another double life, like my poetry/biography oscillation and Norwich/London split, which itself echoed the Oxford/Hull divide of years before.

As I finished my spiel, one of the telephones on Hayden's desk shook into life: it was a secretary in the prime minis-ter's office downstairs, saying that she'd seen me come into the building, told the prime minister, and now Blair wanted to say hello. I took my leave of Hayden, an assistant whisked me back down the famous stairs, past the portraits of former

prime ministers silently pleading with posterity, and next thing
I knew I was chatting to a woman – from Belfast, to judge by
her accent – who was standing with her arms crossed outside a
door off the Cabinet Room. She was obviously a guard of some
sort but seemed ill equipped to repel terrorists; in her red jacket
and sensible black skirt, she looked more like an attendant at a
holiday camp.

'So,' she said, 'you're going to see the prime minister.'

'That's right.'

'And why's that?'

'Because I'm the poet laureate.' I'd never said this aloud
before, and it sounded ridiculous. For the first time, and by
no means the last, it occurred to me that a position I'd always
thought was in some way exalted was also in fact complicatedly
comic.

The Redcoat uncrossed her arms and looked at me narrowly.
'Would that be the new poet laureate?' she asked. 'Or the old
poet laureate?'

'The new one,' I said. 'The old poet laureate is dead.'

At which point a door burst open, and Tony Blair jumped
out. Shirt sleeves, wide smile, youthful Bambi eagerness: the
youngest prime minister since Lord Liverpool in 1812. "Ello,'
he said, dropping the 'h' as though he expected us to talk with a
kind of rock-band off-handedness; then, when he'd eyed me up
and down, and realised that might not be quite right, instantly
refigured himself. The tone-change was so swift and complete,
it made me wonder whether Blair had any fixed personality at
all. But the enthusiasm was impressive, and the energy, and the
frank good humour when we walked next door and Blair introduced me to the Cabinet, who were assembling for their weekly
meeting. Neil Kinnock, who rushed up with a puppy-dog

warmth, and remembered the dinner we'd had with Antony Sher; Gordon Brown, with his head tilted slightly to one side as though unbalanced by the weight of an exceptionally large brain, and his fingernails so badly chewed, I felt surprised there wasn't blood dripping onto the carpet. I said hello to everyone in turn, and was about to walk out into Downing Street when someone said I'd better leave by the back door, in case a journalist saw me and worked out that I was the new laureate (not the old one). As I skulked away across Horse Guards Parade, I began to realise that my life was no longer my own.

---

I was in Adelaide when news of my appointment was leaked to the newspapers – someone in Blair's press office needed to distract attention from a government cock-up and thought this might do the trick. What was it that Ted had said about wanting to go to Australia and burrow into the ground like a wombat? Now I was in Australia myself, but sitting on the bed in a hotel room at two in the morning and feeling skinned alive because the phone never stopped ringing. Some of these calls were from friends being friendly. Most were from journalists who were keen to make their stories interesting by stirring up controversy. Was I the best choice? Who would have been a better one? I felt some sympathy with them: they had a job to do, and a part of me shared their doubts about my suitability. Another and larger part of me felt something like defiance. I'd accepted the position because I knew what I wanted to do with it: to be a safe pair of hands, yes, but also to transform the position by modernising it. Call by call I explained what I meant, and at last the phone fell silent. By this time, I could barely remember why I'd ever wanted anything to do with the whole business in the first place.

———

Hayden was right – there were no official duties. But there was the Gold Medal for Poetry, which had been instituted by George V in 1933 and given most years since then, on the recommendation of a committee chaired by the laureate. A medal which was indeed made of gold and featured a muse-figure designed by Edmund Dulac. Shortly before his death, Ted had recommended that the Australian poet Les Murray be awarded it, but Les hadn't been in England for the last little while, so still hadn't received his medal. The Palace decided the presentation should follow my own first audience with the Queen.

I'd given readings with Les a couple of times in the past, admired his poems, and thought this would make things easier when we met in Buckingham Palace. It did in a way. At least we felt united by a common cause. But it was still hard to concentrate on the flunky who briefed us about the ceremony ahead. For one thing, this flunky was wearing such an extremely tight-fitting Royal Air Force uniform, his words emerged from between his lips in a highfalutin' bat-squeak. For another, the words themselves – once deciphered – sounded mostly ludicrous: when and how to bow ('Neck bow, not a bow from the waist'); when to talk ('Never begin a conversation, only join in when invited, or when appropriate'); and how to address the Queen ('The first time as Your Majesty and thereafter as Ma'am to rhyme with jam, which you two poets won't find hard to remember'). The longer we listened, the more confused and nervous we felt; eventually I started wondering whether I could even remember how to walk and draw breath at the same time. Still, it was easier for me than Les. I was at least used to wearing a suit and tie; if our previous meetings were anything to go by, Les, who was enormous, was more inclined to baggy pants, a crotch-length jersey, and a shapeless hat. Now, hunched on the slippery satin-clad sofa outside the double doors to the room where we were about to be received, he'd also squeezed himself into a suit. He looked desperately strained.

———

The flunky summoned me, Les whispered good luck, the double doors flew open, and off I went, my legs miraculously still working as I trekked across the miles of carpet to where the Queen was standing beside a small grey armchair and a highly polished table with what looked like an electric bell, a Bakelite nipple, set dead centre; there were two other chairs nearby – one beside her, the other facing her, and both of these were very pretty, very French, and disturbingly flimsy-looking. Don't worry about that now, I told myself. Just make sure to sit still when the time comes. And meanwhile remember the etiquette: neck-bow, shake hands, and wait for her to say something.

———

My mother had once taken me as a child to watch the Queen drive down the road near our house in Hatfield Heath – the local papers must have been tipped off, and they'd encouraged people to stand on the pavement and wave flags. I could still remember the mixed excitement and boredom of waiting, then the police motorbike outriders and the feeling of seriousness they cast over everything, then the large and boxy-looking black car with a Union Jack wriggling on its prong above the radiator grille, the Queen's snapshot face in the window, her gloved hand waving, and almost immediately the empty road and hedge opposite again, where everything seemed looser and thinner than it had done a moment before, with the wind blowing straight through.

———

When I'd been invited to sit down, and stole a glance at the Queen now, forty-odd years later, she looked almost identical: the same smooth and faintly luminous skin, the same farcically old-fashioned hairdo, the same grumpy pout. Was she grumpy, though, or was that just what her face did in repose? I couldn't tell until she started talking – but that was another odd thing. For someone who'd been making polite conversation since before I was born, she seemed surprisingly awkward, oddly short of subjects, as it were. I thought I could help with that – I may not have been the most gregarious person in the kingdom, but I knew how to chit-chat and I'd grown up around horses, for God's sake: the Queen liked horses. But I remembered that I wasn't supposed to speak until spoken to, and kept quiet, my hands clasped in my lap. Eventually the silence broke. 'I'm afraid I don't read much poetry,' the Queen said. 'I have so many of those blessed red boxes to read – my government keeps sending them.' Realising I was now under licence to speak, but with an odd sense of disembodiment, I heard my own words begin surging off my tongue, saying that I knew what she meant. But this was obviously nonsense, so I stopped, then started again: I told her I'd seen her passing in her car when I was a child; I organised my memories and turned them into a little story.

'Oh, that's rather nice, isn't it?' the Queen said, in such a quiet voice she might have been talking to herself. It made me feel sorry for her, in the same way I might feel sorry for any old lady who seemed tired of doing things she didn't want to do and resented the weight of her years. But that was nonsense too. The Queen was the exact opposite of 'any old lady'. Even so: why couldn't we just pretend to be talking like normal people; I could start on the horse thing, and tell her that I'd grown up in the country. She'd like that, wouldn't she?

Everything stayed as it had been in the beginning: constipated. The Queen repeated that she didn't have much time for reading, as though by using the word 'poetry' even once, she had incinerated all other possible topics of conversation, and this time I said smarmily that if she read only one book of poetry a year – this year, a book by Les – then she was doing better than most other people in the country. She gave a weary little smirk, then fitted her mask tightly in place again. 'Yes . . .' she said, adding a peculiar hump to the middle of the word, then letting it trail off and sink so slowly, it sounded nothing like an opinion by the time it eventually died.

I wanted to pay my respects to Ted; I'd heard on the grapevine that the royal family as a whole, and Prince Charles and the Queen Mum in particular, had been friendly with him: the rumour mill said that he and the Queen Mum used to go fishing together, and that Prince Charles had commissioned a memorial window to Ted in the chapel at Highgrove. This made him an impossibly hard act to follow – but maybe a little easier if I explained that Ted and I had been friends? 'Oh yes,' the Queen told me, with an almost invisible head-dip and pout. 'I believe that Ted Hughes and my mother did see quite a bit of each other. Actually, I'd like to have a poet laureate who paid attention to *me*.'

The double doors on the far shore of the carpet burst open again, the Queen and I both stood up, and Les rocked on the threshold while the flunky called out, 'Mr Les Murray.' Then Les rolled slowly forward, his suit rustling, his face tweaked into a rictus of anxiety and pride. Should someone make an introduction? I waited for a moment, realised it should be me, and flapped my hand from the Queen to Les and back again, managing not to say aloud, 'The Queen, Les; Les, the Queen,' then stepped away. I'd had my turn.

The Queen shook Les by the hand and told him she was going to give him the medal now, immediately, because in the past, when she'd met other poets like this, she'd sometimes for-gotten to hand it over. With Ted, for instance – and in those days protocol required that anyone leaving her presence had to walk backwards until they reached the door, so as not to seem discourteous. After Ted had managed this manoeuvre, bow-ing all the way, the Queen suddenly remembered his medal and called him back to hand it over, which meant that once he'd pocketed it, he had to walk away from her in reverse for a second time. Anyway: here was the medal for Les now, in a beautiful slim leather box. The Queen passed it to Les, and Les opened the lid to look inside – whereupon the medal, seeming to have a mind of its own, leaped from its blue velvet bed and dropped onto the carpet.

The three of us stood gazing at it for a moment.

Who was going to pick it up? The Queen? That seemed very unlikely – in fact, I wondered whether she'd ever picked up anything in her life. Les? That also seemed unlikely, but for a different reason: the tailoring. Me, then. I began to reach down – only to find Les, who was presumably thinking, 'That's my bloody medal,' beating me to it, with no audible damage to the suit.

The Queen indicated where everyone would now sit: her in the armchair beside the little table with the buzzer, me in the gilded number at her side, and Les opposite in an equally frail contraption. Its bandy gilt legs grew bandier, held, and Les leaned forward, waiting as instructed for the Queen to begin the conversation. It took a while, as though she was considering a large number of possible openers and couldn't decide which would be the most suitable. 'Well,' she said at last, in a voice so like her own, so regally old-fashioned, she might have been teasing herself: 'Well. Orstralia.' Les creaked a little further forward. Could he reply now, or was there more coming? No. That was it. He took a deep breath and let fly with his answer. 'Oh yes, your Majesty,' he said, 'Australia's a beautiful place with beautiful cities Perth and Melbourne and Sydney with the Sydney Opera House and beautiful country as well Ayers Rock the Great Barrier Reef and then there are wonderful creatures too the kangaroo of course the Aboriginal people have many different names for the kangaroo and then there's the kooka-burra and the echidna and the duck-billed platypus which is especially interesting because it has a kind of homing device in its nose that allows it . . .' He rushed on for what seemed like several minutes, looking around more and more wildly for a main verb, then realised he was never going to find one and came to an abrupt halt. There was a silence, broken only by the creaking of chair legs. 'Very interesting,' the Queen said at last, and stabbed the Bakelite nipple on the table at her side. Whereupon the double doors swung open once again, revealing the same natty-looking airman: he looked slightly flushed, as though he'd been bending over despite his extremely tight trousers, listening at the keyhole.

Les and I stood up, shook the Queen's hand, then made our neck-bows and turned our backs. It felt rude, so at the door we swivelled round and bowed again, after which the airman closed the doors behind us. A South American ambassador and his wife were already on the launchpad, waiting to be fired in next; they both looked pasty-faced with terror. Les and I raced outside, tore off our ties, and vanished across Green Park to look for a bar.

———

Readings, readings, readings. Talks, talks, talks. Interviews, interviews, interviews. And visits to schools – at least one a week, often more. Hayden was right, a lot of teachers did have a hard time teaching poetry, and they needed all the help they could get. And this help, as well as appealing to the side of me that enjoyed teaching, was also a way to fulfil the promise I'd made to myself about turning the laureateship into a job.

Mostly the teachers were pleased to see me – they'd invited me, after all – and mostly their students had long ago decided that poetry was boring or difficult or posh and silly or senti-mental. Especially the boys, who generally seemed to think it was worse than any of these things – it was girly. But this was my mission now, to sell the unsaleable, and before long I worked out a kind of patter, beginning with a question: did anyone ever come across any poetry in their everyday lives out-side school? The answer was invariably no – why would they have done? – it was bad enough having to read it in class. Then I asked them when they'd last been to a wedding or a funeral,

225

and if they had, was a poem read during the service? Well, yes, it was actually.

One or two students sat up.

I told them about the time I'd been to look at the bouquets of flowers laid on the grass outside Kensington Palace after the death of Princess Diana, the hundreds and hundreds of them, all rotting by the time I got there, so the whole place was stinking. But stinking wasn't the point. The point was: almost every bunch had a little card tied to it, and on most of these little cards there was a message, and most of these messages included a bit of poetry. Very bad poetry, mostly, but poetry nonetheless.

What did that tell us?

We turn to poetry when life feels intense. Exactly. We might learn to talk about poetry in fancy ways, but in truth it's a very primitive thing. Primitive rhythms like heartbeats and pulses, and language that sounds mysterious but touches our heart-strings and makes us cry. Or proper nonsense which everyone loves, and which sounds like pure fun but also makes a kind of sense: ''Twas brillig, and the slithy toves/ Did gyre and gimble in the wabe'.

Or another example. A schoolboy had been murdered at the end of my road the other week – someone their age, maybe they read about it in the paper? Next day, this dead boy's friends started making a shrine in his memory; it was enormous now, I'd passed it on the way here. Candles and teddy bears and photographs and T-shirts. A pair of girl's knickers, too; that was interesting. And dozens of cards, and lots of poetry on the cards. I felt sure most of it had been written by people who hated poetry at school – but see: poetry did belong in life. It wasn't just a puzzle you had to solve so that you could pass an exam.

Then there was the question of how poems are and are not like songs – the songs that some of them played, and the songs they all endlessly discussed and listened to outside school. Most of those rhymed, didn't they, and used rhythms to reinforce whatever they were saying. Why not think of songs as a kind of cousin to poetry, and take things from there?

———

If school-visiting and radio-talking and giving readings comprised most of the 'doing' side of this new life, what about the writing part? Not writing for myself but writing about the royal family – the part which had caused so much trouble for my predecessors and also bothered me in prospect. I reminded myself that Ted used to go fishing with the Queen Mum and wondered if it meant that he'd always been popping in and out of the Palace like a friend. Would it make my life easier if I were somehow able to develop a closer connection with the Queen and those around her? The very idea seemed preposterous. Besides, I had no wish to exaggerate the extent to which I felt 'employed' as a writer. Poetry, as far as I was concerned, was a republic.

Yet here I was at the point of having to write poems about significant events in these royal lives. Everyone said that I didn't *have* to, but everyone expected it, and the newspapers were poised to give me a hard time if I stayed quiet. They had a point, the papers – once again, I could see that. Having said yes to the job in the first place, I couldn't expect to cherry-pick the bits that I felt were easy or fun and ignore the difficult stuff. After all, if I'd been carpenter laureate, and a customer had asked me to make a table, I should have been able to do it.

Know-how and practice; a design to follow. But that was the problem in a nutshell. Writing poetry, for me, had never felt like making a table. I'd always depended more on self-forgetting and accidents than opinions and clear plans; I'd always resisted the idea of writing to a deadline; and I'd always believed that poetry shouldn't so much have a subject as be its own subject – shouldn't walk in through the front door of whatever it finds interesting, but go around the back, or climb in through the window, or drop down the chimney. Surprise! Surprise, and independence of mind. Although Shelley had put it better in 'A Defence of Poetry': 'Poetry is not like reasoning, a power to be exerted according to the determination of the will. A man cannot say, "I will compose poetry." The greatest poet even cannot say it.'

———

Prince Edward was the first up: he was about to get married. Prince Edward whom I'd never met, and knew almost nothing about. So I researched a few things online, found nothing that sparked any useful thoughts, then wrote something short and general about love and marriage and sent it to the papers. When I read them next morning, and saw my poem embedded in a small tomb of comment for and against, I realised that what I'd sensed while fielding those calls in my hotel in Australia was now a permanent fact of my life: at least as far as my 'royal poems' were concerned, I was taking part in a game I should never expect to win. I remembered a lunchtime with Philip. We'd been drinking in the Staff Bar at the university in Hull, talking about the critics who'd attacked his Oxford anthology, all of whom (and especially Geoffrey Grigson) he dismissed as fools. 'It's a mug's game,' he said, banging his glass down. 'Anything to do with poetry. A mug's game. We all have to grow thick skins.' Even at the time, that had sounded like good advice. Although now I couldn't help wondering: if I did manage to grow a thick skin, would it mean that I also coarsened the thin skin I needed to write poems in the first place? Would it in fact prevent me from writing poems altogether?

Ten years. I wanted to do something as laureate that would outlast my time in office – to found some sort of programme or organisation that would benefit poets and poetry. But what? A Laureate's Prize? An annual festival? A series of scholarships? In the end, the answer depended on a happy combination of coincidence and choice. Ever since beginning to read poems at school, I'd been interested in thinking about the ways that sound – pure sound – conveys feeling and sense. It had a lot to do with my English teacher Peter Way, and the day he asked our sixth-form class to write about Eliot's *The Waste Land*. The poem was already nearly fifty years old by then, but still seemed stranger and more difficult than anything I'd read before: I simply didn't *get* most of it. The hooded hordes maybe, but the hyacinth girl, and all that darting from here to there, and the scraps of languages that I didn't speak? Peter Way wasn't surprised. In fact, he seemed oddly pleased to discover that we knew what difficulty was when we saw it, and talked to us about Eliot's notion of the 'auditory imagination', then played a recording of Eliot himself reading the poem aloud: did that help? As the sad voice swooped along, more like someone singing than reading, more like plainsong, the lines that I hadn't understood a moment before started to come into focus. And not just that. They started to move me – I could feel the hairs on the back of my neck standing up. How did that work? Was the sound that words made, irrespective of their dictionary-sense, a part of their meaning? Everyone knew that was true about certain sorts of words – onomatopoeic words, especially. But maybe it was true for language as a whole. I tucked the thought away, and read other poets talking about the same idea. I was on a French jag at the time, and found Paul Valéry: 'In the poet/ The ear speaks,/ The mouth listens.' And I saw that what applied to Valéry's own poems was true for all poems – they use music to sweeten and frame their thought: 'Thought is hidden in verse like the nutritive virtue in fruit. A fruit is nourishment, but it seems to be nothing but pure delight. One perceives only pleasure, but one receives a substance. Enchantment veils this imperceptible nourishment it brings with it.'

Six years later I started thinking about sound in poetry more seriously, when I was writing my thesis about Edward Thomas. Thomas himself had always said that sound-sense and page-sense were inseparable – that was one of the reasons he liked Robert Frost so much: 'the sound of sense' was Frost's big idea. 'The ear is the only true writer and the only true reader,' he'd written, around the same time he first met Thomas. 'You listen for the sentence sounds. If you find some of those not bookish, caught fresh from the mouths of people, some of them striking, all of them definite and recognizable, so recognizable that with a little trouble you can place them and even name them, you know you have found a writer.'

Faber asked me to make a new recording of my poems, and the sound engineer sitting in the studio on the other side of the glass was Richard Carrington: square-shouldered, sandy-haired, bearded, and twinkling-serious. I knew him by reputation – he was the best in the business – and when we finished our work we sat around to talk for a while. Without thinking where it might lead, I told Richard that I thought it was a pity no one had previously recorded poets reading their own work in a systematic way.

'What do you mean?' Richard asked.

I reminded him that the first recordings of poets had been made in the late 1880s (Browning and Tennyson), but since then hundreds of interesting voices that could have been preserved had been lost.

'Like who?'

Like Oscar Wilde, Charlotte Mew, D. H. Lawrence, Wilfred Owen, A. E. Housman, Thomas Hardy. And Edward Thomas of course. And Rupert Brooke. We don't have any of them. Wouldn't Hardy have enjoyed seeing some mechanically minded poetry lover clatter up the drive to Max Gate in a jalopy, promising to make his voice immortal? And what sort of voice did Hardy have, by the way? How strong was his accent – how Dorsetshire did he sound? And if very, did this make him feel like an outsider when he was writing? People tend to think that dead poets all spoke with an RP accent, because that's the voice most actors use when they're reading poems on the radio. But in the Tennyson recording, for instance, there's a distinct Lincolnshire growl in 'Half a league, half a league . . .'. What does that mean it would be like for us to be able to hear Keats, who died sixty years before Thomas Edison invented his machine? Take the 'Chapman's Homer' sonnet, which is actually *about* being an outsider looking in on high culture (among other things): imagine how much better we might understand that aspect of the poem if we could hear Keats reading it in a cockney accent.

Or think about how much we gain from hearing Philip's voice: he may almost never have read in public, but he did make recordings, and they take us deeply into the poems. Not just their mood, carried on the wings of cadence, but sometimes their intended meanings as well. That passage in 'Lines on a Young Lady's Photograph Album', for example, where he stresses the word 'art' in 'But o, photography! as no *art* is,/ Faithful and disappointing': it helps us to understand that Philip (or the speaker in his poem, at any rate) didn't think photography *was* an art, however much he enjoyed it, and however skilfully he practised it. Think about the slowness and concentration of his voice, too, the way it sharpens his satires and bathes his lyrics in longing. Think about something else, too. As a child, Philip's stammer was so bad he couldn't bring himself to ask aloud for a ticket at the train station; he had to pass a note instead. But after his parents had sent him to a speech therapist, he didn't just learn how to talk more easily; he acquired an entirely new accent. A voice with no Coventry in it – unlike his sister, who at the end of her life still pronounced 'chicken' as 'chicking'. Did Philip's new and posher voice bring with it a more mainstream set of values and ambitions? Might it in fact have made him more conservative in all respects – poetically as well as politically? It's not the sort of question that expects a hard and fast answer, but it's worth asking.

As I left the recording studio, I said to Richard over my shoulder that we should do something about all this. Specifically, we should think about using this newfangled thing the internet, collect the voices of poets reading their own work, and make a website where people could listen to them.

———

Out of the blue, a gilt-edged and weighty invitation arrived from Prince Charles, inviting me and Jan to Sandringham in north Norfolk for the weekend; we'd never met him before, not properly, just shaken hands at a reception. Would accepting mean that I automatically turned into the kind of lackey poet I'd promised myself not to be? Not necessarily, we decided, and accepted, making a note of the instructions to bring our formal clothes, because we were expected to dress for dinner.

———

As soon as Richard and I started working together, building what turned into the Poetry Archive, we became friends. He was astonishingly efficient, well organised, and capable. And also astonishingly courteous, warm-hearted, and entertaining. An immaculate person, in fact, and a stickler for accuracy in others. When I first complimented him on this, he demurred and told me a story about the grand old thespian Sir Frank Benson, who in a production of *Othello* once mangled the hero's great speech to the Senate, and ended it by booming to the audience, 'Or words to that effect.' There were never any 'words to that effect' in Richard.

———

Jan and I caught the train from London to King's Lynn, where a chauffeur wearing a bowler hat that looked as though it had been reinforced with metal, like the one Oddjob wears in *Goldfinger*, collected us and drove very fast through the lanes of Norfolk, on tyres that whistled strangely across the road surface and felt unyielding; they'd been fortified to deflect the bullets of snipers lurking in nearby hedges and pig farms. Despite my determination not to feel that my head had been turned, I had the distinct sense of disappearing into a different time-world, where the normal rules of life no longer obtained; a sense that deepened the moment we swept through the gates of Sandringham and crunched to a gravelly halt. I climbed out, made to collect our cases from the car, but was told no, a valet would carry these up to our room – Jan and I should go straight indoors and have a drink before changing for dinner. We found the rest of the house party already milling in the main hall (high-ceilinged, Victorian mock-medieval, with a roaring open fire), and a quick glance round was enough to show what kind of gathering it was. Luvvies and their partners: Jeremy Irons and Sinéad Cusack, Jools Holland, Valery Gergiev, Robert Harris, Richard E. Grant and Joan Washington, Mario Testino, and of course Stephen Fry. We were both given a pint of gin, then another one, and were soon talking enthusiastically about nothing, while Prince Charles and Camilla Parker Bowles (not yet the Duchess of Cornwall) sailed around making everyone welcome. Camilla, I thought, looked like a smarter version of someone my father might know, a smiling country lady. The Prince was more earnest: asking questions, engaged, implausibly modest, surprisingly candid (he almost immediately mentioned how unhappy he had been as a child), and unexpectedly weathered – red-faced, wearing an old-fashioned grey tweed suit with wide lapels, and a shirt with cuffs that ended well below the sleeves of his jacket, as though he was keen to hide his hands, which looked chubby and disproportionately small.

---

Richard and I kept the ground rules of the Poetry Archive as simple as we could: to be included, poets had to have published at least one book and it had to be good of its kind (I convened a panel of other poets to help me make the call about what was good and what wasn't); the widest possible range of voices would be included; there would be a Children's Archive as well as a general site; there would be a strong educational component, but not to the exclusion of fun; all poets would get a fee for making their recording; and the collection would be international, although all the poems had to be written in the English language.

---

The reception swirled to a halt, and Jan and I were shown upstairs to our bedroom, already quite drunk, where we found our suitcase had been not only delivered but also unpacked, and the clothes we were expected to change into for dinner (my dinner jacket and Jan's long dress) had been pressed and laid on the bed. Jan noticed that a loose hem had been mended, too, which made me wonder if the same kindly and invisible hand might also have taken away whatever unwashed things I'd packed, then cleaned and returned them. Perhaps if we were ever invited back, we could bring clothes with seriously stubborn stains and have them laundered? (I later heard that the cars of those who'd driven to Norfolk instead of catching the train had been filled with petrol by the time they left.) We lay on the bed and laughed aloud. Anxiety, gin, extravagance. The air of defiance that surrounded the still-unmarried Prince and Camilla. It all seemed to have produced a mood of mildly hysterical sexiness.

And not only in us. After we'd changed into our appointed clothes and gone back downstairs to the dining room, we found the other guests greeting each other like old friends, oohing and aahing. It turned out the Prince had ordered a pantechnicon to be filled with ornaments and decorations taken from other royal houses, and asked for them to be distributed through Sandringham to prettify it. There was nothing to be done about the pictures on the walls, which were mainly Edwardian portraits of lugubrious Highland ponies hunched against blizzards, or faithful collie dogs sitting beside their stricken masters (also felled by bad weather). But the table itself was magnificent in a mad way – the plates and cutlery almost buried by vast and elaborate flower decorations, which were set in a silver sea of salvers, figurines, plates, jugs, tankards, bowls, candlesticks, and candelabras. All this was riotously at odds with the things that the Prince had spoken about previously (conservation and sustainability and suchlike), but nobody cared. We'd all come to the circus, and by now we were determined to enjoy it.

---

Neither Richard nor I had set up a charitable company before, or any sort of company come to that, but we found a way. The Gulbenkian Foundation gave us £1,000 of seed money to write a business plan; other charities and foundations chipped in;

Charles Clarke, the secretary of state for education, give us a chunk of government money; the Poetry Foundation in Chicago stumped up funds to include a number of American poets; and hundreds of meetings and three years later the Archive was launched at the British Library, with the first president, Seamus Heaney, introducing it all. (Seamus who also contributed £1,000 to the kitty, insisting we tell no one about his generosity.) Soon, a quarter of a million people were using the site every month, and every month they were listening to more than a million pages of poetry. Occasionally, on my way round schools or during the Q and A session after I'd given a reading, people complained that the audience for poetry had all but disappeared. Sure, I said, the sales of books were mostly falling, and the space given by newspapers to the reviewing of poetry was shrinking. But the Archive told a different and more encouraging story. Poetry had moved out of its old sanctuaries into new and less 'establishment' sites. And the result was remarkable, the opposite of what doomsayers thought. The Archive's audience figures proved that there were actually many more people listening to and reading poetry now, not many fewer.

―――――

On the morning after, Jan and I brought our hangovers downstairs to the dining table, which was now comparatively simply decorated, and I talked to the Prince about Ted; the Prince shook his head sorrowfully over the bad Plath press, and said he knew what that kind of thing felt like. Then he talked more about his childhood, remembering the time that he'd come back from boarding school to Buckingham Palace at the beginning of the long summer holidays, but hadn't been allowed to see his mother because there'd been an outbreak of chickenpox at the school and he might be infectious. As he spoke, he fiddled with the signet ring on the pinkie of his chubby left hand. The anxious and unhappy child was still wincing beneath the skin of the adult.

———

Then Jan and I were given our orders for the day: a tour of some Norfolk churches, followed by a picnic lunch at a lodge on the estate. Camilla shepherded some of the guests into her Land Rover, drivers corralled others, and Jan and I ended up in the car with Oddjob back at the wheel, the Prince in the passenger seat beside him, and Jan and Mario Testino and I squeezed in together on the back seat. Testino looked nervous. I thought it must have something to do with those pictures he'd taken of Princess Diana – but he also seemed completely bewildered by the countryside itself, as though he'd never before seen a real field or a real tree or a real blade of grass. As Norfolk flashed past our windows he scoured it for a suitable topic of conversation. A pig farm. That would do. 'Ah!' he said to the Prince, and pointed to an enormous sow suckling its young in a furrow of filth. 'Pigs! Do you shoot pigs?'

We sped onwards, lingered round a few churches inspecting details that Prince Charles must have shown to innumerable other guests in the past, then drove on to the picnic. But wait. Picnic? Surely not just blankets under a tree and a wicker hamper? No indeed. As Oddjob turned off the main road up a grassy track, we saw a handsome log cabin ahead, set beside a pond; there were butlers and maids there already, carrying heavy-looking crates. But what was happening near the water, why did the ground there seem to be moving? As the car stopped and we got out, I looked again. It wasn't the ground moving. It was hundreds of toads, and they were mating. Some in couples, but most in large slithery gangs. Crawling over each other. Shoving and pulsing. Croaking and gulping. Jan and I stared in silence, wondering whether we should pretend not to have seen anything. But Jan had a much better idea. 'What do you think would happen if I kissed one?' she asked the heir to the throne. 'Then there would be a surfeit of princes,' he told her.

———

The Poetry Archive never exactly settled down: it had to keep changing in order to keep growing, and I had to keep chasing money to fund it. It might have started with an over-the-shoulder remark, but now it was the main focus of my laureateship and working for it filled half of every week. Enough! But apparently not. It sprouted two offshoots: Poetry by Heart, an annual national verse-speaking competition for children; and another one-off competition for children to write their own poems, to celebrate the Queen's upcoming Golden Jubilee. I wrote to her private secretary and asked whether the Palace would be willing to hold a reception for the winners and their families, as well as any other poets who cared to attend, and he invited me to come to Buckingham Palace so that I could say more about what I had in mind. On the appointed day, halfway through our conversation, a flunky burst into the room looking panicky, and said the Palace staff had to go to their assembly points *now*, and I had to leave and go home *now*, because there was an emergency. Somebody must have died, I thought. The Duke of Edinburgh? Should I start thinking about the poem I'd have to write? At the front gate, I asked one of the policemen on duty what was going on. The policeman wouldn't look at me but kept staring at the sky; he said terrorists had flown two planes into the Twin Towers in New York, and there might be other targets elsewhere in the world, including the Palace. Now we were both looking up, watching a passenger plane circling in the stack as it prepared to land at Heathrow.

———

Those royal poems, though – they were still the problem: destined before birth to seem either too distant from their subject or too impertinently close. I wrote them wondering why my stint as laureate seemed to have coincided with much more activity in the royal calendar than there'd been during Ted's time, and knew as I sent them off to the newspapers that I might as well be pinning a target on my back: the Queen Mum's hundredth birthday, the Queen Mum's death, the wedding of Prince Charles and Camilla, the death of Princess Margaret, this or that jubilee, the eighteenth birthday of Prince William. I felt so exasperated by the time the last one came along, I produced a half-baked rap that I hoped would be construed as a joke. In truth it was an act of self-sabotage. I'd had enough. The whole business proved what I'd thought from the start: when it came to writing about the royal family, laureates were damned if they didn't, and damned if they did.

Poems about national events that had nothing to do with the Windsors were a different matter. They felt like a chance to make poetry play its part in whatever large conversation was taking place at any given time, and in that respect fitted the job description I'd designed for myself – to make poetry a part of

everyday life. It wasn't hard to find subjects that seemed suitable: the Paddington train crash, a disastrous outbreak of foot
and mouth, homelessness, school bullying, the catastrophe of
the war in Iraq, and (at their request) the theme of 'liberty' for
the annual Trades Union Conference in Brighton. For the last
one, the TUC sent a car to collect me from home so that I could
read it during one of their plenary sessions, and it turned out to
be the same set of wheels that had brought Tony Blair to give
his speech to the Conference twenty-four hours earlier. Blair
had forgotten to collect his notes when he got back to Downing
Street, and they were still tucked into the back-seat pocket.
When I pulled them out and looked them over, I found that
they included the draft of a ditty that he'd written to lighten his
other more prosaic remarks. The rhythm was all over the place,
but never mind. Hadn't I been saying that it was part of the
laureate's job to encourage poetry to grow in unlikely places?

# Part Seven

---

## 2002–2021

Jan and I took the children on holiday to Menorca; we'd done it every summer for the last decade and more, staying across the harbour from Mahón in a cottage near the water that her parents had bought after the war. In the past we'd been happy here, as happy as anywhere. Now, because of the trouble I'd brought into our marriage, I didn't know whether I wanted our life to accelerate, or slow down, or stop altogether.

On one of the last mornings before we flew back to London, Jan and I left the house early and drove for half an hour to Es Grau on the north-east coast of the island, then walked barefoot through the pine wood down to the shoreline, then among the dunes, then along the wide, open beach between clumps of lily and sea holly, before stopping to watch a heron fishing where shallow river water oozed into the bay. Sunlight and stillness. Bright chalk fragments in the dark brown current, and bubbles rising. The heron's priest-like poise seeming to stretch the minutes, then stretch them further, so that for a moment I thought we might be able to escape our life altogether. But no. The beak lunged and stabbed, the head lifted again, and the fish bulged as it sank down the long throat.

We put on our shoes, turned back towards the car, and started the engine – the battery had been playing up during the last few days, and no wonder: this was the house jalopy; it had been on its last legs for years. But today there was no problem and off we went, retracing the journey we'd made at sunrise. I wound the window down to catch the aniseed scent of fennel plants growing wild at the roadside and feel the heat bouncing off the gravel. This time tomorrow, I was thinking, we'd be on our way to the airport. And a week from now, or a month from now, or six months from now, we'd have to face the future and decide whether—

The engine stopped. Nothing spectacular, no clanking or rending, just the usual affable rumble one minute, and silence the next. I yanked on the handbrake and glared at the empty road ahead. Typical. Today of all days. Now we'd have to ring for a tow truck and spend hours in a garage, not swimming with the children as we'd promised.

But wasted time was the least of it. As we sat wondering who to call, a rapid popcorn crackle broke out under the bonnet, and a tongue of smoke poked through the dashboard, followed by a single inquisitive flame. Was there a fire extinguisher some-where? Of course not. There were only things that were bound to make matters worse, not better. Burnable things. Sweet wrappers and lolly wrappers and straw hats and smears of sun cream and pizza boxes and beach umbrellas and swimming trunks and paperbacks and a million grains of sand that year after year had been happily rubbed, picked, brushed, fanned, flapped, smoothed off our own and the children's bodies, as we dried on our way back from swimming.

For a second or two I stayed put, mesmerised, while frag-ments of Louis MacNeice's poem 'Brother Fire' fizzed unbid-den through my head: 'When our brother Fire was having his dog's day . . . suckled with sparks . . . sizzling air . . . O delicate walker, babbler, dialectician Fire,/ O enemy and image of our-selves . . .' Then Jan and I were scrambling out of our seats, lunging forward to rescue a basket of towels from the boot, flinching back again. Then further back, as the fire strengthened and took hold. By now we were almost excited – after all, neither of us was hurt, we had a story for the children, and we could already hear a fire engine on its way (someone must have seen the smoke and reported it). But then the blaze suddenly wasn't exciting any more, it was frightening, and, as a larger explosion puffed through the engine, the bonnet flew up and a breeze from the harbour leaped inside, rubbing its hands among the flames. They flickered through the dashboard, licked around the speedometer and the fuel gauge, cracked the glass, and gripped the steering wheel.

I'd often seen films – who hasn't? – with scenes of burning cars, and never quite believed them: cars were made of metal, and metal didn't burn. Now I could see that everything was fuel for destruction. The delicious oils slathered across the engine parts, the rubber of the windscreen wipers, the rims holding the windows in place, the numbers and needles in the dials, the cloth of the seats and the foam inside them, the roof padding, the mats in the footwells, the dirty yellow paint of the bodywork, the tyres, and most scrumptious of all, the petrol tank. Harvest was everywhere, and fire was ravenous. It wanted the car gutted. It wanted bareness and emptiness. It wanted there to be nothing left, and didn't care how ugly nothing might look, or how useless it might be, how entirely without a future.

By the time the fire engine arrived, the flames had died down and the car was a shell, its scorched moon-skin giving odd pings and groans as it began to cool. Jan and I hardly dared look at each other. We were both people who enjoyed things being understated, and now the God of Symbols had risen from his bed at the roadside, parted the barricade of scrub, planted himself four-square in front of us, and screamed obscenely in our faces.

---

Eventually I moved into a flat around the corner from our old house, and five years after that Jan and I got divorced. In the short term, at least, I threw myself more busily than ever into laureate work – it was a way of not thinking. At the same time, thinking was exactly what I needed to do: I wanted a better understanding of the havoc I'd caused, and since I had very little appetite for talking about it with anyone, I thought writing might help. Even though putting words on a page had never been simply cathartic for me in the past, it had at least allowed certain kinds of self-interrogation. Prose had, anyway – poetry had always been too glancing, and too strongly averse to using reason alone. So prose is what I went back to, angling away from biography and writing instead about my own childhood, bracketing the account of my early days with a description of my mother's accident.

The accident, which I felt sure lay at the root of everything. Looked at from one angle, it seemed like an act of completely random violence. Seen in a different light, my mother had seized on disaster to rescue herself from aspects of her life that she felt were disappointing, only to find that it produced grotesque multiplications of suffering. In a different setting, I'd done something similar, also with catastrophic results.

---

I sent the completed manuscript of the childhood book to my father: it was meant to be a peace offering because my father had hardly spoken to me since I'd left home. Eventually the phone rang.

'I've finished,' my father said, like a child in a bathroom.

'Great, Dad,' I said. 'What did you think?'

My father hesitated; this by his own admission was the first book he'd ever read all the way through, yet in some sense he knew the story already: he was one of its main characters.

'Hilarious,' he said at last, with a heavy sigh.

———

There was a Jubilee service at St George's Chapel at Windsor, and I'd been asked to write some words to be set to music – normally it would have been music by the master of the Queen's music, Malcolm Arnold, but he was too ill to work, so the chapel choirmaster had stepped in. Once the plans were in place, the Palace wrote to say the Queen expected to be in the congregation and wondered whether I'd like to attend. I was still trying to build a bridge back to my father, and asked whether I could bring him with me: my father was an old-school monarchist, and I knew he would very much like to meet the Queen. (During my childhood he used to leap to his feet the second she began her annual Christmas broadcast on the television, and stood to attention throughout, his thumbs aligned with the seams in his trousers.) Yes, I was told, that would be fine – and all I had to do then was persuade my father to travel across London. Normally this would have been like getting Lot to revisit Sodom and Gomorrah, but the incentive of a royal meeting turned out to be irresistible, and now we were sitting side by side in the chapel listening to the choir singing the choirmaster's music. The words I'd written were inaudible, and not printed in the programme either, but my father and I pretended to enjoy ourselves. We were together, at least, and the Queen had given me a nod and a smile when she came into the chapel; my father had seen that and given me a nudge.

Then it was time for the interval, and a flunky appeared, saying the Queen was waiting in an anteroom and wanted to thank me for my poem. I asked: could I bring my father along too? No, I couldn't, my father's name wasn't on the list. I remonstrated. I'd explained weeks ago that my father would be here, and I'd been assured we could meet the Queen together. But still no. I tried again: my father had come a long way; my father had fought for King and country in the last war; really, it would mean a lot for him to meet the Queen. But again no – and now would I be so good as to follow along quickly, the Queen was expecting me.

My father gave a wan smile: it was OK. But it wasn't OK, it wasn't OK at all, and yet I couldn't do anything about it: the Queen was the Queen. I apologised to my father, followed the flunky into an anteroom that was writhing with suits, and waited my turn. When the suits eventually disappeared, because the second half of the concert was about to begin, the Queen beckoned me over, thanked me for writing the poem, and told me what I already knew: the music had drowned the words, and she hadn't been able to hear most of them. Nor me, I told her. The Queen made a grimace, looked aside as though she was debating with herself whether to say the regal equivalent of 'it's the story of my life', then frowned because someone behind her had given a little cough to show that it was time for me to leave. As I reached the door, I turned to give my neck-bow, but the Queen was worrying about running late, and had started rootling in her handbag. She brought out her lipstick and mirror, puckered her mouth into a moue, applied the lipstick, and patted her hair. Then the private moment ended, and her public performance resumed. The Queen clicked her handbag shut, stiffened her shoulders with a shrug, and turned towards the door. I'd already gone back to my father before she looked up.

————

I began taking the children to Sunday lunch with my father now and again. None of us enjoyed it, but all of us understood why we went: customs had to be observed, even when they were a kind of lament. 'How tall you are!' my father told the children as they unbuckled from the car. How much older you look, they and I thought, but said nothing of the kind until we were on the way home again. Their home with Jan, and mine elsewhere.

Then Jesse had a homework assignment: find someone in your family who remembers the Second World War and talk to them about it; make a tape recording of what they tell you. This time it was just the two of us who drove down to Essex, and after lunch Jesse and my father retreated into the sunroom – a glass extension to the sitting room, shielded from the lane by a high beech hedge, where my father spent his days smoking and staring into space, or tut-tutting over the *Daily Telegraph*.

I waited next door so as not to be a distraction but craned forward to hear: my father had told me so little about his time in the war, I expected to discover things I didn't know. 'This is me talking to Grandpa,' I heard Jesse say as the tape recorder clicked into action – but their voices soon dropped to a murmur and my attention refocused as I looked around me. This is where my father lives now, I thought – this is the life he made separately from my mother. Deep wall-to-wall carpet. A chintzy plumped-up sofa and oversized armchairs. Side tables cluttered with photographs of children and grandchildren. A tall red glass bird standing to attention by the door, approximately like a heron, and a bowl on the coffee table in the shape of a large seashell – those must both be Susan's ideas. A small shelf of books beside the fireplace and my own among them, the ones I'd sent to my father and which he'd never read. By the window overlooking the rose bed, the desk where my mother had written to me and Kit while we were still at school, and where in the holidays she rattled the sweet tin after lunch, saying, 'Just one each, otherwise your teeth will drop out.'

The sunroom door opened silently, as if remembering had made it happen, and my father stooped through. 'There is something,' he was saying to Jesse over his shoulder, then turned to include me as well; 'I don't think I've ever shown you this.' He knelt by the desk to pull open the sticky bottom drawer, then searched through the albums stacked inside. Their stiff grey pages turned over in my mind – a flicker of small deckle-edged pictures, with my mother's curly handwriting underneath each one: Kit wearing a hat to go swimming in the North Sea because the water was so cold; a terrier sniffing a sugar lump; my mother's pony Serenade standing under the may tree.

My father stood up again, holding a clutch of yellowing Roneo-ed pages, and explained that he'd had a clear-out recently, and found this. I wanted to tell him, and didn't, that he always seemed to be having a clear-out these days, as though he wanted to die with his entire life already tidied away.

'A seating plan of the Nuremberg Trials,' my father said, flourishing the pages with a gleam of triumph in his eye.

This was Jesse's day, not mine, and I wasn't meant to be a part of the conversation. But I couldn't help myself. 'How come, Dad?'

'Because I was there,' my father said. He knew he was telling me something we hadn't talked about before, but judging by the way he was half smiling, he felt proud to remember it now. 'I'd done German at school,' he went on. 'And I was good at it, I spoke it pretty well, and since my regiment was nearby, waiting to be demobbed, I thought I'd go. I mean, it was an open courtroom, anyone was allowed to go.'

'What was it like?'

'Like?' he repeated, showing a flash of the same irritation that had glimmered through my childhood. 'It wasn't like anything. It was unique. I went because I wanted to see those bastards get their just deserts.'

He turned back towards the sunroom, the Roneo-ed sheets of paper with their faint purple script still shaking in his hand, and closed the door behind him.

———

He'd never have put it like this himself, he didn't like thinking of himself as someone who might change, but my father's conversation with Jesse lifted a kind of barrier in him, and now whenever I saw him, the main thing he wanted to do was remember episodes from the war. Perhaps this too was a kind of clear-out – an evacuation of himself that matched the purging of files and folders in his desk drawers. And when the sixtieth anniversary of D-Day came round, and he mentioned that he and Susan were going on a bus trip with a dozen or so other survivors from his regiment, the Essex Yeomanry, to visit their landing site on Gold Beach on the Normandy coast, he asked me to go with him. Once we'd seen the beach, we'd follow the same route east that the regiment had taken in 1944, and end up in Bordeaux, where there would be a jamboree. The Queen again. And President George W. Bush. I didn't have to think to say yes.

I stayed in my father's cottage overnight, and we joined the bus while dawn was still breaking – 'Reveille!' he said, settling down beside Susan and watching the clouds lose their pink as we drove towards Dover. I sat a few rows behind everyone else and listened to them chatting and chuckling as the miles rolled beneath us. They all thought it was absurd that newspapers were suddenly calling them heroes; in their own minds they'd only done what they had signed up to do. But when we reached the landing site near Arromanches-les-Bains, and heard the brass bands playing, and saw the bunting and the buffet, and found the generations younger than their own were all applauding and cheering, their chests did puff out a little.

My father and I left the crowds and walked on the beach, shielding our eyes against the glare, trying to look through the holiday heat-haze and see the past that lay beyond it. It was difficult, what with the children squealing, the jet skis slamming through the waves offshore, the dogs and kites. My father peered around blindly, like someone who'd been abruptly hauled out of a dark cave. He seemed baffled, not so much by the difference between now and then as by the difficulty of believing that what had happened to him here was in fact a part of his own experience. I had my ways of feeling that I was a ghost, and now I could see that he had his ways as well.

Some things squeezed through. My father reminded me that his half-track was in line to be second off the landing craft as it approached the beach, but the Germans had hammered wooden spikes into the seabed to delay the boats in deep water, and when the first vehicle drove down the front ramp it sank: the soldiers inside it were drowned. My father's half-track then rumbled across their roof, and that saved his life. When he reached the water, the tide was low enough for him to keep going until he reached the shore.

'And that's when you changed your trousers!' I remembered.

'Exactly,' my father said, but it was hard to know whether this story amused him any more; it was the kind of thing that also belonged in a different time, belonged with my mother, in fact, who used to tease him in ways I'd never heard Susan do. He changed the subject. There had been a pillbox, he said, over there to the right of the beach, and the machine gun inside it was firing at will, killing soldiers as they clambered through the surf. It might have stopped the landing altogether if Sergeant Palmer hadn't popped a shell clean through the narrow window-slit. 'Good shot, old boy!' someone had shouted, like a spectator at a cricket match, and after that the landing went ahead without delay. By evening the regiment was off the beach and making its way slowly through the bocage in long thin columns, passing fields where dead Friesian cattle were lying on their backs with their legs in the air. The farmers had all fled, and there was no one left to milk the herds.

We left the beach ourselves and the bus took us onwards to Bordeaux, where we'd been booked into student accommodation that belonged to the university: adjacent box-bedrooms, each with a bathroom attached. My father and Susan parked their things, I did the same, and then we walked into town. I couldn't remember the last time I'd done anything as normal as stroll down a street with my father, looking for somewhere to eat, and the strangeness of it made me apprehensive: how were we meant to talk to one another now? With a new kind of candour? I didn't want that, it was too late for me to abandon my defensive ways, and neither did he. When he suddenly grabbed me by the elbow and asked me about Jan, and I told him that she and I were both doing what we wanted to do, he eagerly let go of me again: he didn't believe me for a moment but was glad not to talk about it. He'd done all that he felt was needed, simply by posing the question.

We found somewhere for supper, ate it, stayed within the boundaries of our politeness, then headed back to our rooms in the university. It had been a long day, and my father was tired – he was an old man now, over eighty. I was tired too, and stepped into my room feeling grateful that I'd soon be asleep. But wait. I needed to pee first, so went into the bathroom, then pressed the handle on the side of the cistern and began brushing my teeth. But wait again. The handle of the lavatory, instead of simply resetting itself as the cistern filled, had – what had it done, exactly? There'd been a little scraping noise, and then a clunk. I put down my toothbrush and turned to look. The handle had fallen onto the floor, that's what it had done, and now there was water pouring from the cistern. Really pouring. Arterial water, gushing and gurgling; in just a few seconds it had covered the entire floor of the room.

I remembered crouching in the attic in Kirk Ella with Joanna twenty-five years earlier. That watery disaster had been the symbol of much larger damage – the end of our marriage – and there was no threat of a similar amplification here. My relationship with my father would never end, it would just stay locked in the same civilities for the rest of our lives. And yet as I began to stare along the skirting and search for a stopcock, I realised that what had just happened, despite being so ridiculous, or rather because of it, did tell me something I needed to admit. It forced me to confront the fact that although I'd spent my entire adult life trying to escape my father's world and his influence, the sheer force of his presence still had the power to infantilise me. It was indisputable. Here I was with water lapping around my shoes, thinking that any minute now I'd have to knock on his adjacent bedroom door and say, 'I'm sorry, Dad, I've broken the lavatory.'

So come on! There must be a tap somewhere. I leaned further forward, my face bubbling under water – and yes, there it was. A little metal lever. Definitely a stopcock. I turned it, lifted my head and took another breath, then plunged again and turned it again. And again. And the water stopped. And the level immediately started to drop, as the flood poured away through the drain beneath the shower. Magic. Magic and a miracle and marvellous. As it swallowed the last few inches, the drain gave a few raucous gulps, and I put my ear to the wall and listened. Had my father heard that? But there was no sound from next door, and I told myself that he must already be asleep. Or if not asleep, then dozing in blissful ignorance, because he was a little deaf these days – the result of spending all those years in the war, he sometimes said, firing artillery guns.

---

'Only mediocrities develop,' according to Oscar Wilde. He didn't mean that the best writers don't change and grow; he perhaps meant that writers worth their salt have a central obsession, or a set of linked obsessions, which are large and complex enough to sustain them through a lifetime. Having this obsession is not an absolute guarantee of quality, of course, but it does comprise a foundation and a thousand growth-points – whether or not the writers themselves realise what they are, and prove capable of using them.

It had always been obvious to me that my mother's accident and its consequences had been my obsession – to such an extent that it sometimes blinded me to other and equally formative possibilities. Now, and thanks partly to historical coincidence, I began to see what one of these secondary fixations might be. The sixtieth anniversary of the D-Day landings, as well as other remembrances of the end of the Second World War, overlapped with the start of lengthy commemorations to mark the outbreak of the First. My father's previous life as a soldier would have made me sensitive to these things under any circumstances: he'd remained a Territorial soldier throughout my childhood, and all my original ideas about responsibility and courage – and even maleness itself – had in one way or another taken their direction from his uniformed example. Now, as laureate, I was invited to write poems to honour these anniversaries, and for the first time since taking up my role, I felt there was a fruitful coincidence of public duty and private compulsion.

But there was also a risk. As I often said to my students, writers' instincts to identify with the experience of people other than themselves – even when they mean only to sympathise – can easily lead to ugly or embarrassing appropriations. Especially when the 'other experience' is extreme or painful. So how could I possibly write poems about people fighting in a war, when I'd never done such a thing myself? When I was a baby boomer whose great good fortune had been to be spared – so far – that kind of danger and devastation? Clearly, I'd have to discover an exceptional kind of tact, or another way of approaching the subject, which could be combined with tact.

I was asked to write a poem about Harry Patch, the last surviving British soldier to have fought in the First World War, and after reading an autobiography that he'd co-written with Richard van Emden, I went to see him in his nursing home in Wells in Somerset. A sparrow-man, chair-bound but not bed-bound. A soldier for whom the remote war-past was more vivid than the present. A witty, self-deprecating survivor, whose sudden celebrity was the result of biological chance rather than intention or ambition – as he kept saying during our conversation, he hadn't meant to outlive all his contemporaries, he must just have eaten a lot of vegetables. But a distinguished man too, who used his eminence to chastise warmongers and to emphasise the suffering of war rather than any kind of glory.

As I talked to Harry, and then as I wrote my tribute to him, I realised that if I could use as many of his own words as possible and think of my poem as a kind of collaboration rather than a solo effort, I might not only catch most accurately the flavour of his personality, but also find a way round the problem that had been bothering me. Yes, it would certainly display a sort of vulgarity if I pretended that my own response to war was as authentic as the thoughts and feelings of someone who'd actually been caught up in one; but no, it was not impossible to approach the subject if I relied primarily on the words of people who had been there. If I created a kind of found poetry, in fact.

Once I'd finished the poem about Harry Patch – five unrhymed sonnets – the subject of war, and this collaborative way of writing about it, wouldn't leave me alone. And after several months a pattern began to emerge. I was writing a series of poems set in various wars during the twentieth and twenty-first centuries, from the First World War to the conflict in Afghanistan, and wherever possible I was basing the poems on the words of soldiers who had been involved in those conflicts – some previously silenced or ignored (the victims of PTSD), and most of them ordinary Joes. These ordinary Joes were generally the voices that spoke most powerfully to me, because these were the men that knew best the reality of close contact with an enemy, who remembered most accurately and feelingly the weight of a rifle, whose descriptions of fear and relief were most compelling because they were the least inhibited by codes of class and custom.

Very soon my interest in pursuing these poems developed into something like passion – at which point I began to ask myself: why? Was it just relief at finding a subject that met the writerly requirements of my laureate life, but had nothing to do with royal weddings and whatnot? Certainly. But there was something else to it as well: something to do with my father. In every account of conflict that I read, in every soldier I talked to, I saw his image as well as theirs. Which meant that every time I felt moved by their stories and their losses, I thought about his story and his losses. But the poems that I was writing now were not just elegies; they were celebrations of my father. Celebrations of what he had done as a young man, and attempts to show that I appreciated him in ways that neither of us would have been able to say aloud. At the same time, they were also almost opposite things. They were forms of apology for the ways I'd disappointed him, and attempts to cross the distance that had always existed between us.

I made these war poems into a sequence called *Laurels and Donkeys* and ended it with a series of adapted conversations with soldiers serving in the Desert Rats, who at the time had been led to believe they would be the last British troops to leave Afghanistan. The idea was to turn these conversations into poems, which would then become a radio programme for the BBC – and once my producer and I had flown to Germany, then set out on the road towards the camp in which the soldiers were now based, Bad Fallingbostel, near Hanover, I realised that this time my father was even more obviously a part of the process of composition than usual. As our car whizzed along the tree-lined roads, and the black shadows of leaves flickered across our faces, I remembered him talking to my mother during my childhood, saying that as his regiment advanced through the Falaise Gap and into Germany in late 1944 and early 1945, he had passed Belsen concentration camp, not previously knowing it was there, and been alerted to its existence by the smell of burning flesh. Now, suddenly, there was the same name on a sign at the roadside: Belsen. By the time we'd arrived at Bad Fallingbostel and settled into the rooms the Desert Rats had made available for us, present time and historical time were already woven tightly together in my mind. Over the next several days, and during the months following in which I turned the interviews into poems, I felt for the first time in my writing life that my father was sitting beside me, and each of us understood what the other was saying.

---

Busy as it was, my laureate life had a peculiarly static quality, for the simple reason that it could never escape the obligations that came with the role. But now that my ten years were nearly up, things suddenly became more fluid again: I resigned from

UEA and was appointed to set up a creative writing MA programme at Royal Holloway College, University of London; I
began looking around for new occupations to take the place
of school visits and readings. But one last thing, before any of
these things became my next routine. The sherry. The notorious butt of sack, which had been given to laureate after laureate
since John Dryden's day. There was still no sign of it, so I wrote
to my contact at the Palace – Sir Michael Peat, the Keeper of the
Privy Purse – and asked him where it had got to. No joy there.
Michael told me that the sherry had nothing to do with the
Palace: it was a present from the Sherry Institute of Spain, and
if I wanted to do any tippling, I'd better write to them about it.
I did, and pronto. I don't like sherry much, but a perk is a perk.

It turned out that Graham, the man from the Institute who'd
organised Ted's sherry for him, and was due to sort out mine
as well, had been ill – but he was better now and quickly made
arrangements for me to spend a weekend visiting various
bodegas in Jerez. 'How much sherry is there in a butt?' I asked
him. 'About 650 bottles,' he said. 'And would that be arriving
annually or was the gift a one-off?' 'A one-off,' Graham said,
which in its way was a relief.

I went with my girlfriend Sarah, a young American novelist,
and Graham met us at the airport in Jerez, then took us out
to supper, where he introduced us course by course to various
different kinds of sherry before depositing us back at our hotel.
By this stage Graham still seemed to be managing perfectly
well despite his recent illness, and so was Sarah: she'd been taking things steady. My own head felt distinctly stripey, but this
wasn't something I wanted to mention to Graham, and neither
was the fact that sherry had somewhat off-putting associations
for me – not vicars and maiden aunts in the classic way, but

awkward pre-lunch conversations at home with my father, or anxious supervisions at Oxford. I'd never seen it as one of life's great disinhibitors. Rather the opposite, in fact. More as a signal that difficulties were on the horizon.

Next morning, after an uneasy night, Sarah and I left with Graham for a tour of half a dozen bodegas, and because I felt embarrassed by not feeling 100 per cent, and conscious of Graham's own professional excitement (as well as his wish to celebrate recovering from a serious illness), I set about tasting with exaggerated enthusiasm: swilling and swirling and not spitting out as much or as often as I should have done. By midday, the sound of another large iron gateway scraping open, the sight of another blindingly hot yard, and the sweet scent of another lofty warehouse had become parts of a dream-kaleidoscope that wouldn't stop swivelling; the notes that I'd been taking on each sample, which I intended to examine later so that I could make my final choice, looked like foam on a wave. But it was OK: if I was doing myself no good, at least I could pause during lunchtime.

Except I couldn't pause, because Graham had kindly arranged for a local sherry-producing grandee to join us in the restaurant, and the grandee had lined up further varieties of sherry for me to taste, and it would obviously be rude not to try them. 'Further' in this case meaning a new example with every course – which, because lunch was tapas, meant several courses. About a dozen.

The meal ended. I went to the gents and stood with my forehead pressed to the cold white wall-tiles for as long as seemed reasonable without causing Graham and his friend to think that I'd passed out, then lurched back into the afternoon. There were three more bodegas to visit before Sarah and I

were released back to our hotel, and although I was now getting better at spitting out after tasting, a good deal of sherry
still managed to slosh into my system. By the time we made it
back to our room, I was carrying my head in my hands, and
my bed was indistinguishable from the several others shimmering alongside it. I lay down very carefully, set the alarm
on my phone, fell heavily asleep, then woke with a headache,
swallowed a handful of Nurofen, and crept downstairs to the
restaurant for supper. Graham beamed at me across the table:
he'd remembered several other kinds of sherry we still hadn't
tried yet, and luckily the cellar here was exceptionally well
stocked.

At breakfast the next morning, I wondered: did the Spanish
drink sherry with their croissants? Astonishingly, it seemed
they didn't, so I tossed back a litre of coffee, then fell in step
as Graham led me off to tour the last few bodegas. After a few
hours of conscientious spitting, and what appeared to be a successful attempt to turn my grimaces into expressions of dis-
criminating judgement, I announced my decision: an oloroso.
Graham seemed pleased, and took me off in a taxi to inspect the
warehouse where my barrel would be stored: my butt. A beautiful and ancient barn, immaculately swept, with bright scurries
of breeze blowing through it and the alcohol scent enfolding
me like a mummy-cloth. And a long row of barrels, with my
own nearest to the door. Would I like to write my name on it?
It's what previous laureates had done, and here was a stick of
white chalk. Sure. I scrawled away, and there it was, my butt
next to Ted Hughes's butt with Ted's signature on it, which was
next to John Betjeman's butt with his signature, which was next
to – what was this, not Cecil Day-Lewis's butt, as it should have
been, but Bill Clinton's butt: there was his name as bold as you

like. How did that get there? No one had any idea, but it wasn't hard to guess. I patted the rough flank, thanked all and sundry, walked out into the sunlit yard, and turned to my own head, which was rolling alongside me in the dust: could we go home now? My head nodded at me.

A month later the consignment was delivered to my flat in London by a driver who gave a look that complicatedly entwined envy with pity. I opened one of the cases and removed a bottle to examine the label, which my daughter Sid had designed for me, and which showed two fish swimming side by side: 'I thought they looked like us,' she'd told me. Then I put the bottle back and stared at the mountain of cases. I'd have to ask Richard Carrington to store them, because there was no room for them here, and Richard had an empty shed in his garden. We could give some to friends and auction the rest to raise money for the Archive.

---

My father rang to say that his back was hurting – he'd been to the doctor, he'd had some tests, and the diagnosis was bone cancer. 'BONE CANCER,' he shouted, holding his phone several inches away from his mouth – something he'd done all his life, to show how much he disliked using it. 'What does that mean?' I asked, meaning what was the prognosis. Well, said my father, it wasn't the Black Spot: a few rounds of chemo and he'd be home again; this wasn't going to kill him. As his words sank in, and despite his best efforts to seem phlegmatic, I heard a note in his voice that suggested otherwise, half sad and half eager. It told me that my father wanted to die. He'd seen a way out and he was going to seize it.

I caught a train to Chelmsford, and a cab to the hospital took me past the barracks where my father had done his square-bashing when he joined the Territorial Army after the war. He'd remained a Territorial until the mid-sixties – he'd eventually become lieutenant colonel of his regiment – and since then he'd missed the disciplines and structures and camaraderie of military life. Besides, in his self-deprecating way he'd always known that he looked good in uniform: handsome and indestructible. Now he was hunched in a too-small plastic chair beside his bed in the ward. Bare bruised ankles and scuffed red leather slippers. Dark green paisley dressing gown. Neatly brushed and parted hair, and the hairbrushes – wood-backed, a pair – crouching on the bedside cabinet. As I stared down, I wondered whether we were going to embrace – I wanted to, but as adults we'd never shown our affection in that sort of way, never hugged or kissed each other, hardly ever touched at all, in fact. Although suddenly my father was half lifting his arms towards me, so I bent forward and our faces collided. For a split second I remembered how he used to come into my bedroom after dark when I was a child, smelling of London and cigarettes, asking me what I'd done with my day; when I touched his face, the rasp of his cheek was like electricity. Then the memory faded, and I pulled up a chair to sit opposite, glancing around at the waxy-looking apples in their cardboard bowl, the yellowish water in the flower vase, the rusty carnations. Eventually I faced forward and met my father's eyes. They looked paler than before; the blue was fading.

'Hello, old boy' – that was what my father called me now – old boy – 'Sorry about the chair. And sorry about . . .' He let the sentence dangle and nodded sideways, indicating the neighbour on his left, an almost-skeleton whose head was flung back on the pillow, mouth recklessly agape. Was my father asking, 'I'm not like that, am I?', or was he warning me, 'I'll be like that soon'? Both, maybe, and there was no easy reply to either. We stalled and smiled: good manners had always been our refuge. Good manners and skimming across surfaces.

'Do you watch the telly?' I asked him, playing true to form.

My father pointed at the screen on a stalk above his bed: his arm was flecked with black scabs where the nurses had attached the machinery for his chemo. 'Pull it closer,' he said. 'It's very clever you know, it's a computer as well as a telly.' His voice was touched with wonder; he and Susan didn't have a computer at home.

'Have you used it?' I asked.

'God no!'

'Would you like to know how it works?' Without waiting for an answer, I pulled the screen towards us, typed in 'Poetry Archive', and began showing my father round the site – he'd never seen it before. But his pale eyes soon glazed over. All I was doing was leading him through a labyrinth he didn't understand, into a labyrinth he didn't care about.

I logged off. 'What is it, Dad?'

His eyes locked on my own for a moment, then swivelled away again. It was nothing. Just weariness – weariness which was now everything and overwhelming. I helped him to his feet, and as we shuffled sideways towards the bed, I felt his thin arm-bone through the sleeve of his dressing gown. Suddenly I remembered walking round the hospice garden with Philip: there was the same hard contact; the same sense of reaching through a living body and touching the skeleton inside.

Next day the doctor was waiting for me in the corridor outside my father's ward, holding a grey patient file in one hand; he looked concerned. It wasn't so much the cancer, he explained – that was serious, but it needn't be fatal. It was more that my father seemed to be depressed. Was there any particular reason? I wondered where to start: the lonely and emotionally frozen childhood; his parents' divorce; the war; his mother's suicide; my mother's accident; her endless-seeming time in hospital; her death; his own gradually deepening isolation. If the doctor knew about these things, he'd understand very well why my father might be depressed. But my father himself would have been horrified if I'd so much as alluded to them. He would simply not have recognised his life in these terms.

'I wouldn't go there,' I said to the doctor; 'he won't thank you,' then turned away and continued into the ward. The bed next to my father was empty now, but my father didn't seem to have noticed; he was lying on his back, eyes wide open, staring through the ceiling.

The doctors found him a room in a hospice closer to home, only twenty minutes by car. It was a glorified bungalow with a dozen pale blue rooms, but my father preferred it here; he had privacy again, and liked looking at the flowering pink cherry outside his window.

'Have they given you everything you want?' I asked, when I arrived for my first visit.

My father rolled his eyes; he could still make whatever I said to him sound stupid. 'Hardly, old boy,' he told me. 'But if I can't have everything, what I'd like instead is a huge photograph of the view at home, on a stand or something at the end of my bed. I want to see the things I know.'

I promised I'd get him some photographs tomorrow, but as I was saying this my father lost interest and closed his eyes: he was slipping away fast now. Had he even noticed that it said 'Andrew' on the panel above his bed? It was his first name, true, but he'd always been called by his second name, Richard. It was like the Gillian/Gilly business with my mother; she'd also been given an illness-name that was not quite her own.

I mentioned the mistake to my father, even though he now seemed to be asleep, and his eyes snapped open at once. 'Bloody ridiculous,' he said, in his resolute soldier's voice. 'Ridiculous. You're Andrew, aren't you?'

'Yes, Dad, I'm Andrew,' I told him, then added, 'but my turn will come.'

My father gave a dry chuckle, and I thought: at least he still knows what's going on. Then I thought again and changed my mind. 'At least he knows what he's doing' is what I meant. Which was killing himself. There was no sign of struggle, no knife or gun or pills, just an almost invisible act of will. A decision that looked like surrender but in fact was adamant. Once upon a time it had been him against the world. Now it was him against himself. He was tired of the world. If the nurses had been willing to let him turn his face to the wall, he'd already have done that.

———

Time buckled and my normal life was suspended, all its chores and responsibilities pushed to one side, and all its other worries on hold. Now, as my father fell silent, the minutes closed around us more tightly than ever, and then tighter still when his wife Susan stopped visiting the hospital: she didn't want to remember my father as an invalid. I told her that I understood, but kept to myself the thought that her absence suited me fine. It wasn't as if I'd had a sudden rapprochement with my father, or a healing heart-to-heart. And it wasn't as if our last conversations had been easy: there'd still been that frisson of disapproval in my father's voice, and the occasional tremor of confusion in my own. But still. As our minutes together became hours, they amounted to more life than we'd shared in years, and they felt priceless to me.

---

One long day passed, and then another. My father was concentrating entirely on breathing now, but each tug at the air sounded gentler and shallower than the last. Then his eyes flicked open again, and he stared straight ahead. 'Just remind me,' he said, with the impatience of someone interrupting a different conversation that he wanted to get back to. 'How are the children doing?'

I told him – their ages, their jobs, their partners – and reassured him that they were happy.

'So everyone's all right then?'

He meant were they doing all right without me living at home, but I didn't want to get into that. 'Yes, Dad,' I said. 'Everyone's all right.'

My father nodded a fraction, then suddenly lifted his chin. 'And you,' he said, with peculiar slow emphasis. 'Never be blackmailed.'

It was so unexpected I thought that I must have misheard, and replayed the sentence in my head a second time, listening carefully. But I hadn't misheard. 'Never be blackmailed' was definitely what he'd said. 'Yes, Dad,' I told him in a stumble. 'I mean no, Dad. Of course not. What . . .' 'What do you mean?' I was going to say, but there was no point. My father had used up the last ounce of his energy and slipped into his doze again.

I leaned back in my chair. Really, though: what had he meant? Was he talking about Sarah? He couldn't have been: he knew nothing about her and nothing about our life together; he'd always refused to speak about her or meet her. Or was my father talking about his own life and his marriage to Susan – which had now lasted longer than his marriage to my mother? He loved Susan, no doubt about it, but did he also somehow feel trapped by her? It seemed possible. In the confusion of his grief after my mother's death, and in the web of courtesies and social codes that governed his existence, I could just about imagine that he might have made Susan a promise he then felt that he couldn't break, because his sense of decency wouldn't let him.

'Dad?' I said, still trying to understand – then gave up. My father had set off without me: the worry-lines in his face were beginning to flatten and smooth, and his arms were stretched straight at his side, as if he were lying in bed at attention. Old soldier. Brave man. Poor long-suffering soul.

I stood up and kissed him on the forehead, inhaling the childish sweetness of his skin, the smell of Bay Rum in his hair, his warmth. Then my brother Kit and a nurse came in, the nurse saying that we should pop out and get some supper, because nothing here was going to change for a while. We did as we were told, and drove to a pub a couple of miles away. Exactly as we found a table and sat down, my phone rang, and the same

271

nurse told me that my father had taken his chance while our backs were turned. He was dead.

By the time we got back to his room, the nurse had already brushed his hair, laid him flat in the bed, lifted his hands from his sides and folded them neatly over his chest, and pressed a red rose between his fingers. I knew my father would have hated that – shop roses – so I took away the flower and crammed it into my jacket pocket, feeling a little jab of pleasure as one of the thorns scratched me. I wanted to feel marked by the moment. I wanted to be scarred by it for life. Then I looked into my father's face for the last time: the strong nose and jaw, the handsomeness, and the suntan from working in the garden. Noble. It had never been a word I used much, but there it was. My father looked noble.

And relieved. My father had done what he'd planned to do. He'd set himself free.

———

That night I stayed with Kit, who was living in a rented cottage near the hospital – a cut-off place at the end of a potholed lane, opposite an ancient church. We had a drink, then I walked across the lane to sit in the church by myself for a while. Damp plaster and musty prayer books. Cold stone. I didn't want to talk to God, I wanted to talk to myself – but my first sentence was a cliché: I was an orphan now. I looked around at the moonlight slopping through the long windows, at the eagle holding the Bible on the back of its faintly gleaming wings, at the little urns and angels and solemn words on the wall-tablets, expecting the world to seem larger than it had done a few hours ago, and my place in it to seem smaller and more precarious.

But the opposite was true – not because I felt nothing for my father, but because I felt closer to him than ever before. Previously when I'd thought about the shape of my own life, I'd always reckoned that my mother was my foundation stone. The sheer drama of her accident, its shock and brutality, and its long aftermath of anguish had surely shaped my character more decisively than anything or anyone else. But now that my father was no longer someone I had to fear, or dance around in a prolonged waltz of obligation, or take the trouble to ignore, I could see that his life had been the larger force. Larger, longer, more insistent, and a great deal more complicated in its effect. I thought of our relationship as a play in five acts: Absence, Fear, Anger, Impatience, Sorrow. The last act, Sorrow, was the one that had started with his illness, was still running now, and would persist into the future. Sorrow was the most comfortable act to watch, and it contained the scenes where my father was most loveable.

I left the church and walked back through the darkness to my brother's house. While we ate supper, Kit told me that the church might seem like nothing special, but it was famous locally because it appeared in a picture by Thomas Gainsborough called *Cornard Wood* – two hundred and some years ago, Gainsborough used to live up the road in Sudbury. I knew the painting – I'd seen it in the National Gallery in London: a wood of golden oak trees enclosing a sultry metallic pond, and a rutted track left of centre, where a couple of donkeys stare into space and a few locals go about their business. One man, wearing a pale straw hat (although the skies are grey), with a bag slung over his shoulder and a dog at his heels, is tramping towards a village in the distance – a minuscule white house touched by a single beam of sunlight, and an equally small church with a grey spire. A church which was this church – the one that I could see through the window of my brother's kitchen. The church I'd just been sitting in.

I couldn't explain why, but it comforted me to think that I was living in a place that also existed in a picture; it strengthened my feeling that being an orphan would not be as hard for me as it is for some others. I stood up from the table and looked at the black walls looming across the lane. I was at the centre of the frame, and the travelling man was still toiling along the rutted track towards me. I'd spend the rest of my life waiting for him to arrive, and while I waited I'd continue to grieve for my father, the saddest person I've ever known.

---

I wished that I'd asked Susan if I could have my father's watch: I'd have liked to spend the rest of my life hearing the same sound of time passing that he'd heard, and see every morning the same divided-up face that he'd seen. Susan might not have wanted to give it to me, but I should have asked, at least. Now here I was beside the grave, staring at the coffin while people threw handfuls of earth onto the lid, thinking I could hear the tick-tock on my father's wrist. Then I thought again. His watch was old, the kind that had to be wound up every night, and this meant it would already have run down and stopped at some random time. And now it would keep that random time until damp crept through the walls of the coffin, and the face spoiled, and the strap rotted, and the watch slipped from the bones of his wrist, and the hands dropped off, and the metal decayed, and the intricate dials and cogs scattered through the earth.

But I mustn't think like that, it made me lose my balance.

In fact, look: I'd already lurched backwards, and now I was standing on my mother's grave. I stepped forward again, took a last look down at my father's coffin, and said goodbye. Now I needed to get back to his cottage. Susan would need help passing round the tea and sandwiches.

———

Six months after my father's funeral I was invited to a poetry festival in Waterloo village in upstate New York – the kind of place that would belong to the National Trust if it were in England: autumnal woods, antique industrial machinery, and an immaculately restored canal. The first event was a discussion about poetry and sound, which I reckoned would be easy going: I could talk about the Poetry Archive. I climbed onto the stage and found my place: Jorie Graham on my right, and to my left the Palestinian poet Tara Muhammad Ali, with his translator Peter Cole, then the Korean poet Ko Un, with his interpreter Kyeong-Soo Kim, nearest to me.

Kyeong-Soo. There wasn't enough time to introduce myself as I shuffled my notes, but I did take in very beautiful black hair, a very beautiful concentrating face, a very cool tweed trouser suit, and very funky black boots with a rib on the toecap like a seam. 'Hello,' she said. 'You must be Peter.'

'No,' I said. 'But Peter is my middle name.'

Then the discussion started – Tara gravelly, Jorie torrential, Ko Un pattering, and Kyeong-Soo's voice surprisingly deep and commanding. But I was suddenly finding it difficult to concentrate on what was being said; I was thinking that if Kyeong-Soo had called me Peter, it must be because she didn't recognise me, and probably didn't know anything about me either. She wasn't here to pontificate about poetry as some kind of expert, she was here to interpret. Very good, I thought. That meant she had no preconceptions based on the laureateship or any public version of myself. She was free to like me – if she chose to do that – for what I was, and not for what I was supposed to be.

———

A year later, Kyeong-Soo rented out her apartment in Brooklyn and came to live with me in London. Kyeong-Soo with her wild-child beauty, her old-soul wisdom, her bravery, her modesty, her quirkiness and consideration. She may not have previously been much concerned with poetry, but she brought poetry back to me – because I found that loving her made me feel more loving towards the world in general: more tolerant of its annoyances, and more interested in its appearances. I'd always believed in principle in the power of so-called ordinary things to fascinate and inform, but now I wanted to honour these feelings more deliberately and turn them into a gift. To convert love into attention, and attention into poems which were a kind of thank you for the love which had triggered them in the first place. Did this mean I no longer thought that all poems were elegies? No. It meant that love poems found some of their intensity from knowing that time was their enemy.

I wished my father could have met her – but my father would never have understood; he would have said, when Kyeong-Soo and I got married, that third marriages were only for people who wear astrakhan coats and gold jewellery. Her own father was buried in a hill-cemetery outside Seoul, and soon after our wedding we flew out to visit him, placed soju and food on the gravestone in the traditional way, then knelt down and bowed our foreheads to the ground. I smelled the damp earth and breathed it in. Kyeong-Soo had travelled a long way to become so comfortable with her dead, and for the first time in my life, I began to feel at peace with my own. When we walked back down the mountain together, past the dumpy grave mounds half hidden in mist and the straggling vines, our own ghosts and the ghosts of those we loved were floating quietly beside us.

———

Mostly I did my remaining laureate business alone; neither of us wanted to feel that Kyeong-Soo was ancillary. Besides, she had her own work to do – interpreting, mostly, and studying for a PhD at the University of London. But then an invitation arrived from the headmaster of a school in Mongolia: would we like to fly out there together, so that I could talk about poems with his students? Really? Mongolia? It was like being invited to outer space – which felt like somewhere I might enjoy looking round for a while. During ten years as laureate, I'd done as much for poetry as I knew how, and often felt deeply rewarded by it. But the manifold committees, initiatives, gatherings, and performances had also taken a toll, and now I wanted privacy and wide horizons again. I thought that if I couldn't remember what these things looked like, Mongolia would remind me.

———

A couple of months later, Kyeong-Soo and I peered through the window of our plane and saw the clouds open below us to reveal a layer of smog as thick and neat as the potato on a shepherd's pie. Ulan Bator. Once we'd landed, our host explained: when the Russians had been here in Mongolia, they'd built power sta-tions in a ring around the outskirts, and now that they'd gone, the chimneys were still pumping out filth. Because it was a val-ley city, there was nowhere for this filth to disperse; by the time we reached our hotel, our eyes were red and pouring tears.

I did my work in the school, then it was Sunday and everything shut down. What would we like to do? Hang out with our host and watch some yellowing videos of *Midsomer Murders*, or go sightseeing? It wasn't a real question – a trip to the steppes had already been organised for us to see the Przewalski's horses, the native Mongolian breed snatched from the edge of extinction, and now thriving in the wild. I'd looked at pictures of them before leaving home: stocky, thick-necked animals with large bony heads, straw-coloured coats, and black manes and tails. Primitive-looking and beautiful. Some of the last wild horses left in the world.

Our driver Kwan revved into the choking traffic stream, then stop-started through the streets and suburbs of Ulan Bator for the next three hours. Crawling, hooting, barging, spurt-ing, cursing, bellowing, sighing, while a frieze of breeze-block men and their bowed wives unfurled on either side. Children wiped our dusty windscreen with dustier rags. An old man tot-tered past clutching a sheep. Another, younger man held a goat steady above the drain at a street corner, with a knife raised above its head. Then we reached the edge of the city proper, where unfinished houses gave way to miles of shanty village: fluttering trash, roped-together plastic, hammered tin. The road which had hardly been a road in the centre of town was now a daredevil potholed track.

Then suddenly it ran clear and smooth. A tarmac ribbon skimming across shallow hills, and these hills absolutely bare as far as our eyes could see. Mile after mile after mile of billowing green nothing, with occasional broken-down trucks, or tents with families squatting around smoky fires, their gypsy colours flickering.

There was no sign at the roadside, but Kwan knew when to turn, and after that there was no tarmac, just a bare track crossed by a herd of sheep sometimes, or a rabbity creature scooting into its burrow, with a mist of very fine sand surrounding the car and a long plume swaggering behind us. Thirty-five million years ago this had all been under water – these lolloping hills and bristly outcrops had been weathered by ocean currents as well as wind and rain. It was exhilarating; I'd never before seen so much time made visible.

After an hour or so we came to a clump of tents. Yurts, I wanted to call them, but Kwan said no, 'yurt' was a word the Russians had used, so the Mongolians didn't call them that, they called them gers, rhyming with 'years'. We parked the jeep and climbed out into the silence. Pure silence, I thought at first, then retuned to the wind and the voices coming from one of the gers, the largest one, which had a fancy portico. We were going to eat here, Kwan told us, then sleep in one of the other tents. Kwan himself would doss down in the car and take us to look for the horses in the morning. He lifted the flap and we stooped inside.

Pork and borscht to eat, and hooch to drink – fermented mare's milk. I'd heard about this, how potent it was, so drank my first bowlful cautiously. Astonishing. Like the early stages of that scare with my tumour. I couldn't feel my legs. But never mind, I thought, the numbness would soon wear off, and anyway a troop of waiters was bringing our food now. Their boss spoke Korean and explained to Kyeong-Soo that although the night ahead was going to be very cold, we'd be warm in our ger because there was a stove that he'd already lit, and he'd creep back in around midnight and top it up with coal. We wouldn't hear a thing.

The bed turned out to be a four-poster – tourism! – but there was no canopy, so when we lay down we found ourselves staring directly at the roof of the ger, which rose into a crown of small plastic lantern windows. We listened to the wind rake the endless acres surrounding us, watched it pluck at the canvas of our walls, then turned out the light. A million stars immediately rushed into the windows overhead – a million stars, and the acid-green eyes of a wild cat, which had perched on the roof and was now staring ravenously down at us. An incubus. Fuseli's *Nightmare*. I rolled away, expecting the mare's milk would knock me out any minute, but that was when the wolves began howling, maybe very close, or maybe in the far distance, it was hard to tell. Kyeong-Soo and I listened for a moment – the extravagant hunger, the primeval despair, the theatrical longing. I thought of the phrase my father had used whenever he found himself even vaguely isolated: 'the middle of nowhere'. I knew what it meant at last. It meant here. Tomorrow morning we would see the horses, and watch the golden eagles flying above them, and hear the wolves again, and each of these things would be a marvel. Meanwhile, this was marvellous too. I looked back to the lantern window. The cat had vanished, and the stars were blending into a single wash of light, an overflow of years that spilt weightlessly across our bed.

———

As I fell asleep, I remembered my first visit to Spurn Point thirty-odd years previously. Today I'd had the same sense of rushing into purified space, with the same ancient song of the Earth filling my head. Back then I'd been thinking about self-annihilation, and a part of me had despised myself for resisting it. Now the idea of extinction was dreadful – partly because I felt in step with my life, and partly because I had a better understanding of my past. I thought of Philip – Philip in Mongolia! – and the lines of his that I liked best. I said them under my breath, but loud enough to set them loose and have them travel over the steppes, where they had never been before:

> Truly, though our element is time,
> We are not suited to the long perspectives
> Open at each instant of our lives.
> They link us to our losses: worse,
> They show us what we have as once it was,
> Blindingly undiminished, just as though
> By acting differently we could have kept it so.

---

We were woken up at midnight: it was the boss, who had promised to fill up our stove with coal. And that was good news, because the cold was now so intense our breath was misting around our faces. Less good was the fact that he'd brought a dozen or so friends with him, and they were standing in a huddle at the foot of our bed, whispering to one another and pointing at us. Forget Przewalski's horses and wolves and eagles and incubus-cats: they'd always been here and with luck they always would be. Forget deep time. Forget endless death and the icy wind pouring across infinite space. This was the really remarkable thing. This English man in bed with this Asian woman.

When Mick Imlah died, time recoiled and landed me back in Oxford, where I'd first met him through Alan: black hair falling into his eyes, and a soft Scottish voice mixing poetry with the everyday – everyday sports, especially. He was the only young writer I knew who had that kind of reach – for the rest of us, poetry was a thing apart – and although we used to tease him about it, we admired him for being so unapologetically himself. So unpretentious and yet so exceptional.

For a while Mick's life seemed to be tracking my own: when I gave up editing the *Poetry Review*, he was appointed as one of the editors in my place; when I parted company with Carmen, he took over as poetry editor there too. By then, Chatto had already published his first collection, *Birthmarks* – although persuading him to hand over the manuscript had been one of the hardest tasks of my publishing life: his perfectionism meant that I almost literally had to tear the pages out of his hands. It was funny-maddening, like his refusal to learn how to use a typewriter, but it was also a serious proof of character. His life was his own, and he was organising it to suit himself. Which meant, among other things, that no one who knew him was surprised it took him twenty years to publish his second collection, *The Lost Leader*, no matter how impatient we were to read it.

By the time the book came out, all such thoughts had become both trivial and more touching than ever: Mick had been diagnosed with motor neurone disease. Mick of all people – the most handsomely athletic and healthy-looking person that most of us had ever come across. The last time I saw him, at a party given by his friend Jane Wellesley to celebrate the publication of *The*

*Lost Leader*, he was already in a wheelchair. Everyone knew that he didn't have many days left, but Mick greeted us with stoical calm, absorbing our sympathy, then turning it back to us as kindness while he inscribed copies of his book. Kyeong-Soo and I had recently got married: 'How do you spell your name?' he asked her, looking up from his chair. She told him, and Mick's hand crawled across the title page leaving its trail of clear script: a message to posterity. As I moved away, then looked back across the room, I thought of how John Taylor and John Hamilton Reynolds must have felt when they saw Keats in the days before he sailed for Italy. Their friendship with him remained a touchstone for the rest of their lives; Reynolds even asked for it to be mentioned in the inscription on his grave-stone. Mick would have laughed and rolled a dark, disbelieving eye if I'd told him this, and he'd have been right – the compari-son was too extravagant. But it came back to me when Kyeong-Soo and I walked into Magdalen College Chapel a few weeks later and sat down for his funeral. Of all the writers I'd met, Mick was the one treated most unkindly by time, the one whose talent was most brutally extinguished.

There was no ceremony when I stood down as laureate, no audience with the Queen and no formal handover. I just stopped one day, and Carol Ann Duffy started the next. Now I was the first ex-poet laureate, but did that mean my life was my own again, even though I'd continue to teach and work for the Poetry Archive? I hoped so, of course, although in the way of these things, it turned out that giving up one thing meant being asked to take on others. Would I chair the Booker

Prize judges and join the board of trustees? Would I set up a government-backed inquiry into the way poetry was taught in schools? Would I take on the presidency of the Campaign to Protect Rural England? Would I become chair of the Museums, Libraries and Archives Council? I didn't like to think what it told me about myself that I so quickly accepted these invitations, but I knew well enough. Either my sense of civic duty was now permanently stuck in overdrive, or I felt anxious that if I said no to anything, I might disappear from view.

———

Kyeong-Soo and I were on holiday in Calabria in southern Italy, and a lot further off the beaten track than we'd anticipated. But that was fine: although I was finding it hard to give my life the slip in any permanent way, at least I'd managed it for a fortnight. Pool-lounging and reading; staring into space; rambling through country where, if we planned things right, we could avoid the pylons and quarries that fed the pockets of the local Mafia.

Then it was late afternoon, and we returned to our room to find my phone fizzing on the counterpane, hysterical with messages. Seamus Heaney had died. I knew he'd been ill: Kyeong-Soo and I had seen him on and off during the eighteen months since his stroke, and realised that he'd lost energy, lost weight, lost his usually perpetual bounce and lift. But the fact of his death still wouldn't fit inside my mind. It was too suddenly sad, too drastic a rupture in the flow of poetry through life. Forty years earlier, he'd been one of the first poets I seized upon when I began writing myself, and since then he'd remained one of the small handful whose new books had continued to feel like major events. In all respects, and despite knowing that thousands of other people must be reacting to the news of his death in much the same way that I was, the loss felt intimate – almost familial – rather than public.

And all the more so because of what we'd had to deal with, then move beyond, in the early days of our acquaintance. When I'd begun working at Hull in the mid-1970s, and was teaching a course on contemporary poetry, it had occurred to me that an anthology of recent work would be handy – something roughly equivalent to A. Alvarez's *The New Poetry*, which Penguin had published a decade or so earlier. Because I was still wet behind the ears, and didn't feel capable of editing such a thing alone, I wrote to Blake Morrison, who was then working as poetry editor at the *Times Literary Supplement*, and suggested we might do it together. I'd never met Blake, but we'd been in touch by letter, and he'd published some of my poems in the *TLS*; he'd also written a short critical book about Seamus, in the same series for which I'd also written a short book about Philip.

Blake liked the idea of the anthology, as did Penguin, and we set to work – agreeing that we wanted to give Seamus pride of place, and planning to use a phrase from one of his poems as our title: *Opened Ground* (like all tyro anthology editors, we wanted to insist on the novelty of the poetry we were promoting). Then, at the last minute, we decided that *Opened Ground* wasn't the easiest phrase to say aloud – that final 'd' of 'opened' bumping against the 'g' of 'ground' – and chose something more straightforwardly descriptive: *The Penguin Book of Contemporary British Poetry*. We both knew that although Seamus now lived in Ireland (having been born in the North), he'd recently allowed some of his poems to be included in collections by British writers. We weren't thinking carefully enough; we supposed, without asking him, that if he'd allowed his poems to appear in these books, he wouldn't mind a selection appearing in ours. He did mind – courteously, which is how he did everything – but definitely: first in a letter to Blake, and then in a letter-poem to the wide world, which insisted: 'my passport's green'. As the weight of his words sank in, and I felt their justice, I could hardly believe that Blake and I had done something which seemed to disrespect a principle we both deeply cared about. It spoiled for me whatever success the anthology went on to have.

To my surprise – and relief – it didn't also stop Seamus becoming a friend. Although, as our paths crossed at lit-biz gatherings and readings, including those organised for the first Arvon/*Observer* Prize, which he helped to judge and which I won, I always felt this friendship was qualified – not so much by the anthology business, which Seamus never once raised in our conversations, but by the self-protection that his extraordinary fame made necessary. It meant there was always a sense of containment about him – part natural shyness, part deliberate reservation – which more or less exactly matched his instinct for generosity.

This generosity deepened after I became laureate, and in the process came to seem more complicated than I'd first thought. Once, when I was reading in Dublin, he invited me and Jan to his house the following Sunday morning, then gave us a little tour of local literary sites: Patrick Kavanagh's bench by the canal, and Joyce's Martello Tower. We were grateful, of course – he'd put himself out for us – yet at the same time I couldn't help thinking he must have better things to do: writing something, for instance. In this respect, his kindness seemed like a form of self-denial. But why? Was it something to do with upbringing and religion – a dominant concern for others? That would certainly fit with the way his poems turned so hospitably towards their readers, and in that respect be something which supported his gift. But at the same time, it put his gift in danger, for the simple reason that it took him away from his desk.

Or was this all too elaborate? I could never quite decide, even when his kindness seemed paramount. Once, for instance, he wrote to say that he was coming to London and had something to give me – and then, as I met him in the foyer of Hazlitt's Hotel in Frith Street, he presented me with a hurley stick. I took it from him feeling pleased but baffled: what did I want with a hurley stick? 'Look at the handle,' he told me, grinning and shifting his weight from one foot to the other – and there was my explanation: a stamp on the handle which showed the name of the manufacturers. Philip Larkin and Sons. In the same spirit, he also sent encouraging words when I began working as laureate, saying that he'd lobbied for my appointment in the first place, then agreeing to become president of the Poetry Archive, then anonymously donating money to it. At a dinner after he'd received the David Cohen Prize, I told him that whenever I felt bamboozled by the public-ness of my new life – significant to me, but far less consuming than his own – I would find my way forward by asking myself, 'What would Seamus do?' He grabbed my arm to interrupt me. 'Head for the hills!' he said. 'Head for the hills!' Which was like him, but not true: Seamus never headed for the hills. Instead, he cultivated a form of negative capability, seeing both sides of an argument, while simultaneously remaining true to himself.

Not that such thoughts found any space in my head as I read through the messages on my phone that evening in Calabria. I felt too purely grateful for what he'd given to everyone who read and met him, and too simply at a loss. Then I remembered his wife Marie and their children, and how their own feelings of bereavement would be riding the general swell of grief – no doubt being comforted by it in some respects, but perhaps also feeling swamped by it in others. It led me to throw down the phone on the bed and follow Kyeong-Soo outside, so that we could swim in the hotel's pool before supper. I watched her dive in. This was southern Italy, I reminded myself, not Tuscany, but all the same. Seamus had always made everyone at home in his own place:

> When you plunged
> The light of Tuscany wavered
> And swung through the pool
> From top to bottom.
>
> I loved your wet head and smashing crawl,
> Your fine swimmer's back and shoulders
> Surfacing and surfacing again
> This year and every year since.

———

A letter arrived from the poet Mary Jo Salter, inviting me to read my poems at Johns Hopkins University in Baltimore, where she was chair of the Writing Seminars programme. In the end I stayed for the best part of a week, checking out the city, meeting other faculty members, visiting the galleries and museums. On my final evening, Mary Jo took me to supper and asked whether I'd ever think of moving to America and joining her on the teaching staff. The offer was so unexpected, so magnanimous, I didn't immediately recognise it as a solution to the questions I'd been asking myself; my first thoughts were only about the difficulties of extricating myself from work in England, and about how much I'd miss my children and my friends.

But I kept thinking about the offer as I flew home, then talked it over with Kyeong-Soo: she'd left her home in America to come and live with me in a country she didn't know; maybe it was time I did the same for her? Maybe in America we'd have a more nearly equal share in the future than England might allow? At some point I flipped back to a conversation I'd had with E. R. Dodds in Oxford almost forty years earlier, when he'd told me about a letter that he'd received from Auden in 1939, in which Auden had said: 'America may break me completely, but the best of which one is capable is more likely to be drawn out of one here than anywhere else.' I was no Auden, and I was also in my early sixties, some thirty years older than he'd been when he left England, which perhaps made me less adaptable. But surely the same principle might apply, and America might set me free – might, in fact, return me to the point I'd reached when I was seventeen and climbing on board the train to Greece and Rupert Brooke's grave. Ever since then, occasionally by accident but much more often by design, my original devotion to poetry itself had slowly been complicated, and in some respects diluted, by my increasingly elaborate commitment to poetry-business of one kind or another. In America, where I would have much more time to write, and be able to lead a simpler and quieter life, I could get back to the beginning, and set out for a second time. When Kyeong-Soo and I finished talking, I emailed Mary Jo and told her that if the offer still stood, I'd changed my mind.

Time sped up and time slowed down: it had always played this trick at moments of special intensity, and now it was happening again. Nothing felt fixed and stable. Sudden lurches forward, sudden halts, sudden side-steps: that was how days worked. One minute I was walking along the bank of the Thames, thinking of nothing but how light played on the water; the next, I was saying goodbye to a friend I might not see for months; the next, I was dreading living three thousand miles away from the children, but reminding myself I'd be back to see them every vacation; the next, Kyeong-Soo and I were scooting off to Baltimore, looking for somewhere to live. We had only a few days to spare, couldn't find anywhere we liked, then on our last morning saw a rowhouse by the harbour in Fells Point, the old ship-building part of town, walked through it for ten minutes, made an offer, signed the contract, and flew home again.

And through it all, throughout this strange bending and straightening of days, the hard fact that I would soon be leaving home kept swerving in and out of focus. Sometimes I accepted it; sometimes I felt that I was blundering through a dream. My mood swung and swerved accordingly. Forty-five years previously, when I'd first met Joanna, leaving my father's house had felt like a natural process. An accelerated process, admittedly, and complicated in its haste, but predictable and eventually moderate: the end of every journey never landed me more than two hundred miles from where I'd started. Leaving my country was another matter. I thought of the anxious wind-whipped faces in the painting by Ford Madox Brown, *The Last of England*, and the poem that Peter Porter had written about it: 'You cannot leave England, it turns/ A planet majestically in the mind.' In my own case, it wasn't distance that bothered me so much as separation by other means. I knew already that no matter how often I came back, I couldn't expect my past simply to wait for me in England, like a boat that remained tied to the riverbank while I wandered abroad for a while. The river would rise and fall, and at some point the boat would drift off without me. The past would change while my back was turned; my children and friends would change; I would change. There would be forgetting and possibly disgruntlements as well. And, as I kept reminding myself, I was sixty-something: switching countries might well be a late shot at expansiveness, but was I sure it might not also be a form of self-destruction, with too little time to discover a new self to inhabit?

This last possibility was the most troubling. Not because I doubted my commitment to making a new life – I felt full of energy to do that. But because the example of my father's later days still haunted me. He'd had worse damages than mine to deal with, and they'd bred resentments which eventually turned him into a kind of hermit. Was I now doing this myself, albeit in a more glamorous-seeming fashion, by moving to America, whereas my father had buried himself in a cottage at the end of an English lane? Mostly I thought not. 'Old men ought to be explorers,' T. S. Eliot had said, and I was taking his advice: my decision was a vote for adventure.

———

Days stuttered. Days stalled. Days drooped and dragged. Then days finally raced into a blur, and a battered red container, its ribs scarred by a lifetime of rattling round the world, clunked down in the street outside our flat. By evening it held everything that

Kyeong-Soo and I owned: every book, every knife and fork, every picture, every stick of furniture except the bed, which we left for my daughter, who was going to become my tenant. Then a man came to collect the cat, squeezed her into a cage, attached a label saying *Missy: Baltimore*, and took her away. The flat fell quiet and we tramped down the six shallow stairs to our basement bedroom, closed the shutters, and tried to sleep. Pub-chat sprinkled along the road outside our window. Cars revved and a burst of music played. A woman ran past laughing. And gradually the silence deepened – the city hush which is never like silence proper, but a colossal atom-storm of miniature and separate noises, all jostling together and almost but not quite cancelling each other out. At one point a blackbird began to sing, confused into wakefulness by the streetlight. Then that stopped as well, and the silence grew deeper still. These were the fluctuations of home, and normally I never noticed them. Now they rushed at me, insisting and imprinting. A part of me wanted them never to end. Another part wanted to shake them out of my head for ever.

———

Fells Point is half a mile square. Brick rowhouses and cobbled streets. Cute, like the East End of London must have been before the Blitz. And noisy – juice bars and smoothie bars and bars proper. But like a village, too, with remnants of the old world: revamped port offices, warehouses turned into loft apartments, and a new brick pathway running along the water's edge past rotting wharves and the remains of boat-building slipways.

Ours is an old house by American standards, 1780-something, and originally built for a shipbuilder or a sailor. So far as I could tell that first morning, lying beside Kyeong-Soo on the mattress we'd thrown down onto bare floorboards, there was a young family living next door to us: I could hear them calling faintly to one another through the partition wall. Or was I imagining things and still hearing dream-voices? Dream-voices like my mother singing in the kitchen when I was ill and taking time off school fifty years ago; dream-voices like my father mucking out the stables across the yard, talking to the ponies to keep them out of his way. 'Good girl, good girl.' I listened harder and thought I could hear a pigeon crooning in the chestnut outside my old bedroom – the one overlooking the ponies' field, where one of the branches swooped down and shone leafless because the animals rubbed their flanks against it, using it as a scratching post. Or were those airy notes coming from the American elm below my window here on South Ann? I climbed off the mattress and looked outside, searching among the leaves until I found it, the marbled head tucking and bobbing. Coo-coo, coo-coo. I blinked my eyes and saw spirals of sunlight and silhouettes. The tree was simplified, and the tree was a labyrinth.

---

I began to explore, searching among the strangeness for familiar things, and on Lancaster Street found sparrows bathing in a puddle of dry dust. I remembered the story of Samuel Schieffelin, who wanted to bring to North America all the birds mentioned in Shakespeare, and failed with bullfinches, chaffinches, and nightingales but succeeded with house sparrows and starlings. Sparrows and starlings. English birds: 'The setting sun will always set me to rights,' John Keats says in one of his letters, 'or if a Sparrow come before my Window

I take part in its existence and pick about the Gravel.' John Keats, whose younger brother George emigrated to America 'to escape the burden of society', and first came ashore up the coast in Philadelphia before heading on west to Louisville in Kentucky. John Keats, for whom sparrows were commonplace, and who had now also crossed the Atlantic inside my head and was standing beside me to watch this cocky breakaway gang. One little bully hogged the centre of the dust-puddle and fanned his wings in a prayer shape, a poor man's bower bird. Stamped his twiggy feet and whooshed up dust to mop the grease in his feathers.

———

Baltimore further afield was a different story. I'd seen *The Wire* and knew the city's long history of injustice and violence, but now there was Freddie Gray as well – the uprising that had flared a month before we arrived. I didn't have to look far to find the causes that I'd previously only read about: they confronted me everywhere, elaborating and at the same time confirming the loyalty that I immediately felt to the city. At the checkout desk in the 7/11 and Whole Foods, at the gas station, in the faces of boys panhandling at stop signs. In 1950 Baltimore was the sixth-largest city in America; since then, its population has shrunk by almost 40 per cent and now it's the thirteenth-largest city. In 1950 the population was 76 per cent white; today it is 27 per cent white – and those who fled took most of their resources with them, leaving a city rife with inequality, haunted by corruption, and grotesquely violent: for the past several years, it's recorded one of the highest homicide rates of any city in America. Kyeong-Soo and I found that we could walk safely for twenty minutes in one direction from our front door, and ten minutes in the others. It meant we had to learn how to live in a bubble – and when teaching began, I found that I was working in a bubble as well. Welcome to America.

But I needed to look harder, more closely, and late in the evening drove through east Baltimore, where everyone had told me not to go. Snapped trees, broken fences, plastic chairs dragged onto wasteland and grouped round a bonfire of tyres. A man running, one hand hauling up his trousers, the other clinging to a disintegrating package, blood on his face. I accelerated away, and when I slowed down again a posse immediately surrounded the car, pressing against the window, looking me over, then scornfully waving me through; I wasn't wanted here. Hookers didn't care though, starting towards me from the kerb at street corners. And dealers the same. I kept my foot down, skirting the puddles of smashed glass. Sodium spillage, then long waves of darkness, then white light again when the moon sailed around the corner of a low-rise and gasped at the scoured sidewalks and bald streets, the starburst windows and fire-gutted roofs, the blistered stoops. I'd never seen anything like it – such rampant decay, such a gigantic seedbed for despair. Ruination for block after block after block. Everything broken, everything. Even the road surfaces gouged and pitted and cratered.

———

For months my homesickness felt like lovesickness – as bad as that; when I thought of my children and dear ones, it seemed as though the tide of my body was running out. Every night I flew in my mind above the London streets and squares, skimming the rain puddles and orange taxi-beaks, the shop blinds and statues in squares. One moment I'd glimpse the bare ankle of someone I love, and the next I felt the sun on the back of my hand as I touched warm skin. Then the kaleidoscope churned again. Here was the Embankment with its slow-moving flocks, and here I was in Soho, and here I was climbing up Parliament Hill, searching for the thimble of St Paul's among the cranes and fancy offices. Then I was back beside the sweet Thames again, eyeing the trophies it had swept from inland – hay-tufts and tree-branches and long scarves of greenery. England basked in my memory like a body, veined with shadow-play. My own shadow was a speck of grit, an irritation in the side of my eye.

———

The house is semi-detached, separated from one set of neigh-bours by a sally port which opens into a narrow yard. Anne and Bill. It means we often bump into each other when we're putting out the trash or fetching and carrying garden things. Anne's a photographer and Bill worked as a contractor until he fell off a roof. Good people. And, as it turns out, keen on horse racing. Was I related to Graham Motion, Anne asked me, soon after Kyeong-Soo and I had moved in; he's a racehorse trainer, she said. Never heard of him, I told her, surprised by how strongly I didn't want to discover a previously unknown American branch of my family, when I was missing my known family so much. Surprised too by how strongly, even after so much time, I didn't want horses playing any part in my life. But Anne wasn't to know this. Graham's a big deal in the Maryland racing world, she went on. The horses he trains have won the Kentucky Derby, the Preakness, all the big races. His stables are up the I-95 towards New York – an empire. I nodded and smiled and went back indoors.

Weeks later I typed 'Graham Motion' into Google, and when his photograph swam onto my screen I found that was I looking at the spitting image of my Uncle Rob, my father's brother. I pushed my chair back from my desk. How much did family matter to me? More than anything but not enough, if my past behaviour was anything to go by, and that probably meant I should leave things be. Besides, why should this Graham bother with me? Given the evidence of his website, with its pictures of winners and stables and colours and trophies, it didn't seem likely that he'd have much interest in meeting an expatriate poet, even if he was a relation.

I logged off, the weeks passed, then simple curiosity got the better of me: I wrote to Graham and introduced myself, explaining that I'd recently left England and was now living down the road. His wife Anita replied by return, invited us to lunch the next weekend, and assembled a dozen of their clan to meet us, including Graham's father Michael. Michael looked so like a slightly aged version of my father – the same stoop, the same deprecating way of talking, the same nose and eyes and mouth, even the same check shirt and V-necked green jersey and brown corduroy trousers – I was almost lost for words. I'd recently been reminding myself that I was a connoisseur of ghosts, but I'd never sat down and talked with one before.

Michael explained that his branch of the family was descended from my great-grandfather's brother Tom, and had moved to the States during the 1950s to work in the horse breeding and training business. So we weren't just loosely connected but closely related. And to prove the point (Michael looked up as the front door opened and a late arrival came into the room), here was Graham's brother Andrew. I moved forward to shake his hand, then embraced him instead, saying his name as he said mine. Andrew Motion. Andrew who was a horse breeder, which was the kind of thing my father would have liked me to be, who had dark hair like my father, who had my father's laugh – a laugh I hadn't heard for many more years than he'd been dead.

We finished our exclaiming and explaining and left the house to walk through the stables nearby, the long row of stalls where the dense smell of hay and straw and dung and sweat took me back step by step into my childhood, and the much smaller and scruffier pony-world that Kit and I had shared. The great effort of my teenage years had been to escape it, and make a different life for myself. Now here I was confronting it again. My instinct was to drive back to Baltimore as soon as possible, but these new cousins were too welcoming, too kind, and simply too nice for that not to seem ridiculous. Didn't I like the past being visible in the present? Well, then. And wasn't it a strange and unexpected comfort to find blood relatives in a country where I'd expected nothing of the kind? Of course it was. As I took in the fire blazing in the grate, the children milling in the kitchen, the family-rumble of tenderness and teasing, I remembered the silence of my father's house. I embraced each member of the family in turn, and said that we'd see each other again soon. Then Kyeong-Soo and I climbed into the car and drove back to our own lives.

———

Did the Brexit vote make it easier to feel sure that we'd made the right decision in leaving England? Undoubtedly. But then

Trump replaced Obama as president, and the resemblances between the US and the UK became more obvious. My instinct, the instinct of almost everyone we met in our solidly Democrat city, was to try and tune him out. But that was impossible; Trump was everywhere, and his torrential sewer-pipe gurning became a part of daily life. We thought about leaving, even though we'd only just arrived, then looked across the Atlantic again and saw what was happening there and hesitated. The sense of living in a nastier world, a less optimistic and almost infinitely more fragile world than the one I'd been born into, was overwhelming. And in America there was precious little of a practical kind that I could do to change anything. I didn't even have a vote.

———

Kyeong-Soo and I drove down to Chincoteague in Virginia, staying in a b. & b. near the estuary. It was midwinter, cold, and the sky was dark by four – but our eyes soon got used to it and found multiple soft lavender colours seeping over the marsh below our bedroom window, then the island of Assateague darkening the horizon. We'd cross over there tomorrow and look for the wild horses. Not wild-wild like in Mongolia but creaturely enough.

I opened the window and heard the land talking – dry creeks muttering, grass scratching, water whining faintly as the current split around the rope trailing off a deck. The ducks were already asleep, camped on their mud-bumps where the foxes couldn't reach them, but the horses on the island were still awake. When I stared at the treeline through my binoculars, I could see their eyes shining. A white blaze here, a black mane there.

But I was making that up, dream-sleeping on islands again, thinking about my mother's horse Serenade and how after the accident she'd stood under the may tree in the field beside the house, questioning me with her eyes whenever I walked past her. What had she done? Why did nobody ride her any more, or talk to her, or pet her? Was she being punished? Poor dumb creature. Her blaze was still there in my mind's eye when I went indoors again, sat down in my mother's empty green chair, and put my feet on the footstool covered with the tapestry she'd made.

Next morning, we drove to Assateague and found a bedraggled-looking herd on the far side of a freshly mown field of barley. As we walked towards them for a closer look, a flock of redwings rose from the stubble, maybe a thousand birds, chattering and whistling while they were airborne, their wings purring, then silent when they landed again and started picking about for food. I watched them admiringly, but also with a feeling of incomprehension, because redwings are not native to England, and these birds had no echo or association for me. If they'd been blackbirds, I'd have remembered the rough grass in the apple orchard of my parents' house. If they'd been crows, the field over the lane from the cottage where my father spent the last part of his life – the grudging triangle of land with its flints and clay-lumps. If they'd been rooks, I'd have seen the elms at Toot Baldon, with their high branches dappling in the sky-streams. But these birds were simply themselves – beautiful, but nothing to do with me. The sky darkened as they rose in their cloud again, and the horses scattered while the Atlantic crashed beyond them.

I looked in the mirror and saw the world at a standstill. Then I looked again and a year had passed: it was July, the hot vacation summer, and Kyeong-Soo and I had found places to swim, sometimes in the old quarry at Beaver Dam, where turtles paddled through the dark green water beneath us, toiling through ruined light-colonnades, and sometimes at Sandy Point near the mouth of Chesapeake Bay. It was always populous there, but we soon discovered a quiet backway to reach it, then parked by the oak wood, cut through the trees past the barbecue burger-smells, and looped along the shoreline to the bay within the bay, where there were never many people. The beach here was a wide strip of hard pale sand, with a grassy promontory to the north and a rock-jetty to the south, with Bay Bridge shimmering beyond it. Grey-blue arch after enormous grey-blue arch, and all as frail-looking as a thinly painted watercolour, although when the wind changed direction I could hear the traffic-rumble and feel its terrible weight.

I stepped into the water knowing that I'd have to walk at least fifty yards before I was out of my depth. At first there was only the faintest current, a dim warmth at the surface, and when I drew level with the fishermen at the end of the jetty, it was still comfortable to stand still and watch: those seabass they were catching were so small, a single strike hoicked them clean out of the water and onto the stones. Just a mouthful! But there were bigger fish too: the last time I'd swum here, I'd had to change tack to avoid a dead rockfish floating sideways through the waves, five pounds at least and stinking. And earlier still? I let my mind drift through the glitter, remembering stories about the early settlers who arrived in the time of abundance. Families who walked dry-shod from their boats to the shore, the shoals of cod were packed in so tight.

When the water reached my chest and the cold began, I threw myself forward, swimming fast until I was warm again. Had anyone ever made it right across the bay? I paused and looked towards the shore of Kent Island opposite. It was a mile off, at least; too far, anyway, with this current and these tankers sailing towards Baltimore. There was one now, beyond the buoy marking the channel: a dead weight of black metal that looked massive even at this distance. I buried my head and began swimming again, warm water-rags fluttering down my shoulders and legs, sun licking my back.

I only knew what happened next when it was already over. Ospreys were nesting on the shore behind me – I'd often seen them in the treetops – and now one had left its roost, floated over the beach, tracked my own line into the bay, seen a fish ahead of me, then swooped down and taken it. Snatched it six inches from my face. Despite the wild flurry and the water drops, I saw the yellow talons exactly, and the muddy-white thrashing wings, the mad-looking eye, the plunge and grab and the beak gaping.

I stopped swimming again. I dangled in the current, treading water as the osprey juggled its load, then gave one two three whomping wing-heaves and lifted away. It was still finding a perfect balance when it turned back towards the shore, and the fish looked like an ingot now, a silver ingot melting and dripping. Conquest! But the bird flew over my head with a look of woundedness, an embarrassed lowness, before it sank into the oak woods out of sight.

———

I'd arrived in Baltimore expecting to start writing immediately about the city and Maryland. But as soon as I began to settle in,

I found myself turning back to England and thinking about my parents. Apparently, and without ever anticipating it, I wanted to write poems that said goodbye to them – or rather, I wanted to write poems that established them as ghosts in my new life, where I could still keep them close.

But not by using the old means. I'd come to America in the first place at least partly because I wanted to stand under the great Niagaran downpour of its poetries, and to feel myself sluiced out and changed by them. No more tightly organised stanzas, or traditionally stichic poems of the kind I'd favoured in the past. Something more akin to the freedom that a great-grandchild of Whitman might feel. Something better acquainted with the barbaric yawp.

Easily said, and comparatively easily done, since decisions about form are consciously made. But what about my old obsessions and instincts? I suspected that in many fundamental ways I might be simply too old to make it new – but did I even want to try? Yes and no. The first poem I finished in Baltimore, a book-length elegy for my parents called *Essex Clay*, and the other two longish poems I wrote immediately afterwards – one a disrupted sequence of lyrics about migration and home-sickness called 'Randomly Moving Particles', and the other a riff on Euripides' play *Herakles*, which was a response to the violence of the city and country which was now my home – proved opposite things. One was that I certainly did want to experiment with new forms; and the other was that all these experimentations and novelties converged on themes that had preoccupied me from the beginning and showed no signs of being exhausted. Age and then the only end of age. Love and its consoling bewilderments. Displacement and resurrection. Ghostliness. Should I have felt disappointed that these things

continued to fixate me, despite the effort I'd made to live differently? Or should I tell myself that the subjects were large and
deep enough to last a lifetime? I didn't need to think for long
before I knew the answer.

———

Writing time is a part of normal time, twenty-four-hours-in-
a-day time, but like normal time it moves at different speeds.
And because writing is solitary, and because I'd organised my
new life to have as few interruptions as possible, I soon realised
that my sense of time passing had changed since I first came
to America. The rhythm of term-time and vacation-time gave
it a broadly definite shape, and so did the visits I made to see
the children and friends in London. But within this new structure, hours and minutes seemed increasingly likely to spring
out of their circle and move at speeds of their own devising.
Something of the sort had begun to happen in England when I
stood down as laureate, and no longer had to meet the demands
and deadlines that came with the job. But I'd so quickly filled
the aftermath with other kinds of obligation, the loosening
effect had been disguised. Now, under the silvery light reflected
from Chesapeake Bay, my time was shaped less by events, as it
had been in the old days, and more by various forms of solitude,
as I had more and more deeply wanted.

But the lack of events made it harder to account for my time.
It wasn't just whole days that passed without me stirring from
my desk, where I'd often be remembering the past and writing
about it, but whole weeks and – during the summer vacation
– whole months. What did I have to show for my existence? It
was the question my father used to ask me every evening when

I was a child and he came to kiss me goodnight: 'What have you done with your day?' He would have understood if he were to ask the question now, and I told him 'teaching'. But 'writing' would have seemed too insubstantial to him, and therefore a waste of time. In my own mind, writing was a way of mapping time, its circles as much as its straight lines. Words on a page were a way of saying 'I am here', but they were only made possible by feeling that I was nowhere.

Then I was given a sabbatical from my teaching and entered a deeper form of self-isolation. What might I do with this timeless time? Begin this book, I decided, and let the past unspool again. I climbed to my study at the top of the house, shut the door, prepared to haul my days back towards me – and suddenly the isolation became even more complete than I'd imagined. The Covid virus arrived; the wheels of the world squealed to a halt; and the air filled with grief and frustration. Sitting at my desk and staring through flimsy spring leaves into the quiet street below, I imagined a set of Russian dolls, each figure smaller and more tightly fitting than the last, with myself at the centre.

My subject was the past, but before I started writing, I found that I needed to anchor myself in the present and remind myself where I now belonged. By thinking about the city and its gigantic complexities, but also about the little things, the details that make a life and a home within that life. The untidy woods of Maryland, for instance – the trees toppled into each other's arms, the trees snapped in half and raggedly kneeling, the trees prone and rotting. And the whole mess draped with vines which are one thing while it's summer, green and flowery, but turn meagre and scratchy in winter, becoming illegible.

———

We barely know Andrew and Joanna, the couple who live across the road from us. But the coincidence of their names! It's early morning still, and here they are fussing on their stoop for a moment before they perch on the top step. They're both dressed in black – black shirts, black pants, black shoes – and Joanna has a purple scarf tied around her neck. Andrew is holding a classical guitar – I had no idea – and after tuning the strings for a moment, cocking his head to one side, he begins a tune. It's some sort of Renaissance ballad, a sweet and simple melody, and even when Joanna starts to sing in accompaniment, the sound remains very thin under the wide sky.

———

Or thinking about that gap in the sidewalk around the corner – a patch of bare earth, and a six-inch-wide tree stump. When I'm walking there, I often set one foot on top of the stump and pause in mid-stride, my memory of the tree resisting me, the bark and sap and splinters and soft damp yellowish hardwood. But I have the freedom of passing through – the gift of that, and the loss of not taking root and casting shade.

———

The music ends, Andrew and Joanna go back inside, and their door closes. Light doubles on the Inner Harbor at the end of the street. Everywhere in the world, as the Covid stranglehold tightens, this morning's sickly longshots become its definite midday casualties. The day casts itself down and the black harbour swallows it, hoarding the heat.

***

Or thinking about American grass – the greenery that dies back in winter, unlike English grass, and lies ivory-white, matted, exhausted. Grass that gives up the ghost, then shoots again with its cutting edges and resistance.

***

Punctually at noon an ambulance arrives; the siren tips off the street. Doors open and blinds tremble. All eyes are on the house opposite: the ambulance men have disappeared inside and there's confusion – small scuffles and a cry – until the ambulance men bend outside again. They're carrying a stretcher, but which of them is it, Andrew or Joanna? It's hard to see at this distance, there's a mask covering the face. Then the men come clear of the tree overshadowing, and I can see that it's Andrew – the mask slipping as his body arches. Joanna stands on the threshold, lifting one hand as the ambulance revs away. She wants to go to the hospital with her husband, but it's not allowed, and she stares along the empty street for a good minute before turning indoors again and closing the door behind her. The earth-brown door.

***

307

Or thinking about a vapour trail overhead – haven't all flights been grounded? It must be military then, something to do with the government. If not Phaeton struggling to control his father's horses before they plunge into the stars, scrape against the Scorpion's tail and the claws of the Great Bear, then plunge towards the Earth and incinerate its forests, scald its rivers dry.

———

The ambulance has torn a low branch off the tree next to Joanna's house, and now a collared dove lands in the crown. A rickety balsa-wood toy, wobbling on its perch although there's no wind blowing. But the song is business-like, like someone doing their chores despite worn-out elbows and sore feet. That forlorn, echoey coo-coo again; coo-coo, coo-coo. Miles away under water, as the virus reduces the amount of sea traffic, whales are discovering the lack of engine noise and modulating their harmonies: they have the whole quiet ocean to fill. Here coo-coo is enough, and the tree is all applause.

———

Or thinking about a painting – Poussin's *Landscape with a Calm*: the hills looming above the villa, the framework of bushy trees, and the foreground with its goats and goatherd (the dog refusing to be drawn). Then my eyes settle on the lake that fills the centre of the picture. The utterly still surface, pale blue as a blackbird's egg. The mirror that shows a distorted version of the hills and villa. What does it mean, this difference between the reality and the reflection? And what does it have to do with those fires on the hillside, one sending up a vigorous smoke-message, the other breaking into flames. Fire! Fire! That must be why the boy next to the wash house on the left of the picture has leaped onto his horse and urged it into a gallop. Fire, again! Fire! From a standing start the horse is already going full tilt, legs stretched like a fairground animal. And the boy's hair is on end, his right arm flung forward and pointing. Fire, still! Fire! The calm has hardly begun and it's already over. Or maybe it never existed in the first place.

———

In mid-afternoon Joanna comes back to her stoop, wearing the same black shoes and black clothes, holding a cup of coffee. She's been told something important – I can tell by the way she hunches forward and stares into the cup, the miniature calm lake. But no one stops and talks to her, so whatever she's thinking she doesn't tell. The collared dove packs up his song and whirrs away. The tree alters its pattern of shadows. The afternoon darkens, and Joanna tips the dregs of her coffee onto the sidewalk, making a meaningless splash-shape.

———

Or thinking about John Donne's poem 'The Calme' – it's one of a pair written in the 1590s, when Donne was in his twenties, busy and ambitious and excited. The companion piece is called 'The Storm', and that's full of terrors, but here Donne is stuck on a ship going nowhere, his mind fidgeting between land and sea, high and low, himself and others. Thinking how buildings melt in fires, how the court moves location depending on the season and the health of the population, how theatres

look when a play ends and the stalls are empty, how stillness
leads to decay:

> As water did in stormes, now pitch runs out:
> As lead, when a fir'd Church becomes one spout.
> And all our beauty, and our trimme, decayes,
> Like courts removing, or like ended playes.
> The fighting place now seamens ragges supply;
> And all the tackling is a frippery.
> No use of lanthornes; and in one place lay
> Feathers and dust, today and yesterday.

Feathers which are left-behind things, beautiful in themselves
but emblems of damage and ruin. Reminders of flight, too,
feathers being angels as well as birds.

And dust. Dust which is the powdered world. Which is sedi-
ment. Which is time's aim and ambition. Dust which fills the
air that I breathe before my time ends. Dust which is my time.

———

At nightfall the news of Andrew's death arrives, skulking along
the street from doorway to doorway, feeding off rumours. It
wears a mask, it touches nothing, but gradually it becomes
more definite. Joanna opens her door and steps to one side;
even now she must keep her distance. But the ghost doesn't care
where she stands. The ghost rushes past her in a flurry, drags
her after him, and slams the door shut. He can't wait to settle
down among his old things, to stretch out his legs and make
himself comfortable.